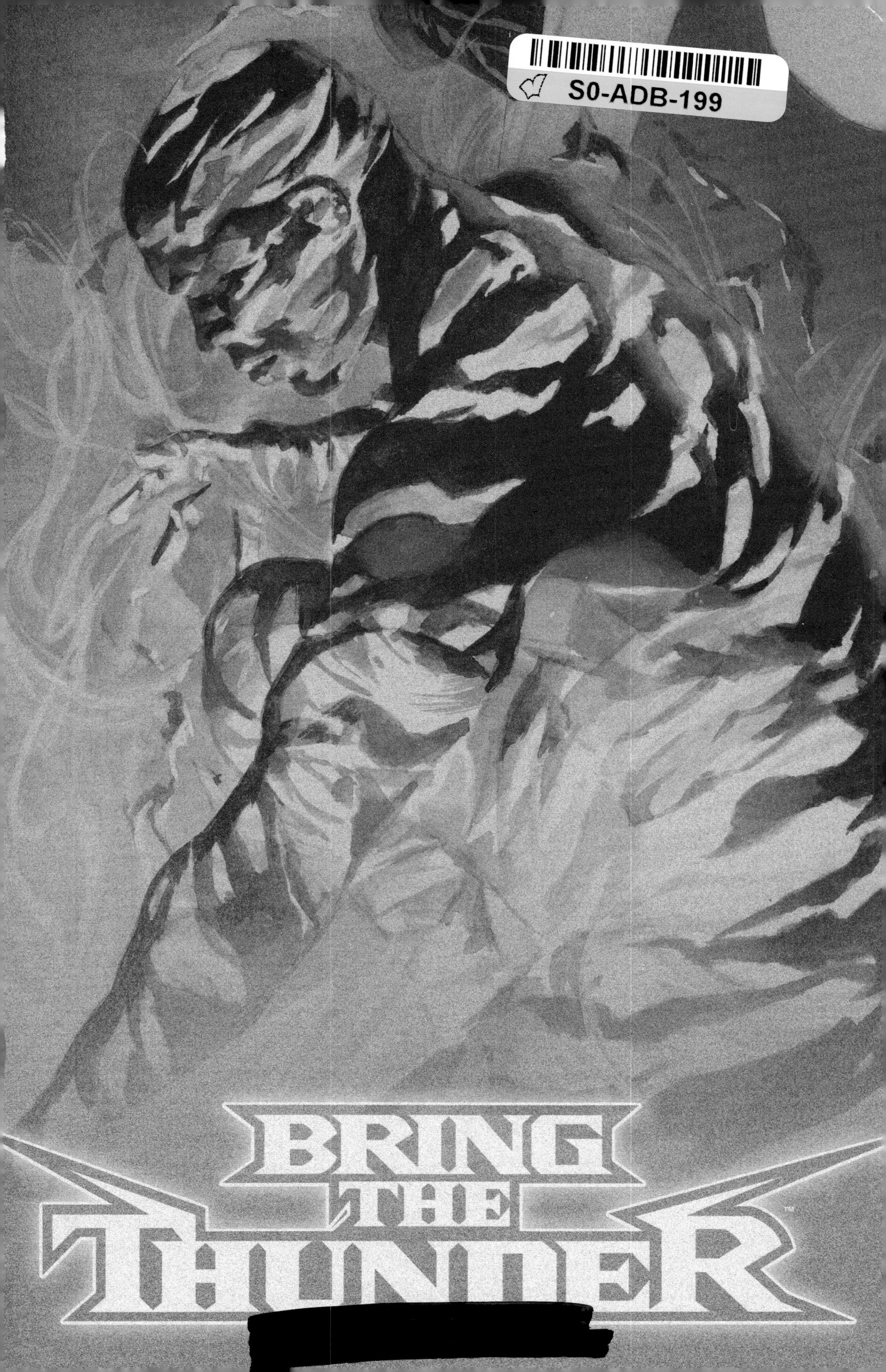

BRING THE THUNDER™

[redacted]

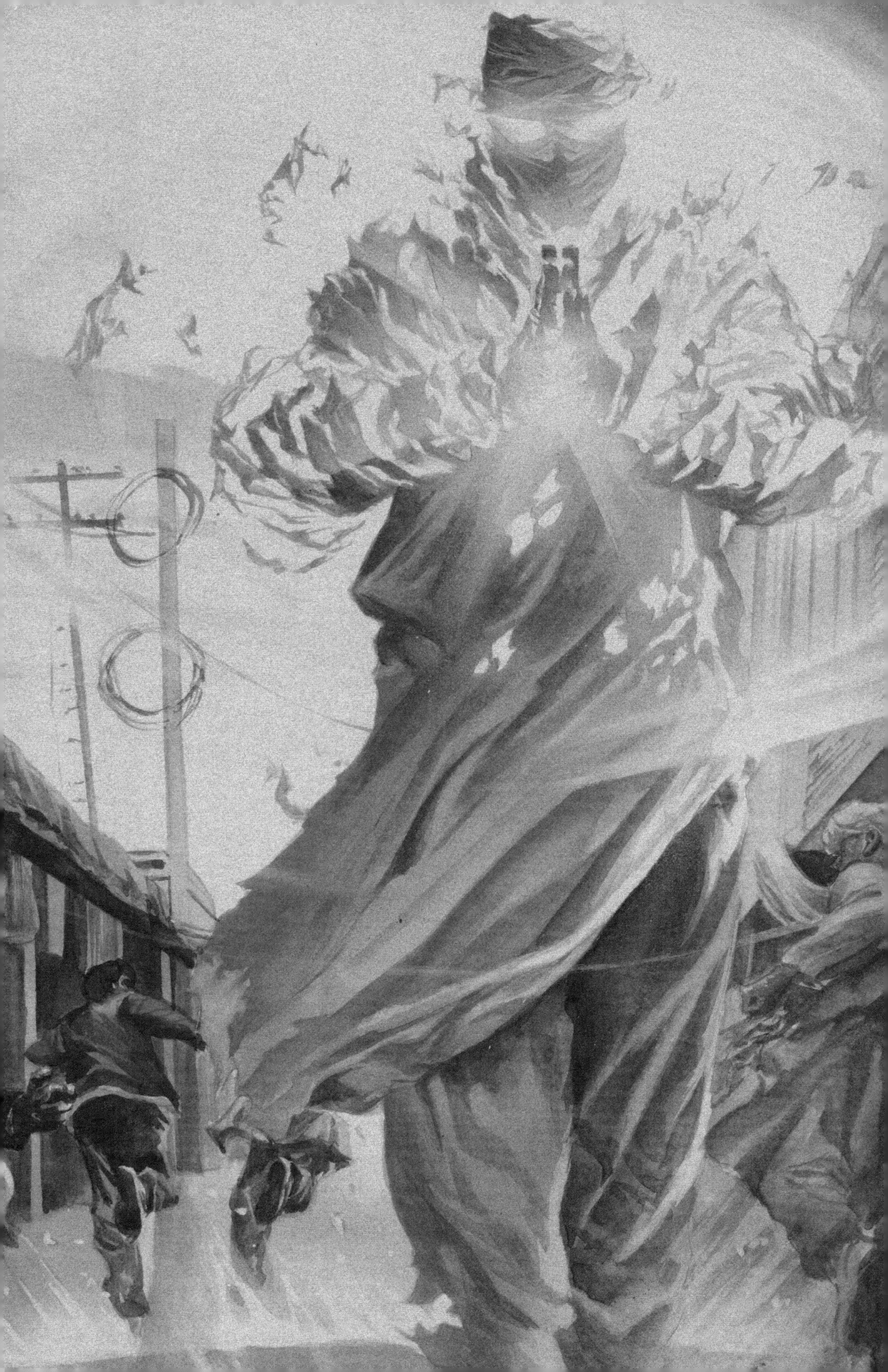

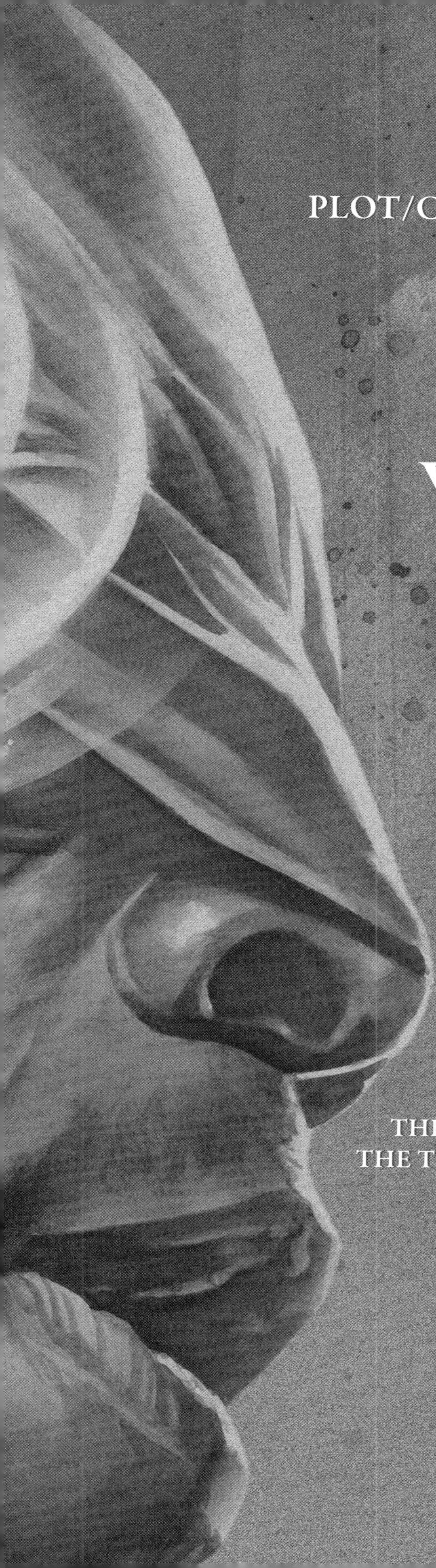

PLOT/CONCEPT/CHARACTER DESIGNS
ALEX ROSS

PLOT/SCRIPT
JAI NITZ

ART
WILSON TORTOSA

COLORS
MARLON ILAGAN

LETTERS
SIMON BOWLAND

COLLECTION COVER
ALEX ROSS

SPECIAL THANKS TO
TONY AKINS
FOR DESIGN ASSISTANCE

COLLECTION DESIGN
JASON ULLMEYER

THIS VOLUME COLLECTS ISSUES 1-4 OF BRING
THE THUNDER BY DYNAMITE ENTERTAINMENT.

WWW.DYNAMITE.NET

NICK BARRUCCI • PRESIDENT
JUAN COLLADO • CHIEF OPERATING OFFICER
JOSEPH RYBANDT • ASSOCIATE EDITOR
JOSH JOHNSON • CREATIVE DIRECTOR
RICH YOUNG • DIR. BUSINESS DEVELOPMENT
JASON ULLMEYER • SENIOR DESIGNER
JOSH GREEN • TRAFFIC COORDINATOR
CHRIS CANIANO • PRODUCTION ASSISTANT

First Printing   ISBN-10: 1-60690-163-X   ISBN-13: 978-1-60690-163-2   10 9 8 7 6 5 4 3 2 1

BRING THE THUNDER™ VOLUME ONE. First printing. Contains materials originally published in Bring The Thunder #1-4. Published by Dynamite Entertainment. 155 Ninth Ave. Suite B, Runnemede, NJ 08078. Bring The Thunder is ™ and © 2011 State Street Films and Savage Tales Entertainment, llc. All rights reserved. Dynamite, Dynamite Entertainment and the Dynamite Entertainment colophon are ® & © 2011 DFI. All rights reserved. All names, characters, events, and locales in this publication are entirely fictional. Any resemblance to actual persons (living or dead), events or places, without satiric intent, is coincidental. No portion of this book may be reproduced by any means (digital or print) without the written permission of Dynamite Entertainment except for review purposes. The scanning, uploading and distribution of this book via the Internet or via any other means without the permission of the publisher is illegal and punishable by law. Please purchase only authorized electronic editions, and do not participate in or encourage electronic piracy of copyrighted materials. PRINTED IN CHINA

For media rights, foreign rights, promotions, licensing, and advertising please e-mail: marketing@dynamite.net

INTRODUCTION

When my old college roommate Alex Ross approached me one day about working together on a project, I couldn't turn him down. Not only is Alex a terrific guy, but also he's one of the most talented, if not the most talented (in my opinion) artists working today. His artwork not only shows his commercial sensibilities, but also injects emotion into the characters' features you rarely see in the comic world. Every year when I find myself in San Diego for Comic Con, I always make a point of it to do my one name drop of the year with Alex; his influence in the comic world is beyond impressive.

For years and years, Alex and I remained in constant contact, updating each other about our various successes, both professionally and personally, and always expressing a desire to work together. Finally, one day, I decided that the wait was over and it was time to do a dream project with Alex Ross.

After we were fortunate enough to bring on Dynamite Entertainment, Alex and myself went back and forth creatively on what type of superhero would connect with an audience that we both relate with. It was an exciting as well as rewarding process to talk story and character with such a strong, creative mind whose years of experience as a visual storyteller were evident from the outset. Once it was settled that the type of superhero we wanted to show was based in reality and, among other things, shared the same problems of the every day man (bills, family, etc.), it was then time to decide on the contemporary issue of our day that our protagonist could tackle. In setting his origin story in the deserts of Afghanistan, our spectacular creative team of Alex, Jai Nitz, Wilson Tortosa, and myself wanted to personalize the story for the reader and convey that this was a hero for this time and this generation.

Obviously, with my and Alex's ties to Chicago, it was a no-brainer to have our hero return home to our hometown with his new found powers. From there, we really wanted to give Wayne (our hero) adversaries that we encounter in our every day lives rather than have him battle the classic comic book villains who often aren't based in reality. Jai and Wilson did an incredible job taking our vision and keeping it as grounded as it could possibly be.

The final reason I am so proud of this project is its ability to add racial diversity to the comic world. From the outset, Alex and I wanted to be sure that we were creating the absolute best story possible, but at the same time, be cognizant of creating a franchise that is based in the principle of inclusion and showing a hero from a background you don't see as often. Speaking personally, it was refreshing to see an African-American portrayed in a heroic light; as an artist, I have always strived to create the same kind of role models that were instrumental in my upbringing and bring those lessons and principles I learned to a new generation.

I thank you deeply for checking out BRING THE THUNDER. It was a labor of love for everyone involved and I hope you enjoy reading it as much as we enjoyed creating it!

Robert Teitel

Robert Teitel is an American film producer.

Teitel is most notable for producing the films Soul Food *(1997),* Men of Honor *(2000), and the three films in the Barbershop series:* Barbersop, Barbershop 2: Back in Business, *and* Beauty Shop. *He is also co-producer of the television series* Barbershop: The Series.

He is a 1990 graduate of Columbia College Chicago. He has been associated with writer/director George Tillman, Jr. since they were students together at Columbia College.

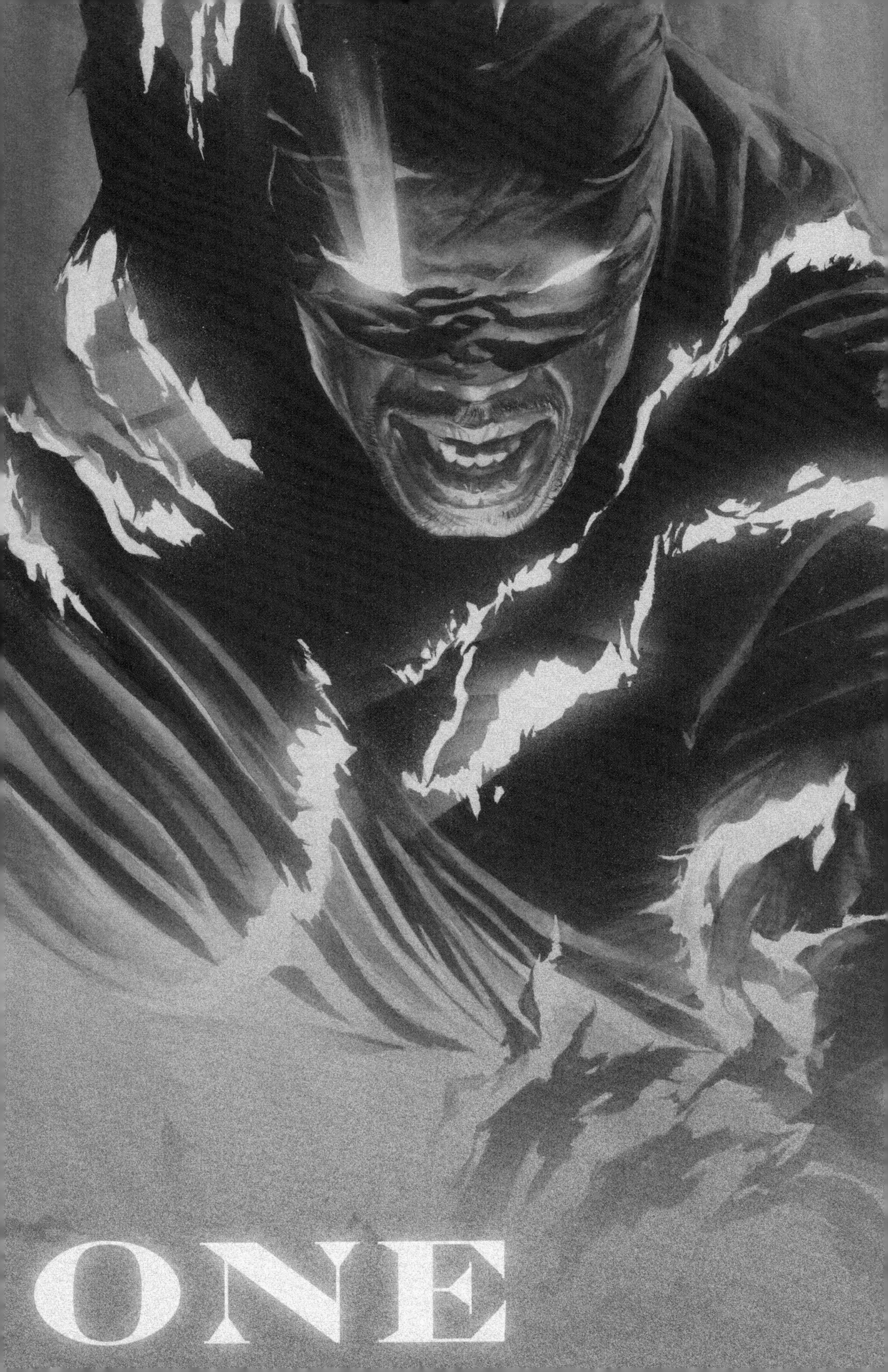

ONE

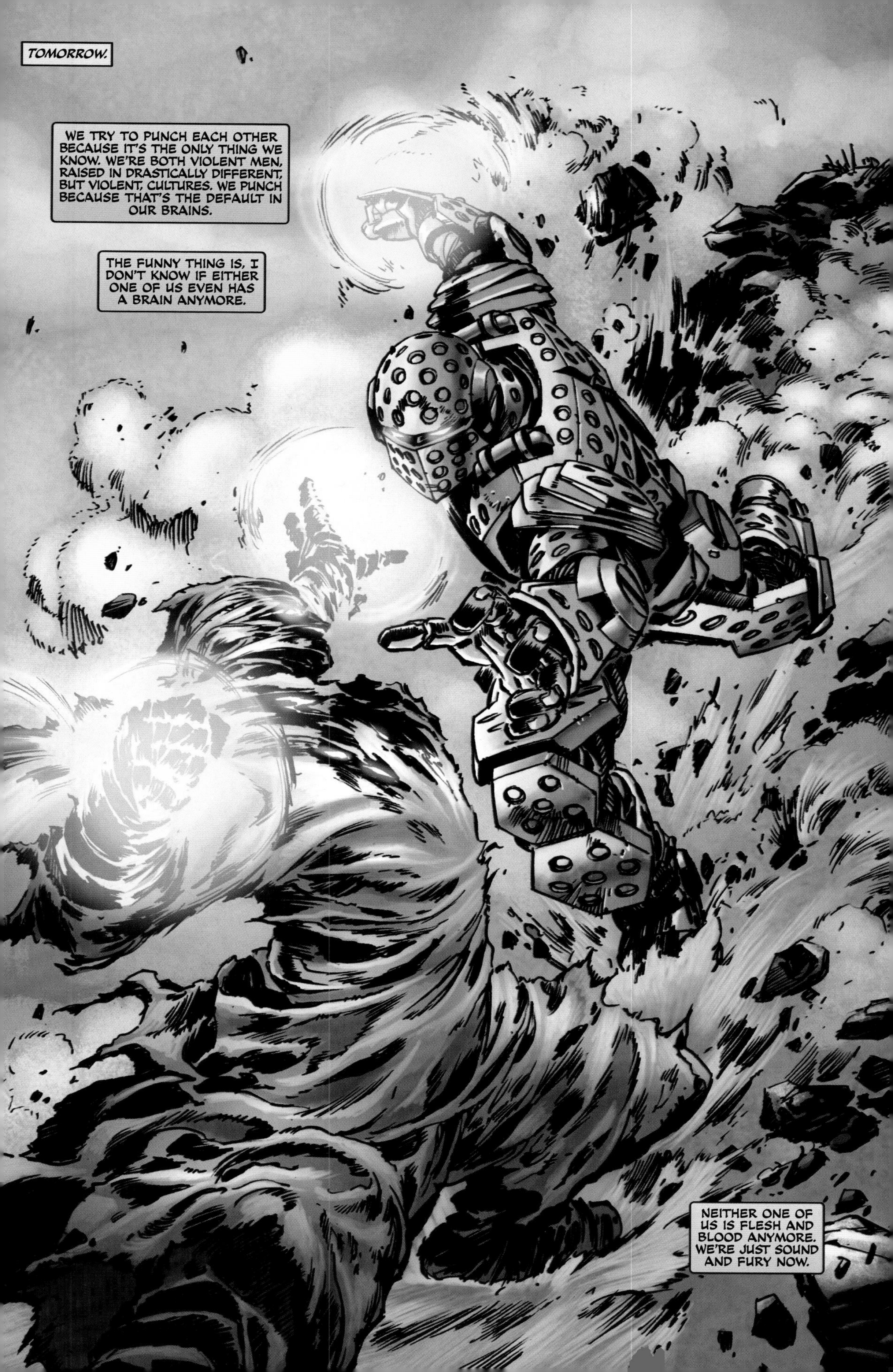
TOMORROW.
WE TRY TO PUNCH EACH OTHER BECAUSE IT'S THE ONLY THING WE KNOW. WE'RE BOTH VIOLENT MEN, RAISED IN DRASTICALLY DIFFERENT, BUT VIOLENT, CULTURES. WE PUNCH BECAUSE THAT'S THE DEFAULT IN OUR BRAINS.
THE FUNNY THING IS, I DON'T KNOW IF EITHER ONE OF US EVEN HAS A BRAIN ANYMORE.
NEITHER ONE OF US IS FLESH AND BLOOD ANYMORE. WE'RE JUST SOUND AND FURY NOW.

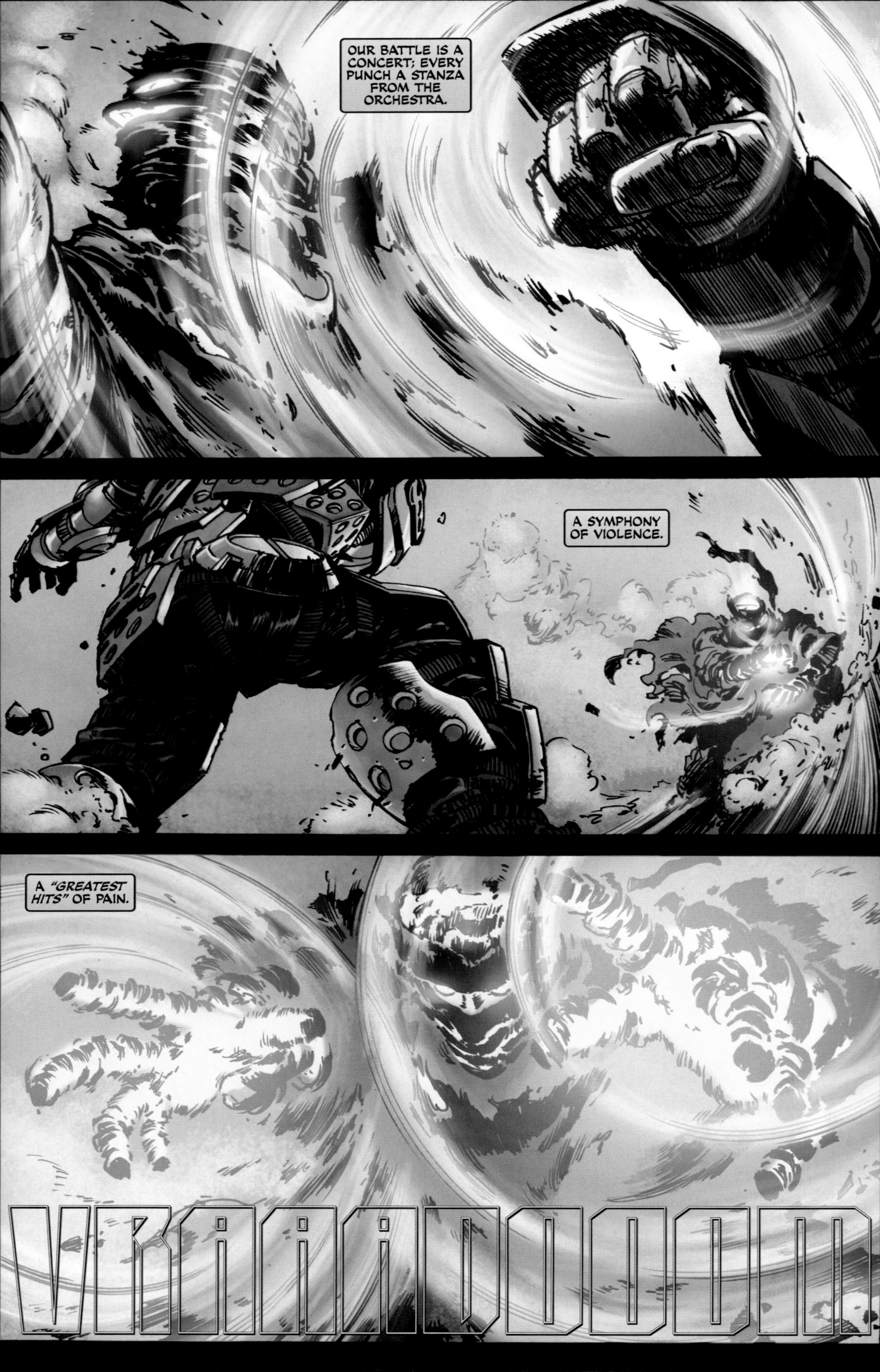
OUR BATTLE IS A CONCERT; EVERY PUNCH A STANZA FROM THE ORCHESTRA.
A SYMPHONY OF VIOLENCE.
A "GREATEST HITS" OF PAIN.
VRAAADOOOM

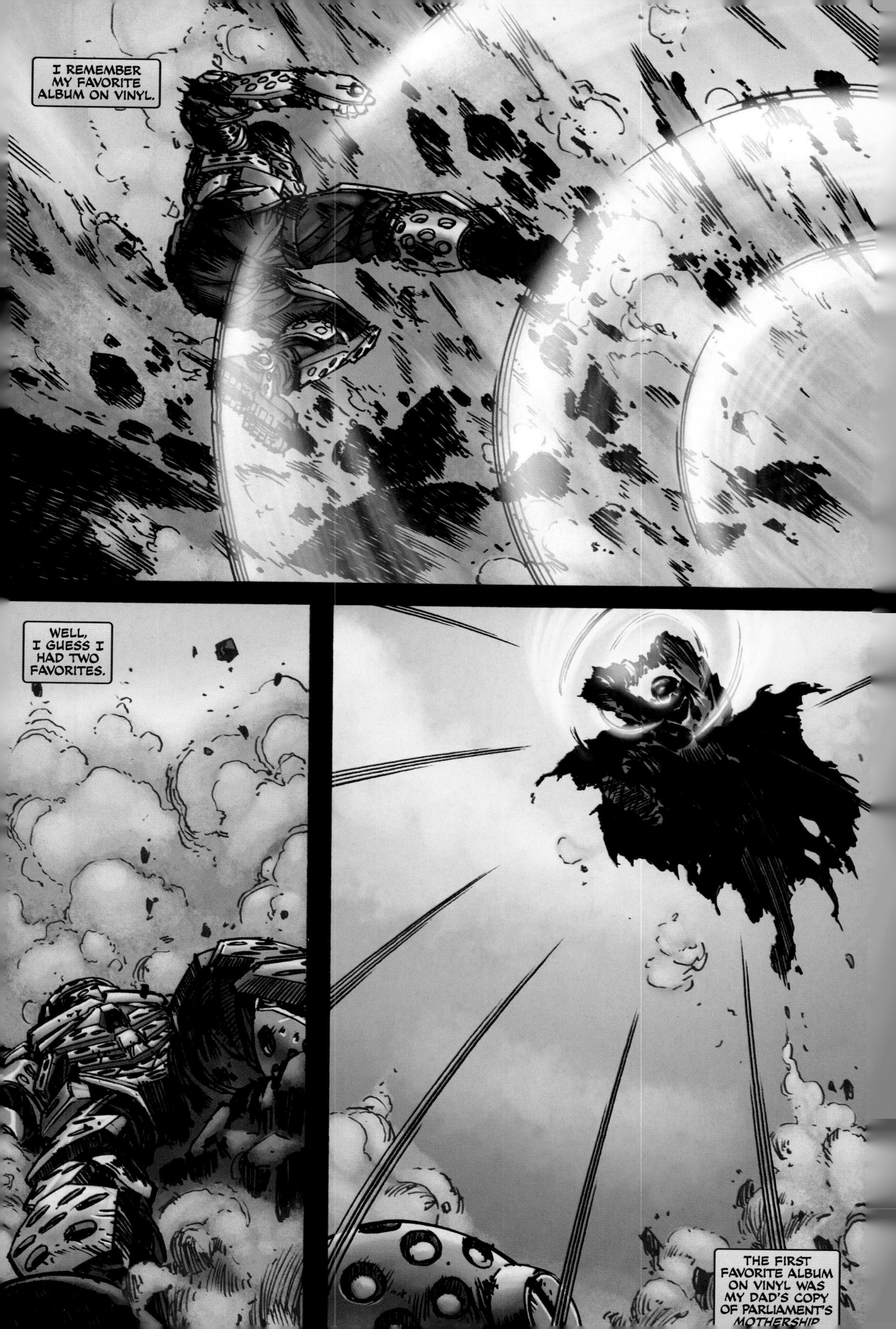
I REMEMBER MY FAVORITE ALBUM ON VINYL.
WELL, I GUESS I HAD TWO FAVORITES.
THE FIRST FAVORITE ALBUM ON VINYL WAS MY DAD'S COPY OF PARLIAMENT'S *MOTHERSHIP*

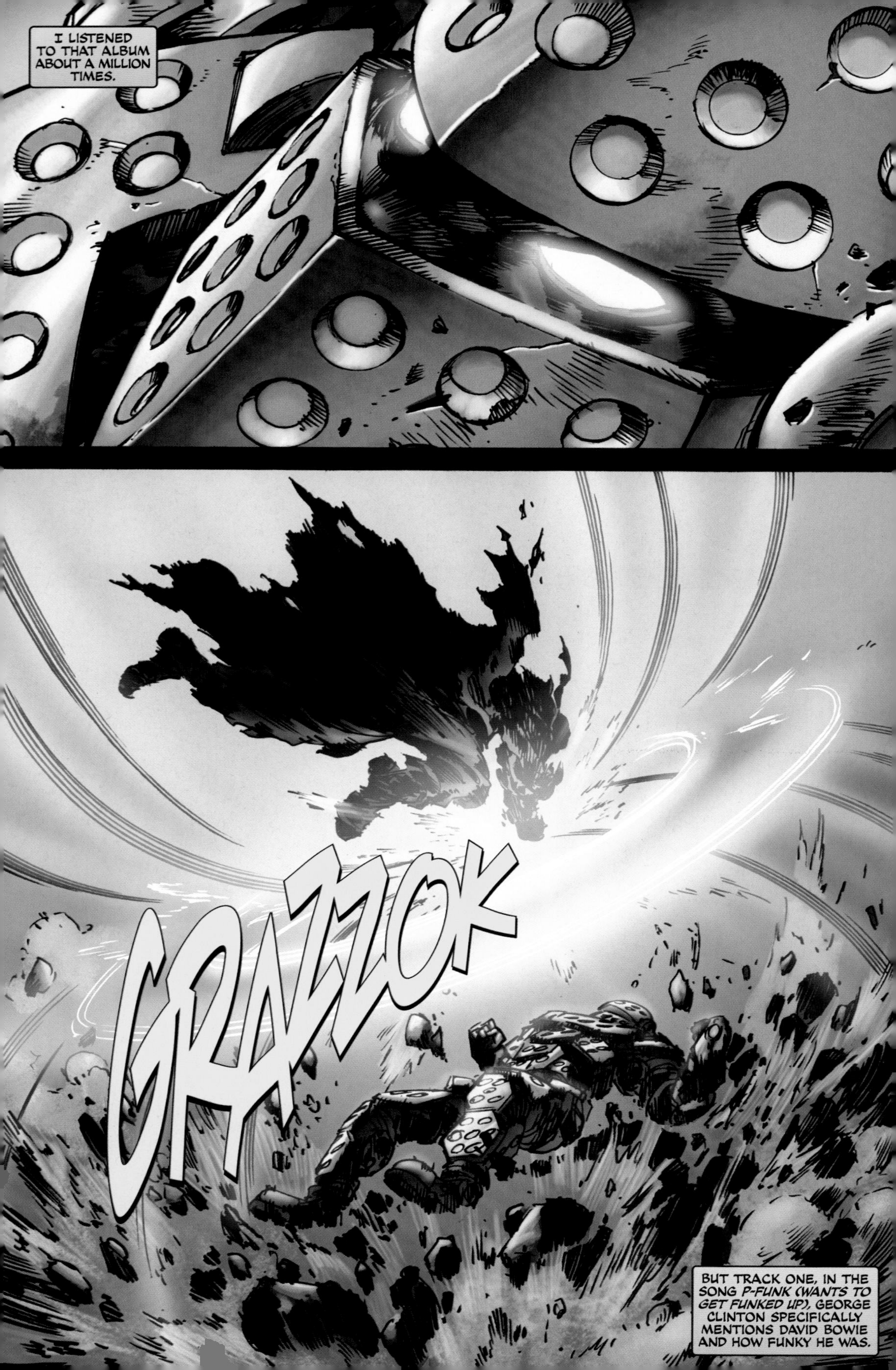
I LISTENED TO THAT ALBUM ABOUT A MILLION TIMES.
GRAZZOK
BUT TRACK ONE, IN THE SONG *P-FUNK (WANTS TO GET FUNKED UP)*, GEORGE CLINTON SPECIFICALLY MENTIONS DAVID BOWIE AND HOW FUNKY HE WAS.

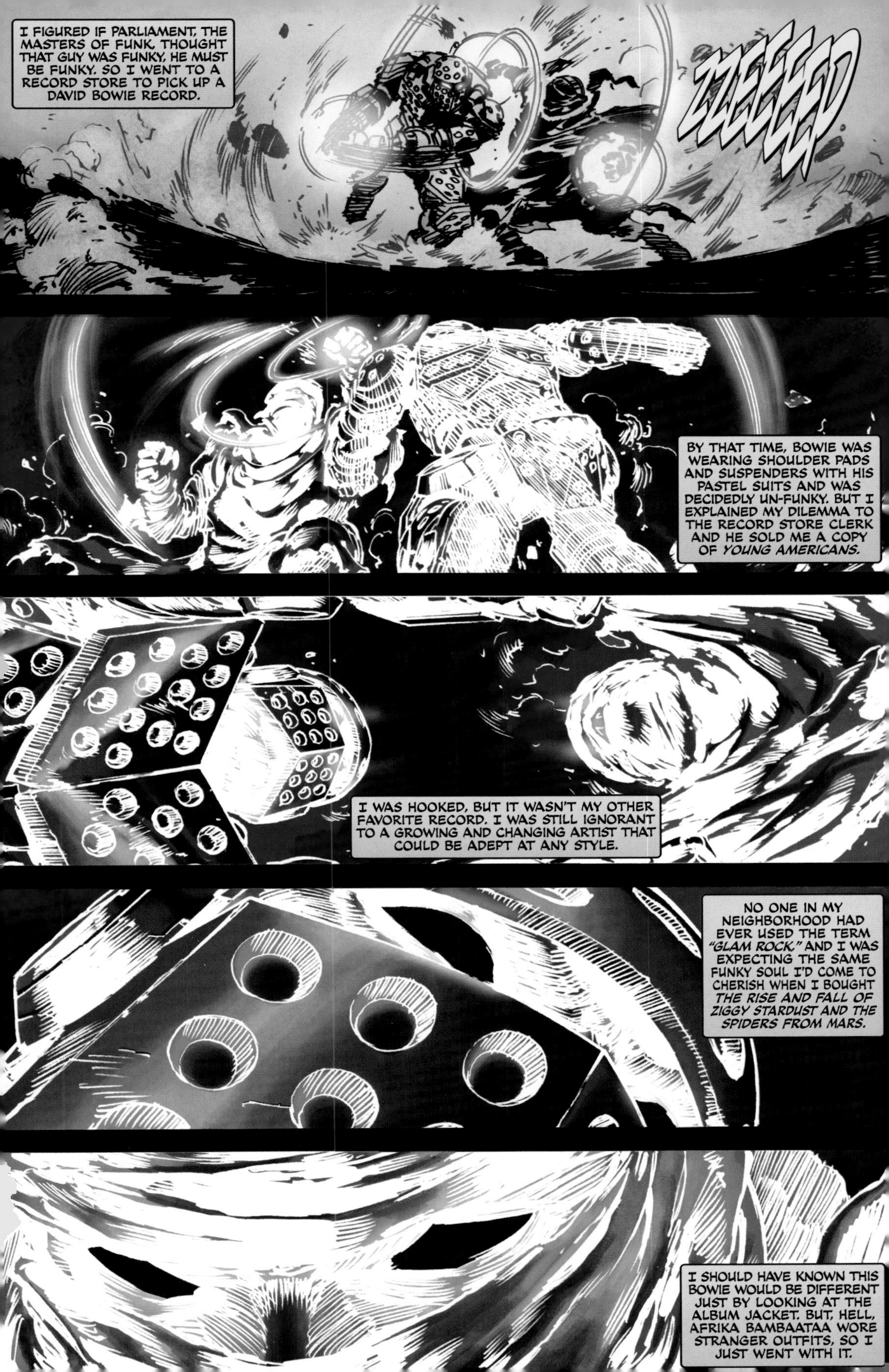
I FIGURED IF PARLIAMENT, THE MASTERS OF FUNK, THOUGHT THAT GUY WAS FUNKY, HE MUST BE FUNKY. SO I WENT TO A RECORD STORE TO PICK UP A DAVID BOWIE RECORD.
ZZEEEED
BY THAT TIME, BOWIE WAS WEARING SHOULDER PADS AND SUSPENDERS WITH HIS PASTEL SUITS AND WAS DECIDEDLY UN-FUNKY. BUT I EXPLAINED MY DILEMMA TO THE RECORD STORE CLERK AND HE SOLD ME A COPY OF *YOUNG AMERICANS.*
I WAS HOOKED, BUT IT WASN'T MY OTHER FAVORITE RECORD. I WAS STILL IGNORANT TO A GROWING AND CHANGING ARTIST THAT COULD BE ADEPT AT ANY STYLE.
NO ONE IN MY NEIGHBORHOOD HAD EVER USED THE TERM *"GLAM ROCK,"* AND I WAS EXPECTING THE SAME FUNKY SOUL I'D COME TO CHERISH WHEN I BOUGHT *THE RISE AND FALL OF ZIGGY STARDUST AND THE SPIDERS FROM MARS.*
I SHOULD HAVE KNOWN THIS BOWIE WOULD BE DIFFERENT JUST BY LOOKING AT THE ALBUM JACKET. BUT, HELL, AFRIKA BAMBAATAA WORE STRANGER OUTFITS, SO I JUST WENT WITH IT.

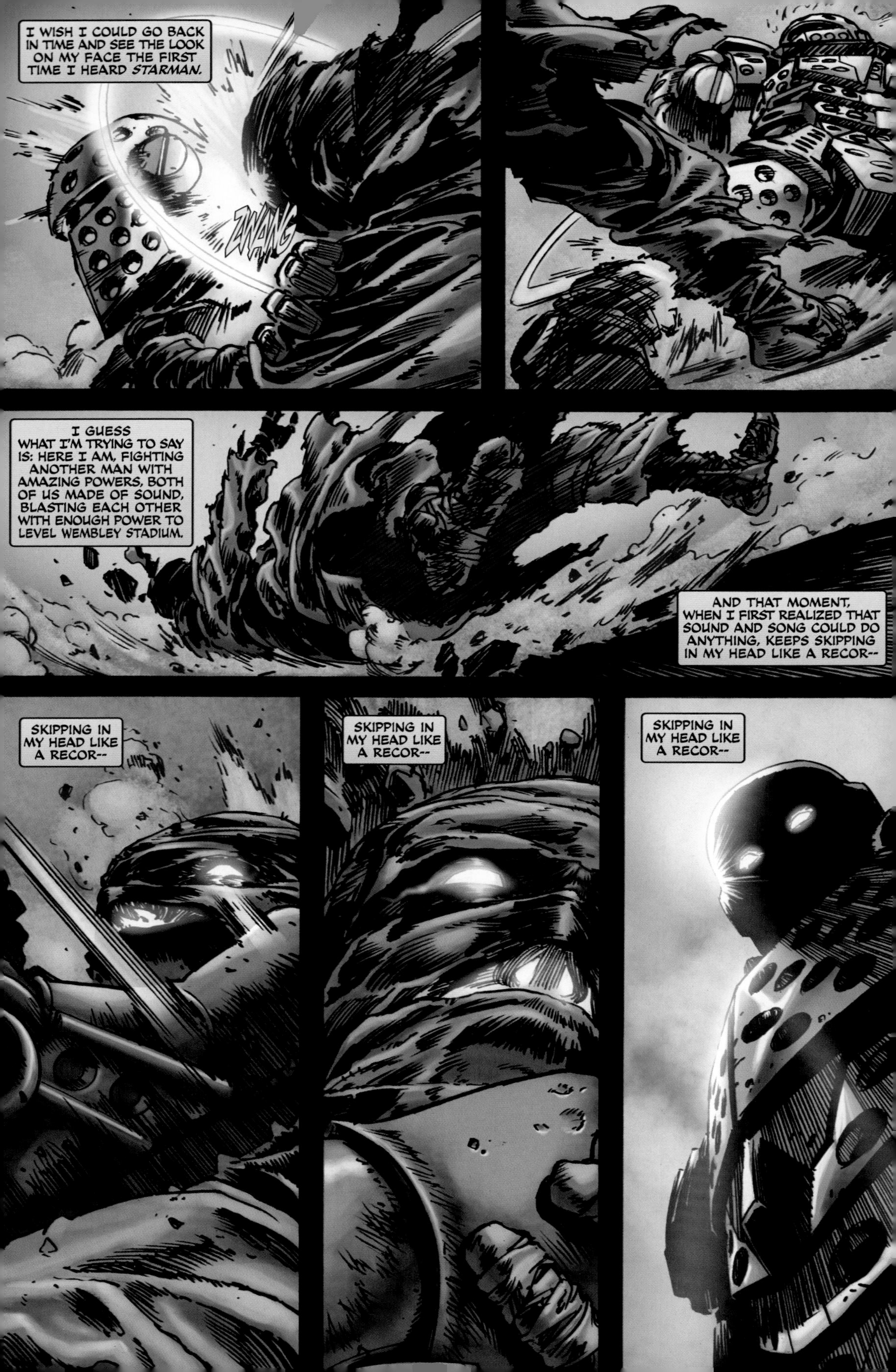
I WISH I COULD GO BACK IN TIME AND SEE THE LOOK ON MY FACE THE FIRST TIME I HEARD STARMAN.
ZWANG
I GUESS WHAT I'M TRYING TO SAY IS: HERE I AM, FIGHTING ANOTHER MAN WITH AMAZING POWERS, BOTH OF US MADE OF SOUND, BLASTING EACH OTHER WITH ENOUGH POWER TO LEVEL WEMBLEY STADIUM.
AND THAT MOMENT, WHEN I FIRST REALIZED THAT SOUND AND SONG COULD DO ANYTHING, KEEPS SKIPPING IN MY HEAD LIKE A RECOR--
SKIPPING IN MY HEAD LIKE A RECOR--
SKIPPING IN MY HEAD LIKE A RECOR--
SKIPPING IN MY HEAD LIKE A RECOR--

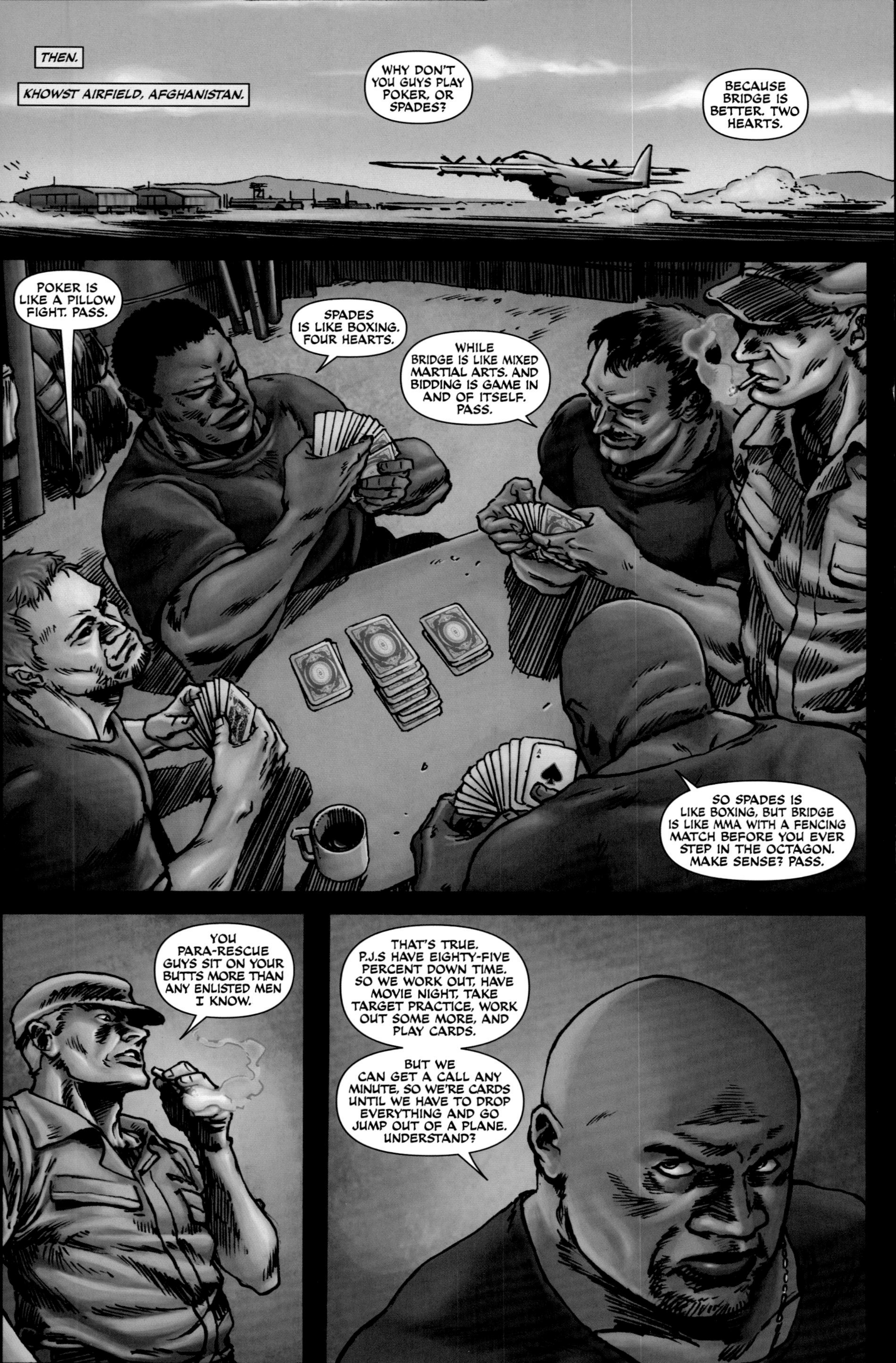

THEN.
KHOWST AIRFIELD, AFGHANISTAN.
WHY DON'T YOU GUYS PLAY POKER, OR SPADES?
BECAUSE BRIDGE IS BETTER. TWO HEARTS.
POKER IS LIKE A PILLOW FIGHT. PASS.
SPADES IS LIKE BOXING. FOUR HEARTS.
WHILE BRIDGE IS LIKE MIXED MARTIAL ARTS. AND BIDDING IS GAME IN AND OF ITSELF. PASS.
SO SPADES IS LIKE BOXING, BUT BRIDGE IS LIKE MMA WITH A FENCING MATCH BEFORE YOU EVER STEP IN THE OCTAGON. MAKE SENSE? PASS.
YOU PARA-RESCUE GUYS SIT ON YOUR BUTTS MORE THAN ANY ENLISTED MEN I KNOW.
THAT'S TRUE. P.J.S HAVE EIGHTY-FIVE PERCENT DOWN TIME. SO WE WORK OUT, HAVE MOVIE NIGHT, TAKE TARGET PRACTICE, WORK OUT SOME MORE, AND PLAY CARDS.
BUT WE CAN GET A CALL ANY MINUTE, SO WE'RE CARDS UNTIL WE HAVE TO DROP EVERYTHING AND GO JUMP OUT OF A PLANE. UNDERSTAND?

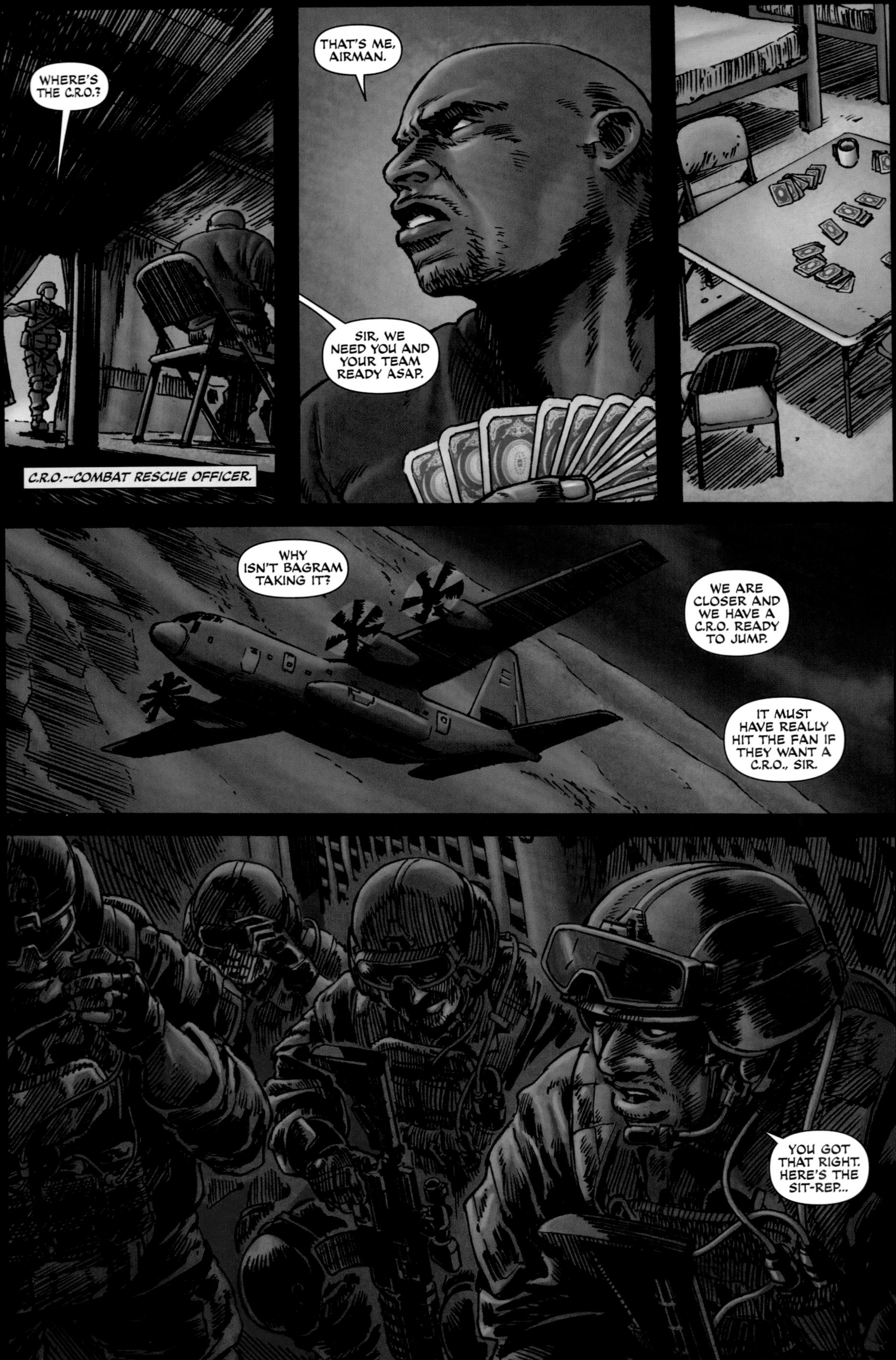
WHERE'S THE C.R.O.?
C.R.O.--COMBAT RESCUE OFFICER.
THAT'S ME, AIRMAN.
SIR, WE NEED YOU AND YOUR TEAM READY ASAP.
WHY ISN'T BAGRAM TAKING IT?
WE ARE CLOSER AND WE HAVE A C.R.O. READY TO JUMP.
IT MUST HAVE REALLY HIT THE FAN IF THEY WANT A C.R.O., SIR.
YOU GOT THAT RIGHT. HERE'S THE SIT-REP...

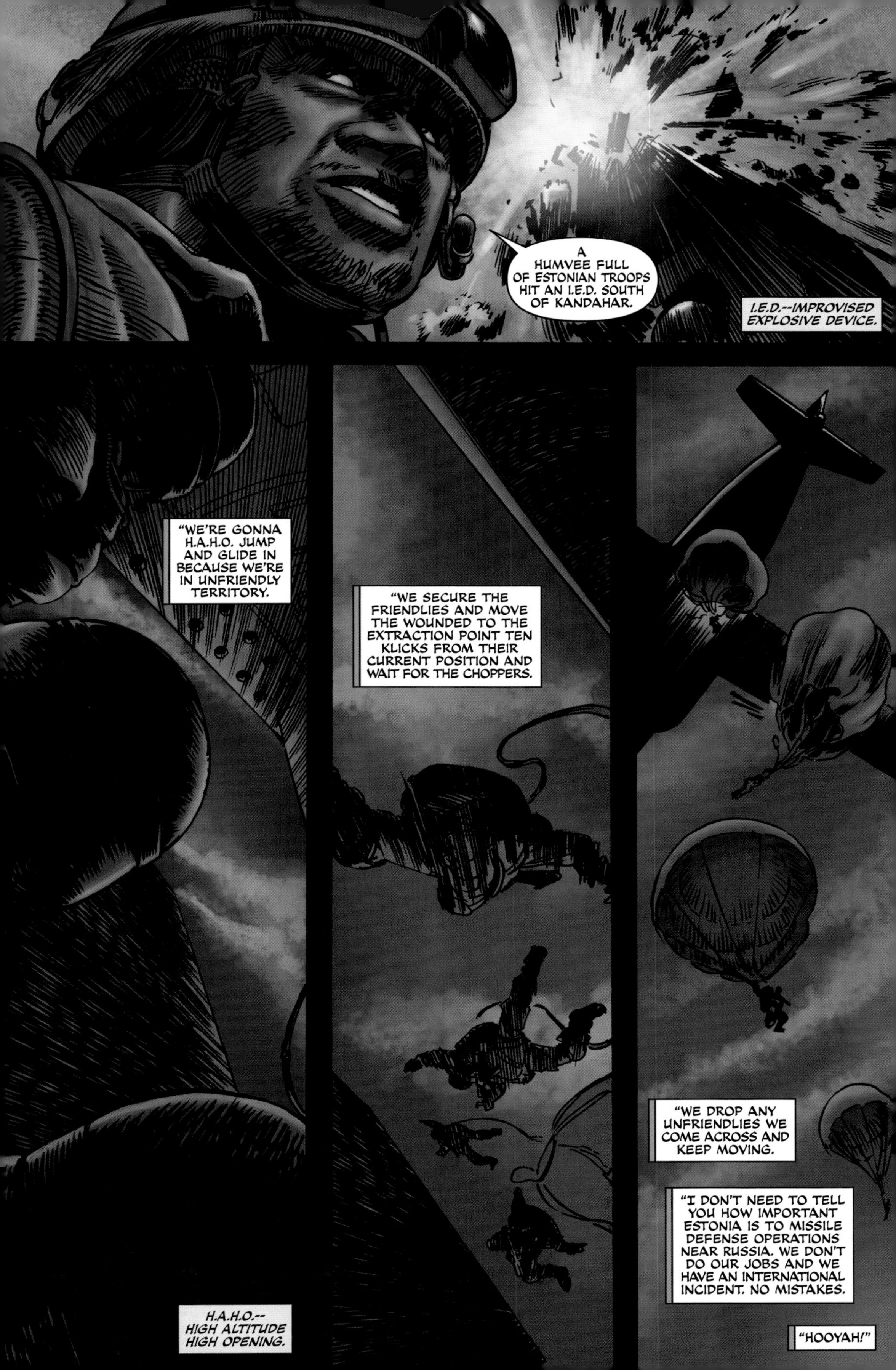
A HUMVEE FULL OF ESTONIAN TROOPS HIT AN I.E.D. SOUTH OF KANDAHAR.
I.E.D.--IMPROVISED EXPLOSIVE DEVICE.
"WE'RE GONNA H.A.H.O. JUMP AND GLIDE IN BECAUSE WE'RE IN UNFRIENDLY TERRITORY.
H.A.H.O.--HIGH ALTITUDE HIGH OPENING.
"WE SECURE THE FRIENDLIES AND MOVE THE WOUNDED TO THE EXTRACTION POINT TEN KLICKS FROM THEIR CURRENT POSITION AND WAIT FOR THE CHOPPERS.
"WE DROP ANY UNFRIENDLIES WE COME ACROSS AND KEEP MOVING.
"I DON'T NEED TO TELL YOU HOW IMPORTANT ESTONIA IS TO MISSILE DEFENSE OPERATIONS NEAR RUSSIA. WE DON'T DO OUR JOBS AND WE HAVE AN INTERNATIONAL INCIDENT. NO MISTAKES.
"HOOYAH!"

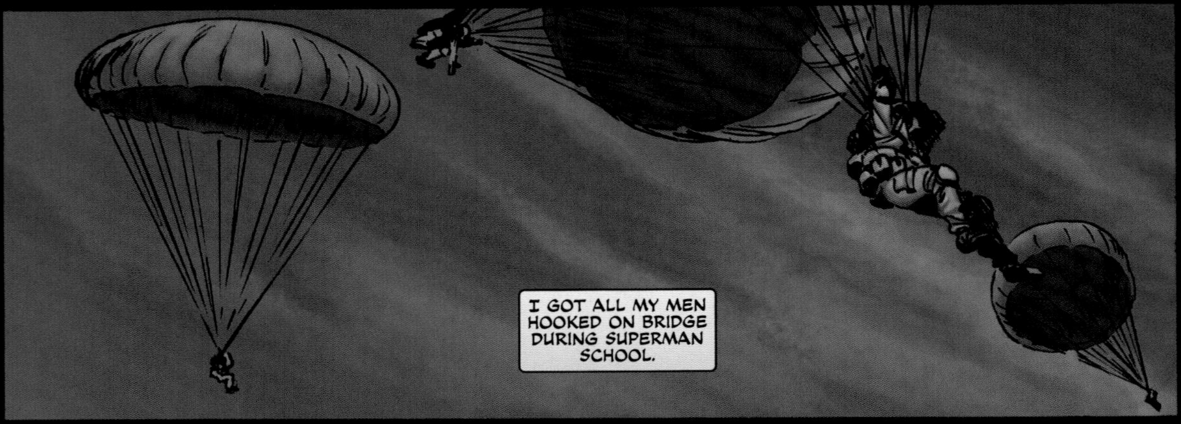
I GOT ALL MY MEN HOOKED ON BRIDGE DURING SUPERMAN SCHOOL.

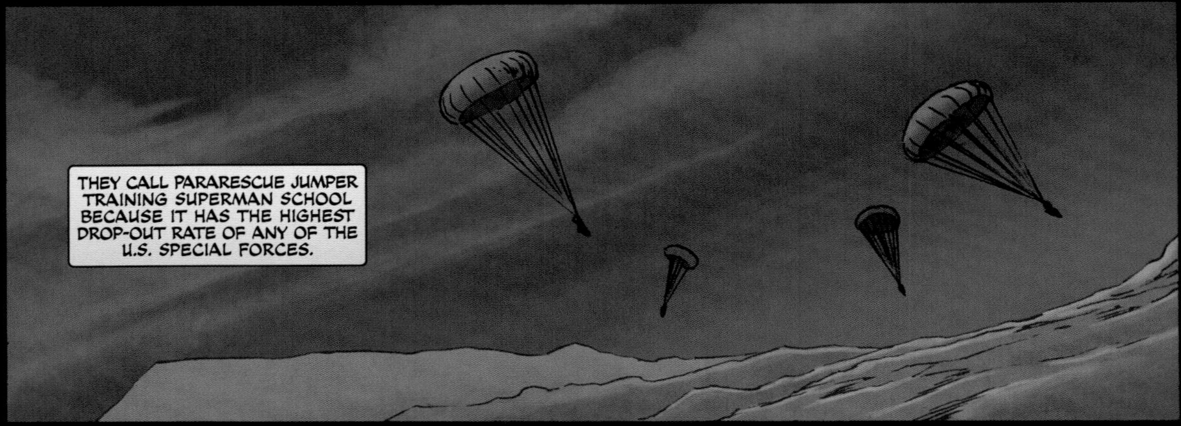
THEY CALL PARARESCUE JUMPER TRAINING SUPERMAN SCHOOL BECAUSE IT HAS THE HIGHEST DROP-OUT RATE OF ANY OF THE U.S. SPECIAL FORCES.

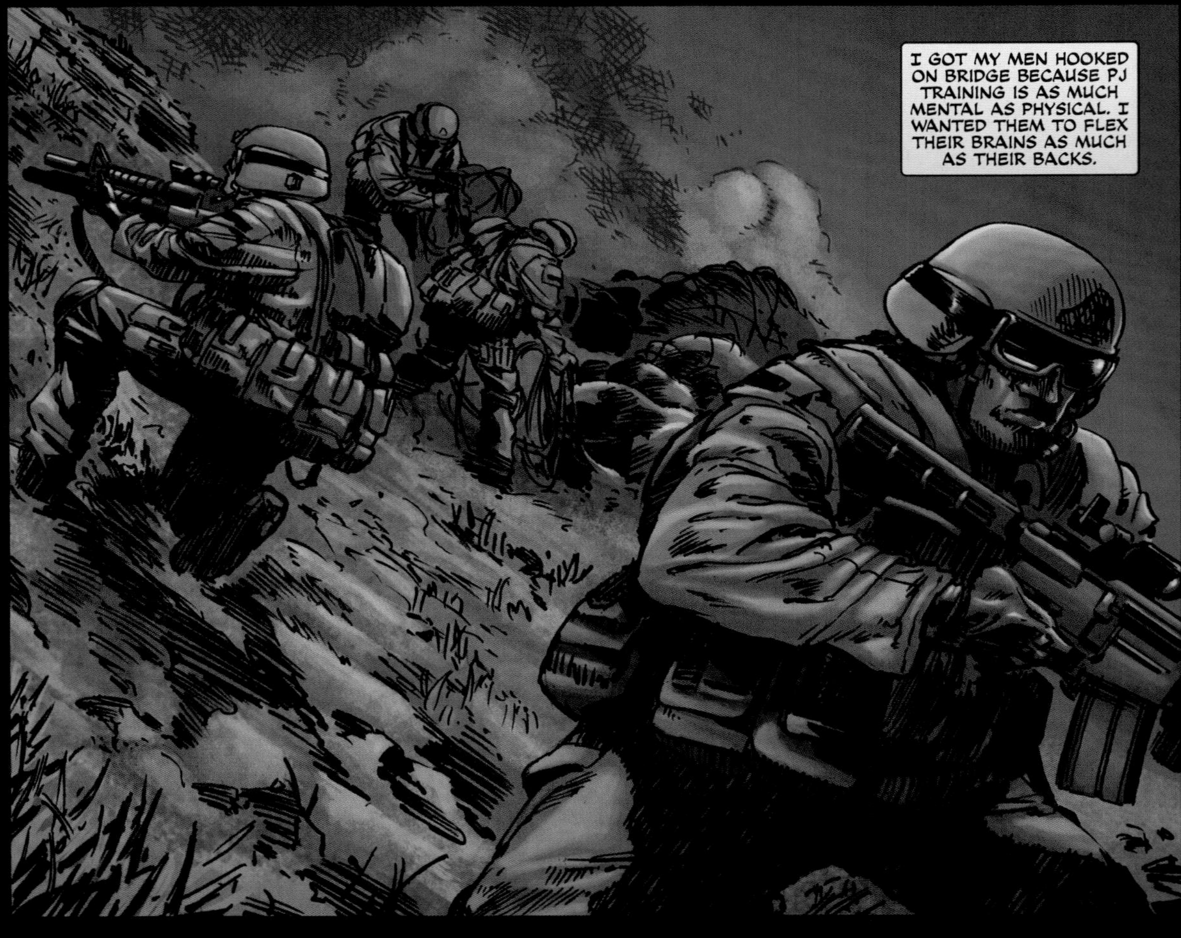
I GOT MY MEN HOOKED ON BRIDGE BECAUSE PJ TRAINING IS AS MUCH MENTAL AS PHYSICAL. I WANTED THEM TO FLEX THEIR BRAINS AS MUCH AS THEIR BACKS.

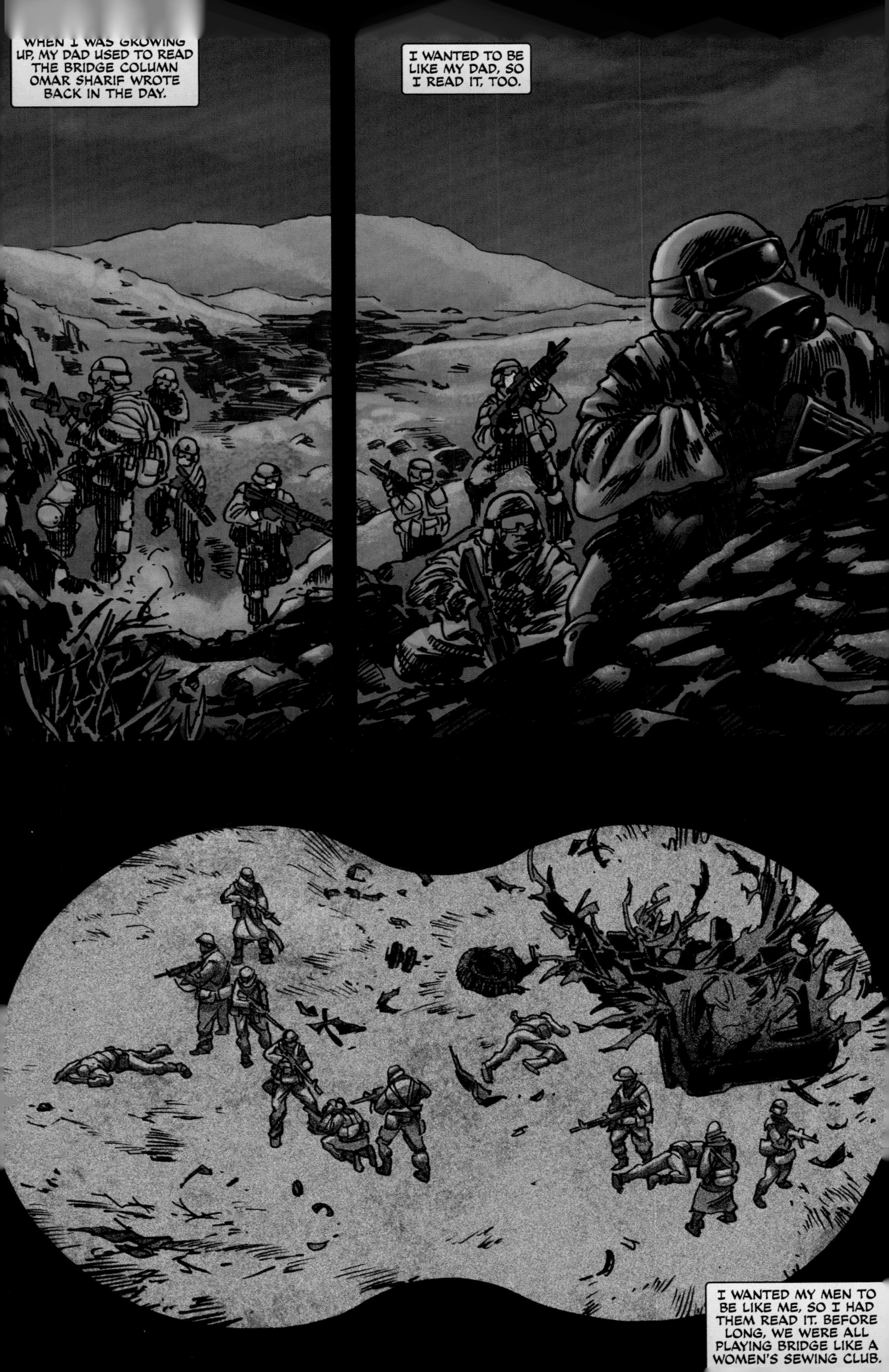
WHEN I WAS GROWING UP, MY DAD USED TO READ THE BRIDGE COLUMN OMAR SHARIF WROTE BACK IN THE DAY.
I WANTED TO BE LIKE MY DAD, SO I READ IT, TOO.
I WANTED MY MEN TO BE LIKE ME, SO I HAD THEM READ IT. BEFORE LONG, WE WERE ALL PLAYING BRIDGE LIKE A WOMEN'S SEWING CLUB.

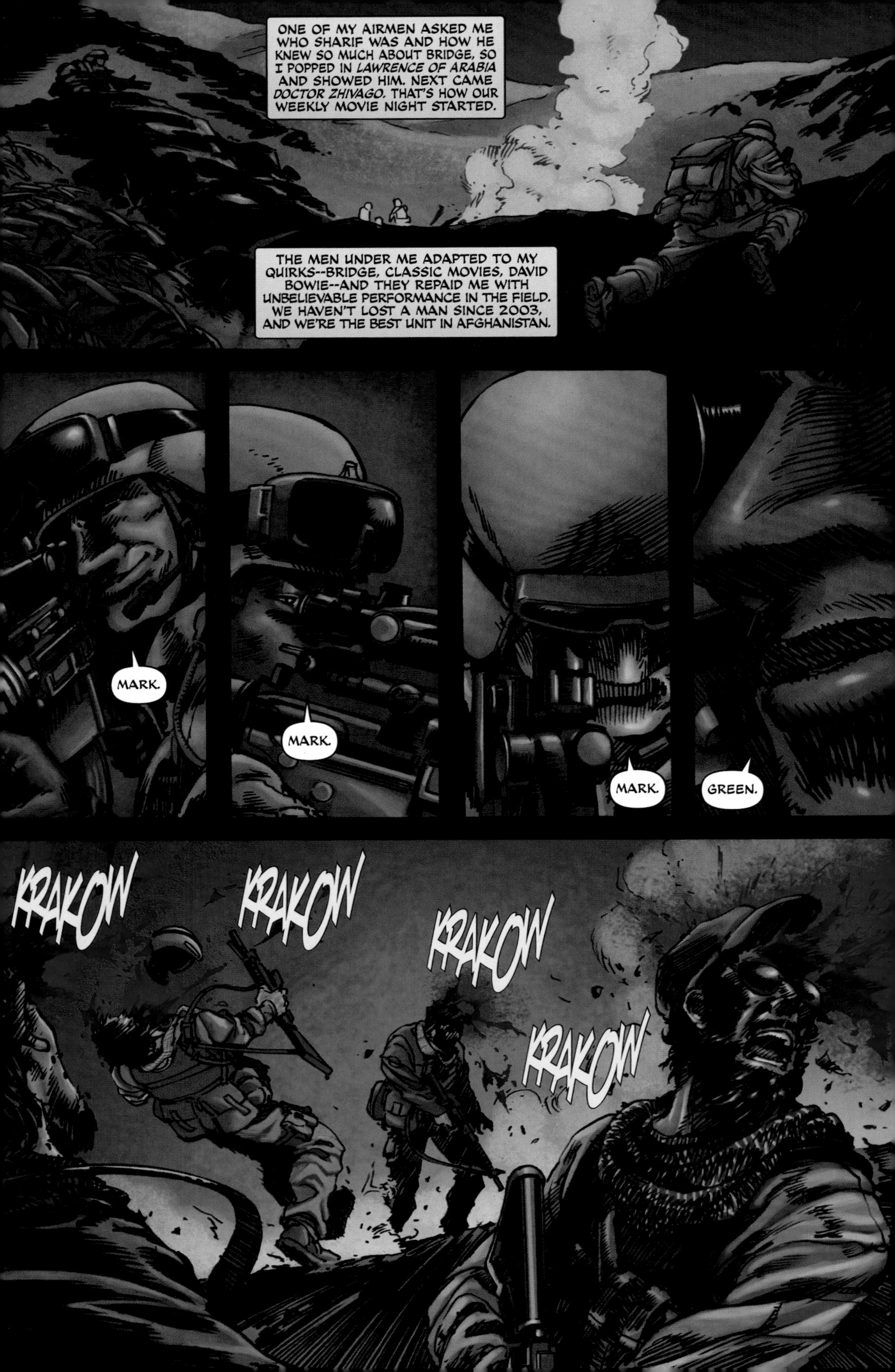
ONE OF MY AIRMEN ASKED ME WHO SHARIF WAS AND HOW HE KNEW SO MUCH ABOUT BRIDGE, SO I POPPED IN *LAWRENCE OF ARABIA* AND SHOWED HIM. NEXT CAME *DOCTOR ZHIVAGO*. THAT'S HOW OUR WEEKLY MOVIE NIGHT STARTED.
THE MEN UNDER ME ADAPTED TO MY QUIRKS--BRIDGE, CLASSIC MOVIES, DAVID BOWIE--AND THEY REPAID ME WITH UNBELIEVABLE PERFORMANCE IN THE FIELD. WE HAVEN'T LOST A MAN SINCE 2003, AND WE'RE THE BEST UNIT IN AFGHANISTAN.
MARK.
MARK.
MARK.
GREEN.
KRAKOW
KRAKOW
KRAKOW
KRAKOW

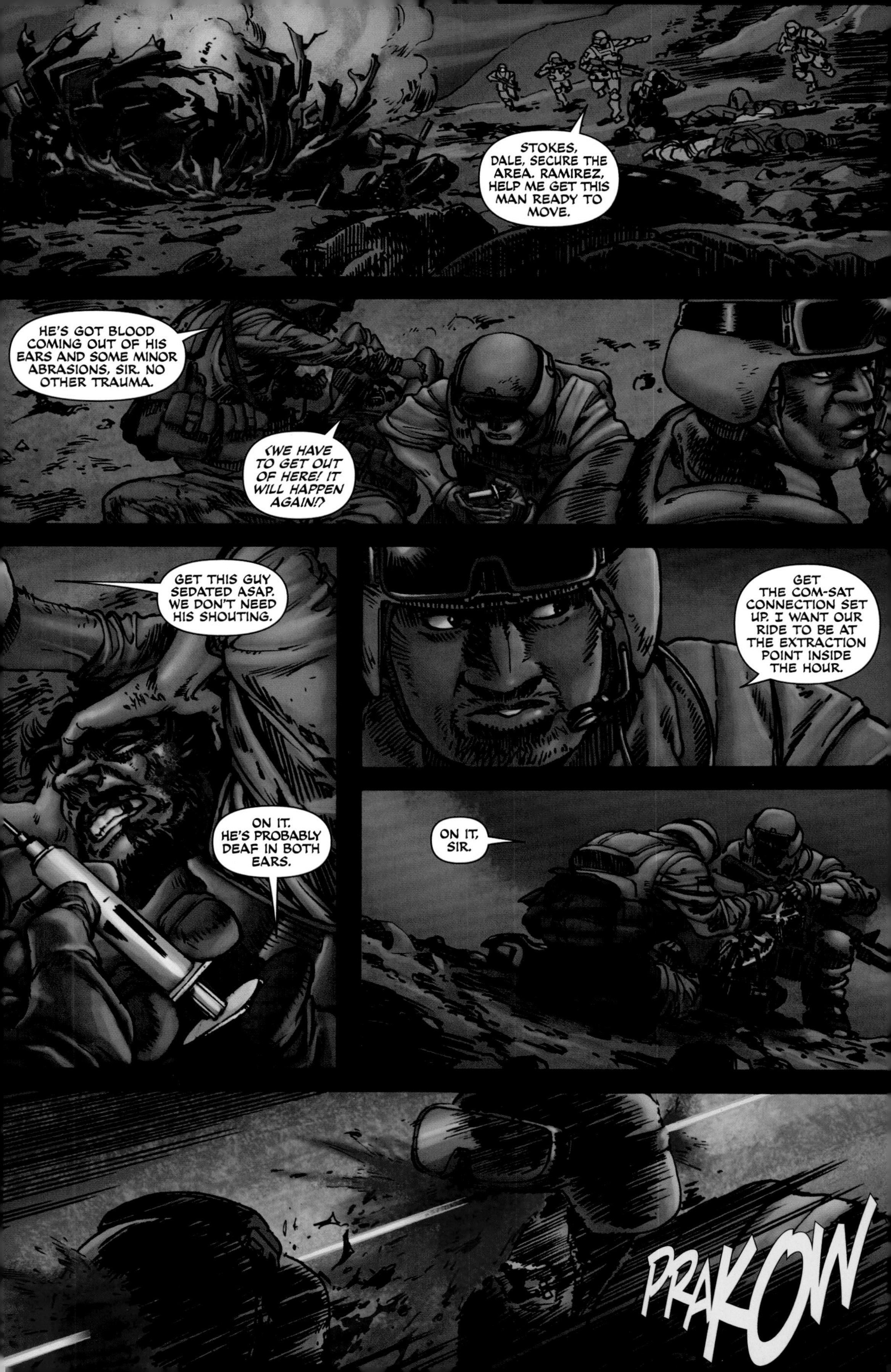
STOKES, DALE, SECURE THE AREA. RAMIREZ, HELP ME GET THIS MAN READY TO MOVE.
HE'S GOT BLOOD COMING OUT OF HIS EARS AND SOME MINOR ABRASIONS, SIR. NO OTHER TRAUMA.
<WE HAVE TO GET OUT OF HERE! IT WILL HAPPEN AGAIN!>
GET THIS GUY SEDATED ASAP. WE DON'T NEED HIS SHOUTING.
ON IT. HE'S PROBABLY DEAF IN BOTH EARS.
GET THE COM-SAT CONNECTION SET UP. I WANT OUR RIDE TO BE AT THE EXTRACTION POINT INSIDE THE HOUR.
ON IT, SIR.
PRAKOW

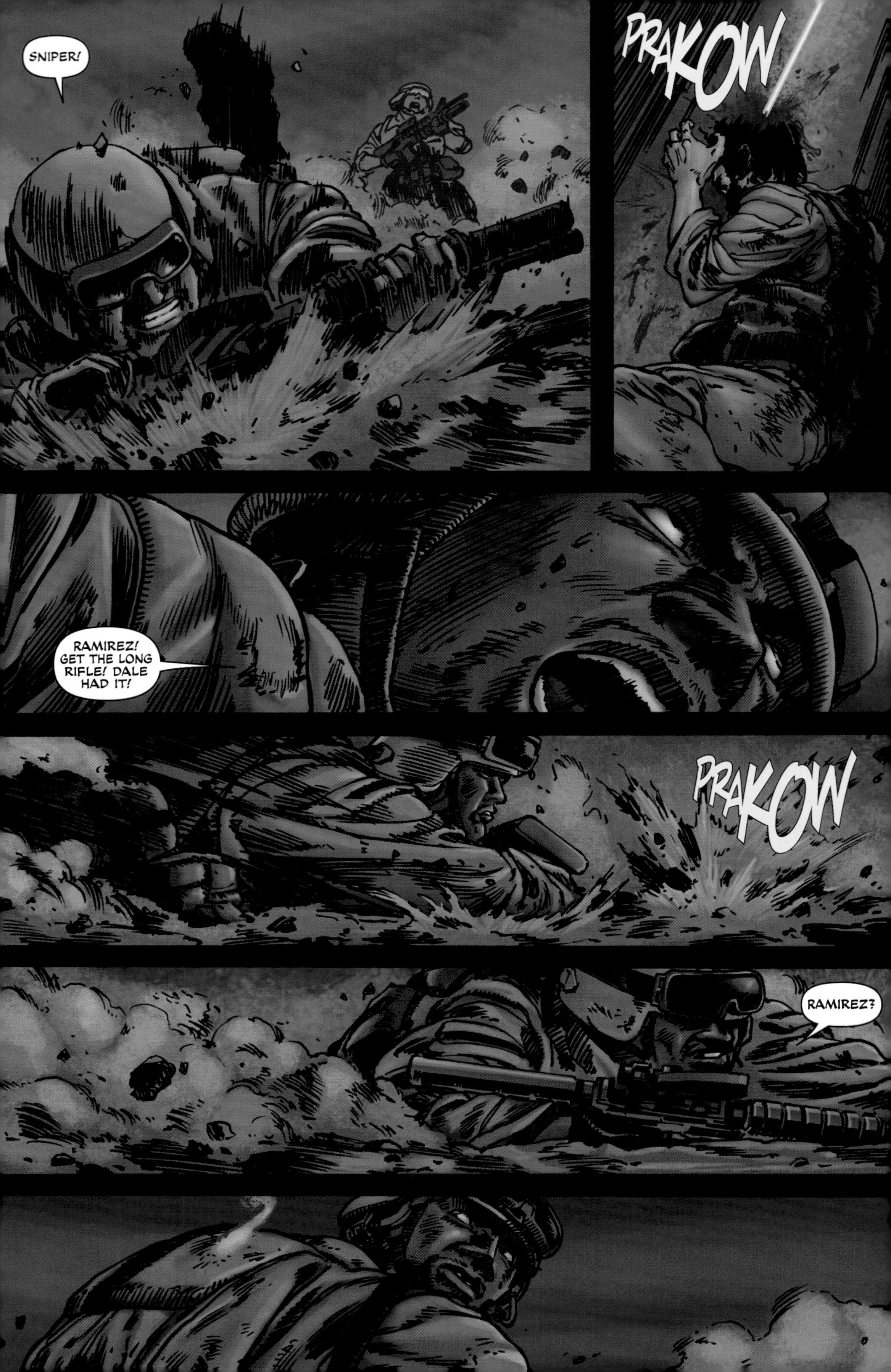
SNIPER!
PRAKOW
RAMIREZ! GET THE LONG RIFLE! DALE HAD IT!
PRAKOW
RAMIREZ?

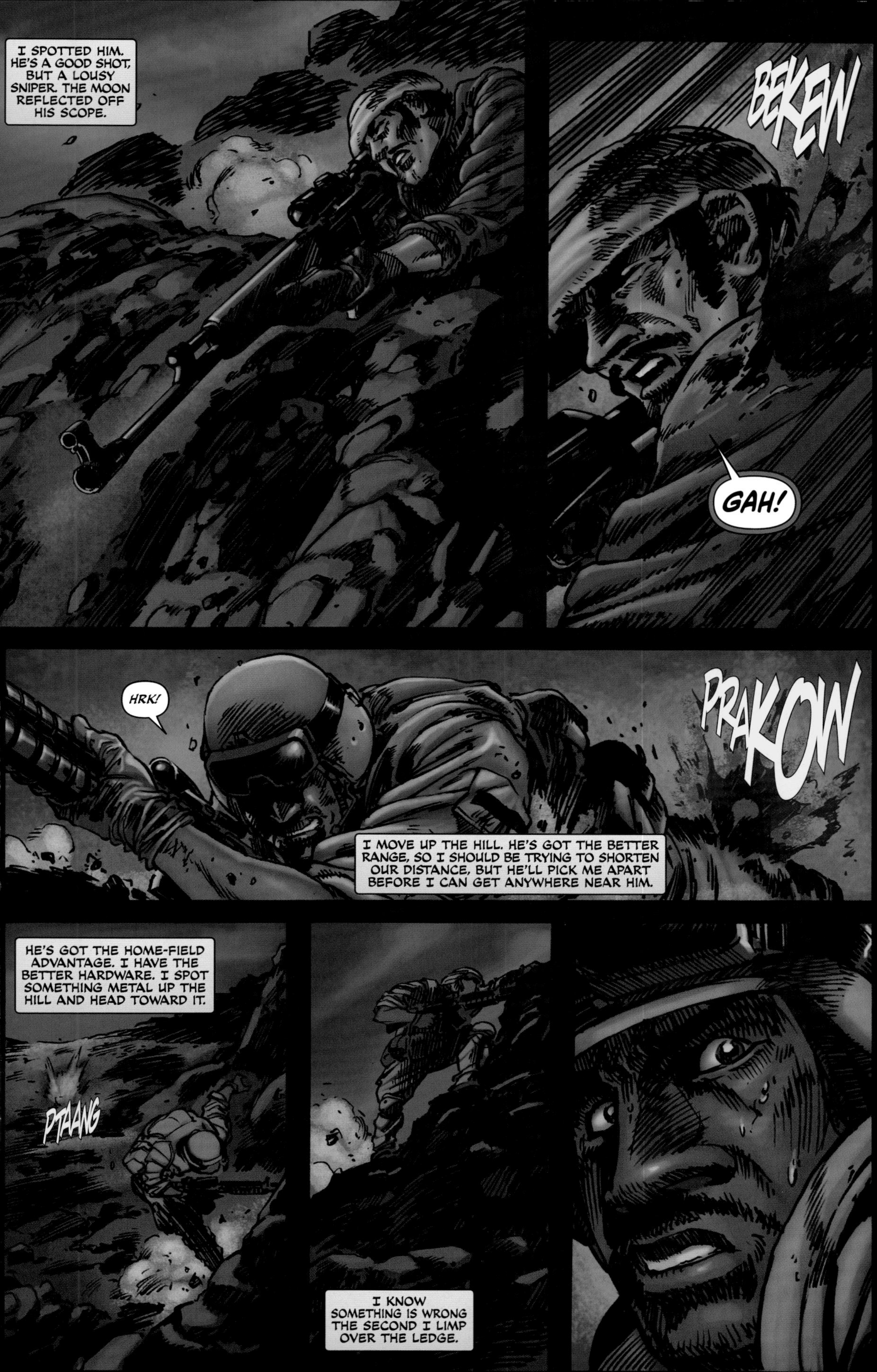

I SPOTTED HIM. HE'S A GOOD SHOT, BUT A LOUSY SNIPER. THE MOON REFLECTED OFF HIS SCOPE.
BEKEW
GAH!
HRK!
PRAKOW
I MOVE UP THE HILL. HE'S GOT THE BETTER RANGE, SO I SHOULD BE TRYING TO SHORTEN OUR DISTANCE, BUT HE'LL PICK ME APART BEFORE I CAN GET ANYWHERE NEAR HIM.
HE'S GOT THE HOME-FIELD ADVANTAGE. I HAVE THE BETTER HARDWARE. I SPOT SOMETHING METAL UP THE HILL AND HEAD TOWARD IT.
PTAANG
I KNOW SOMETHING IS WRONG THE SECOND I LIMP OVER THE LEDGE.

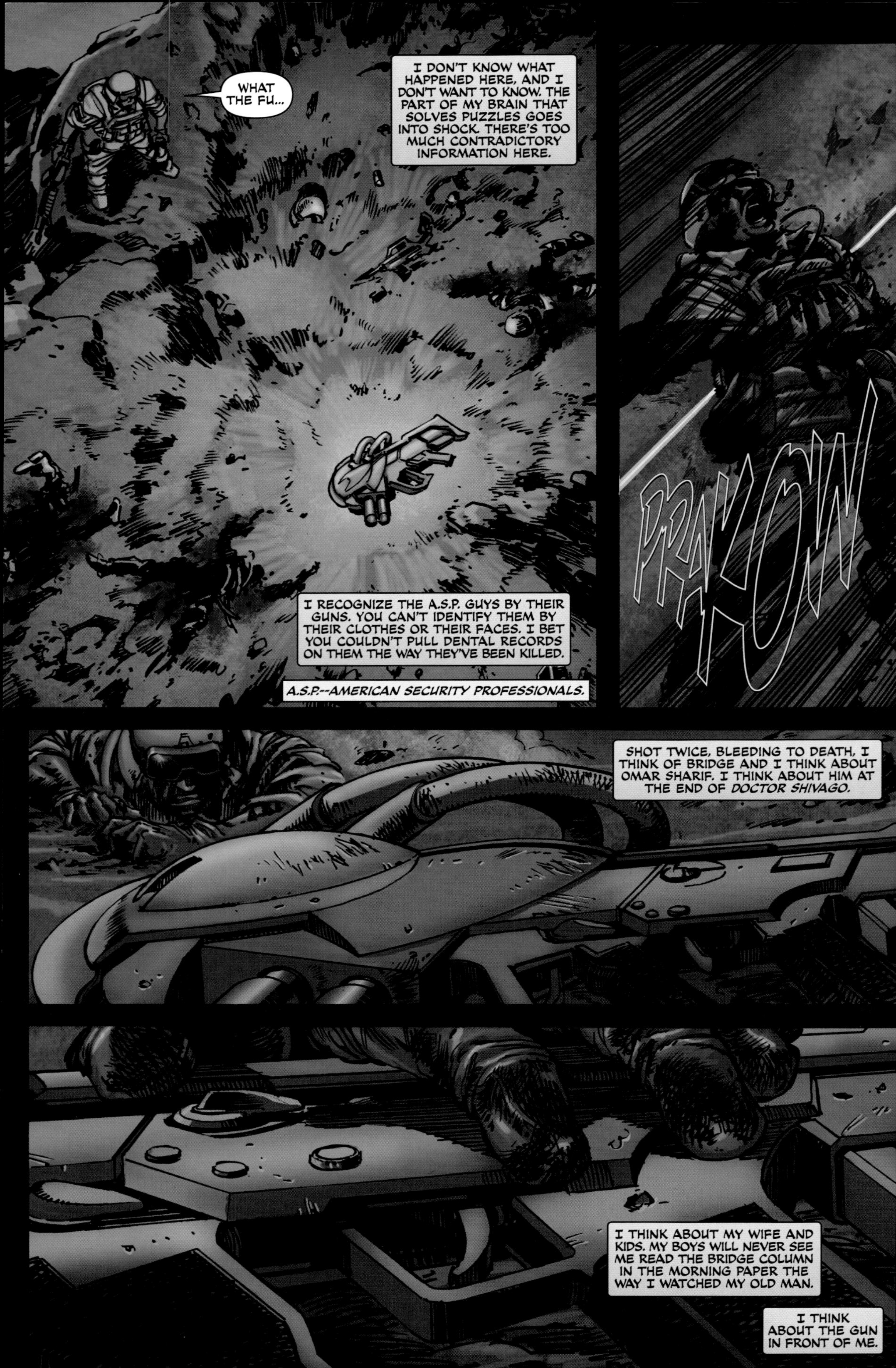
WHAT THE FU...
I DON'T KNOW WHAT HAPPENED HERE, AND I DON'T WANT TO KNOW. THE PART OF MY BRAIN THAT SOLVES PUZZLES GOES INTO SHOCK. THERE'S TOO MUCH CONTRADICTORY INFORMATION HERE.
I RECOGNIZE THE A.S.P. GUYS BY THEIR GUNS. YOU CAN'T IDENTIFY THEM BY THEIR CLOTHES OR THEIR FACES. I BET YOU COULDN'T PULL DENTAL RECORDS ON THEM THE WAY THEY'VE BEEN KILLED.
A.S.P.--AMERICAN SECURITY PROFESSIONALS.
PRAKOW
SHOT TWICE, BLEEDING TO DEATH, I THINK OF BRIDGE AND I THINK ABOUT OMAR SHARIF. I THINK ABOUT HIM AT THE END OF DOCTOR SHIVAGO.
I THINK ABOUT MY WIFE AND KIDS. MY BOYS WILL NEVER SEE ME READ THE BRIDGE COLUMN IN THE MORNING PAPER THE WAY I WATCHED MY OLD MAN.
I THINK ABOUT THE GUN IN FRONT OF ME.

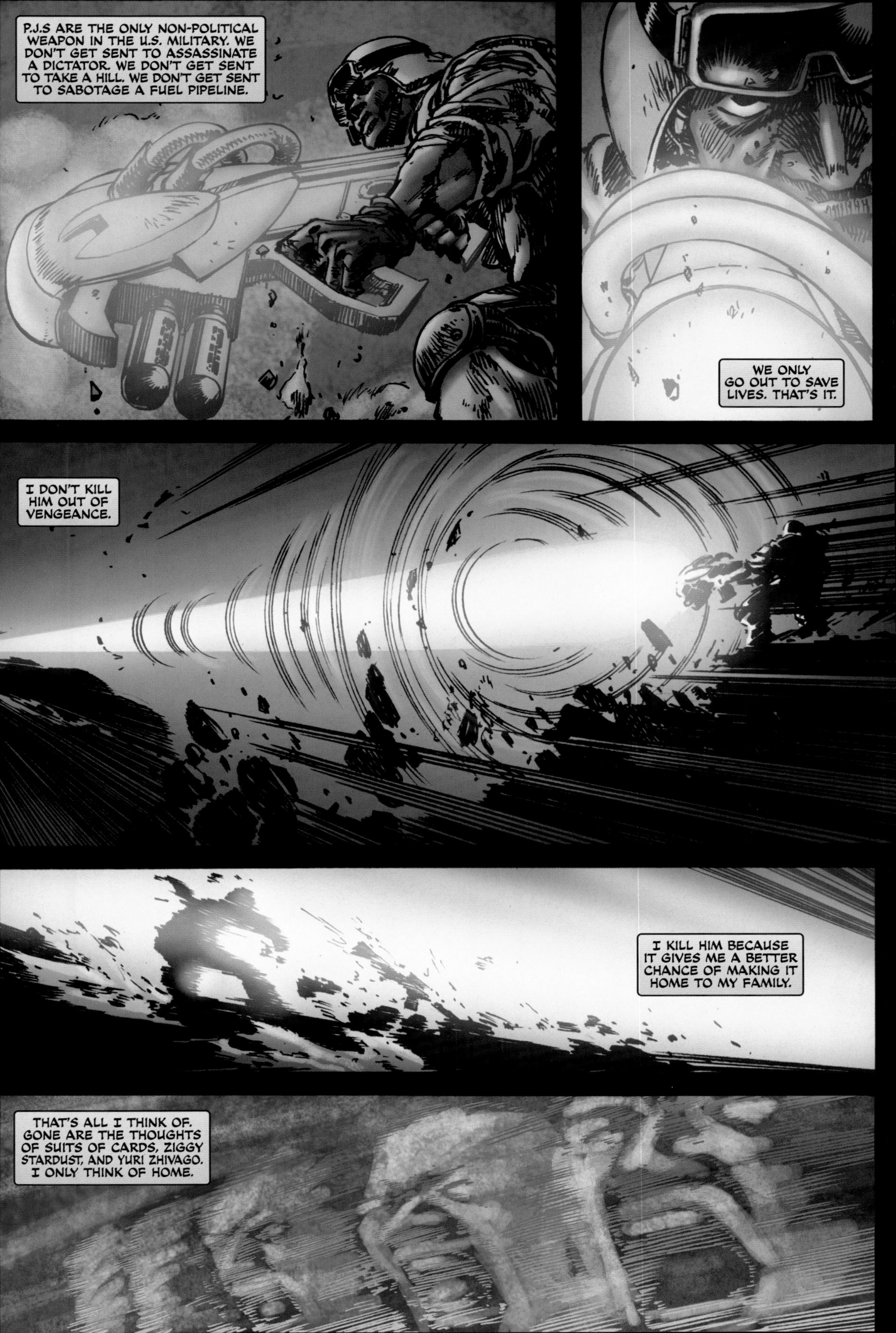
P.J.S ARE THE ONLY NON-POLITICAL WEAPON IN THE U.S. MILITARY. WE DON'T GET SENT TO ASSASSINATE A DICTATOR. WE DON'T GET SENT TO TAKE A HILL. WE DON'T GET SENT TO SABOTAGE A FUEL PIPELINE.
WE ONLY GO OUT TO SAVE LIVES. THAT'S IT.
I DON'T KILL HIM OUT OF VENGEANCE.
I KILL HIM BECAUSE IT GIVES ME A BETTER CHANCE OF MAKING IT HOME TO MY FAMILY.
THAT'S ALL I THINK OF. GONE ARE THE THOUGHTS OF SUITS OF CARDS, ZIGGY STARDUST, AND YURI ZHIVAGO. I ONLY THINK OF HOME.

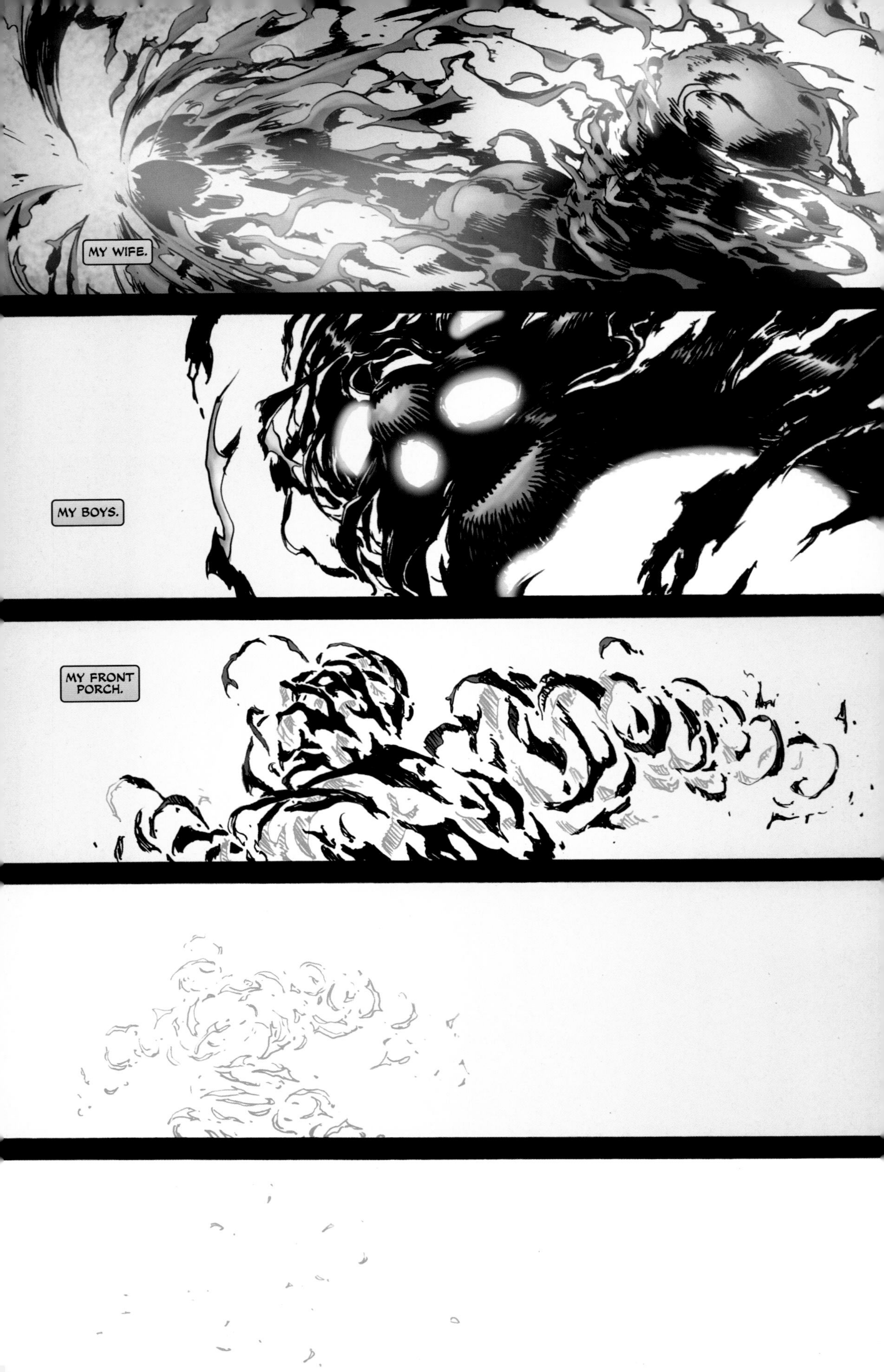
MY WIFE.
MY BOYS.
MY FRONT PORCH.

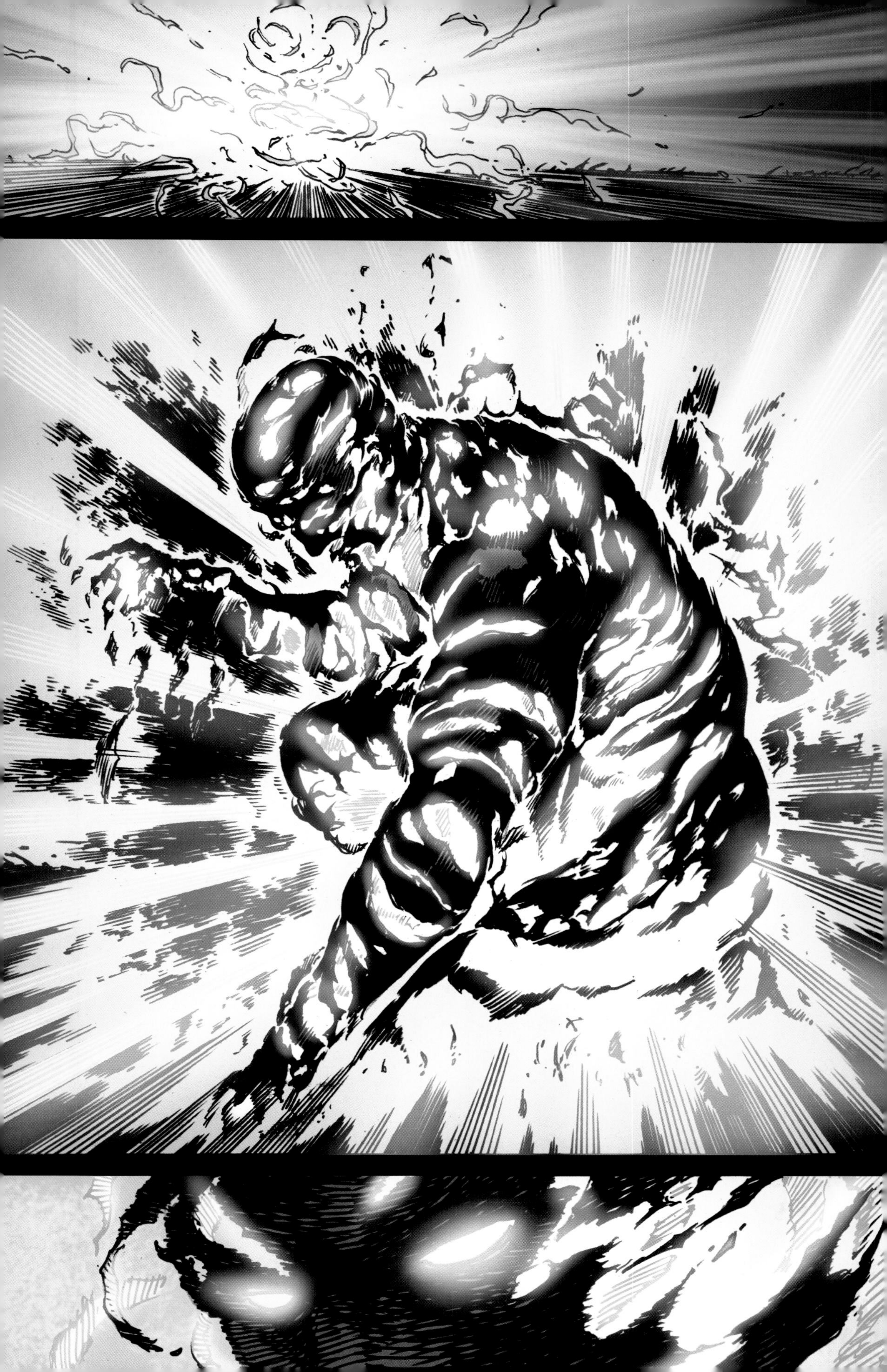

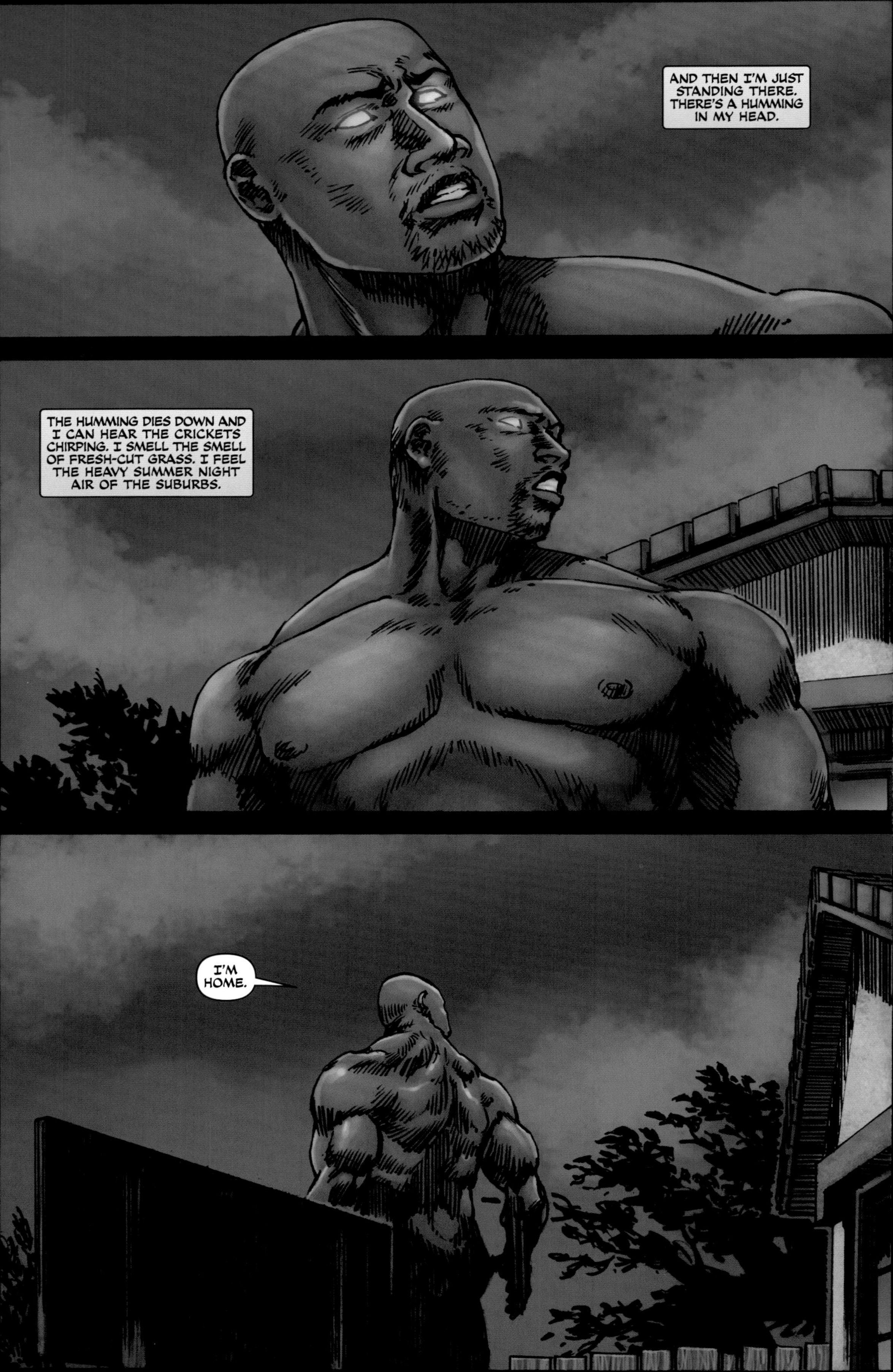
AND THEN I'M JUST STANDING THERE. THERE'S A HUMMING IN MY HEAD.
THE HUMMING DIES DOWN AND I CAN HEAR THE CRICKETS CHIRPING. I SMELL THE SMELL OF FRESH-CUT GRASS. I FEEL THE HEAVY SUMMER NIGHT AIR OF THE SUBURBS.
I'M HOME.

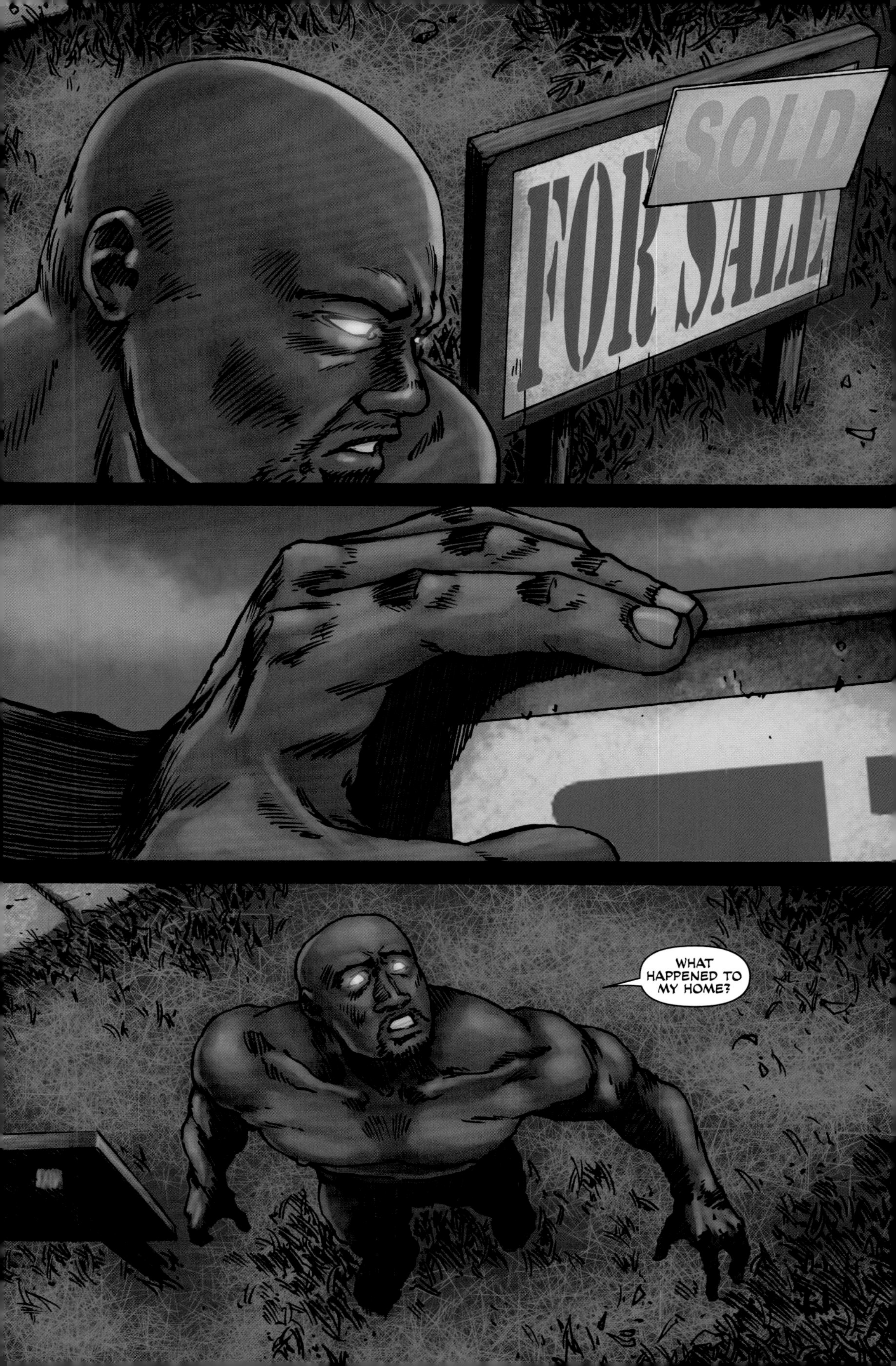
SOLD
FOR SALE
WHAT HAPPENED TO MY HOME?

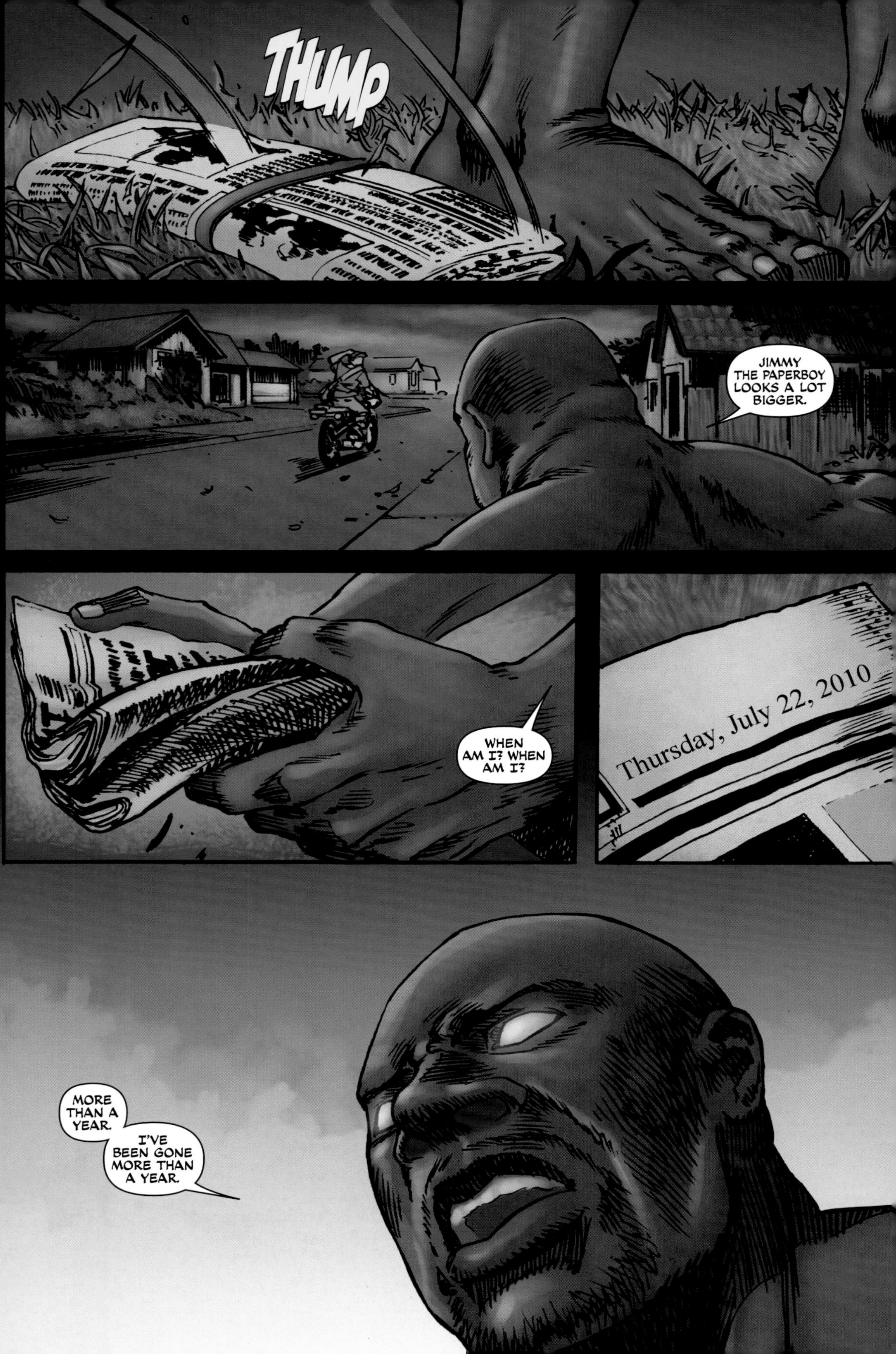
THUMP
JIMMY THE PAPERBOY LOOKS A LOT BIGGER.
WHEN AM I? WHEN AM I?
Thursday, July 22, 2010
MORE THAN A YEAR.
I'VE BEEN GONE MORE THAN A YEAR.

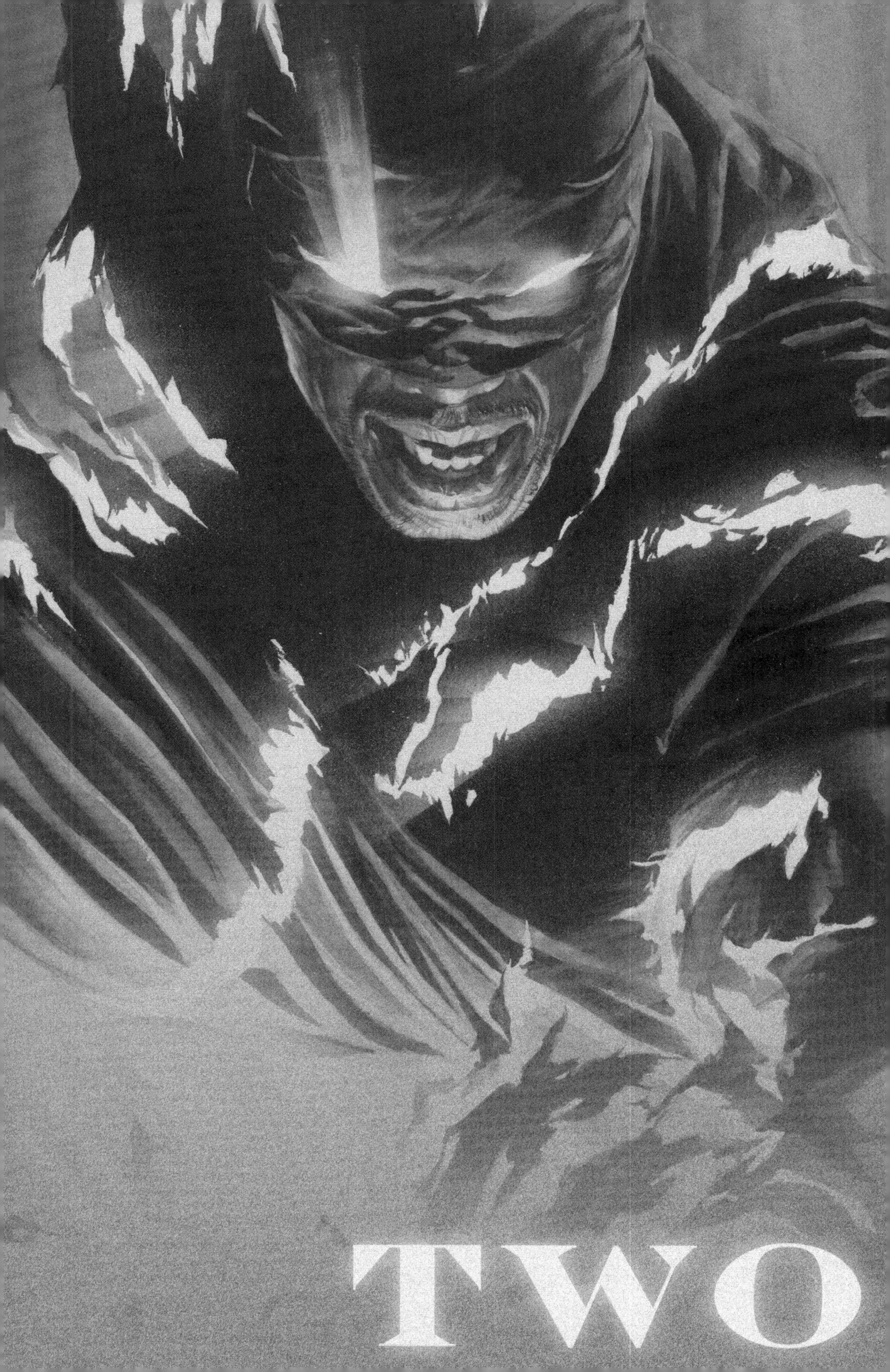
TWO

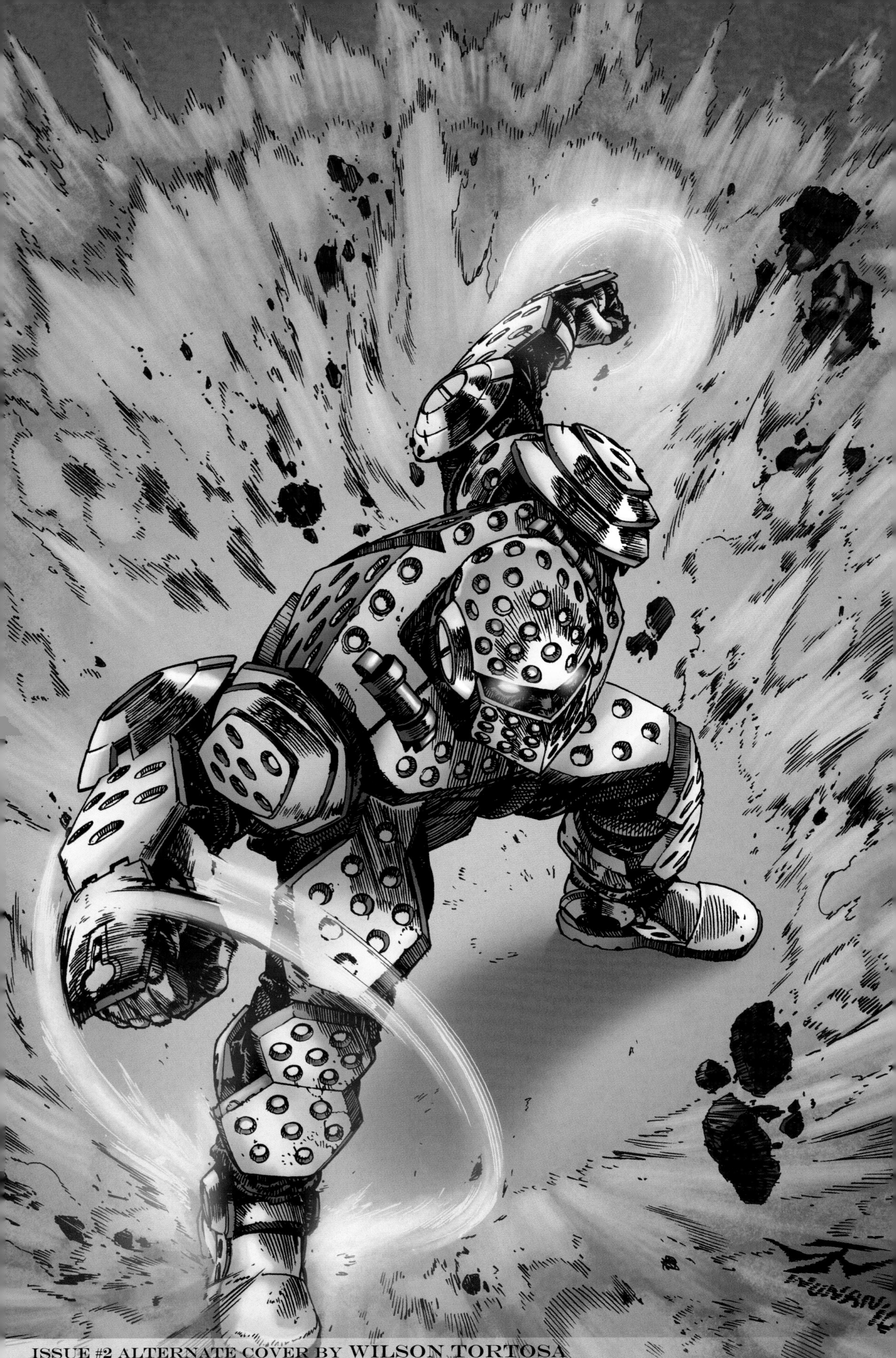

ISSUE #2 ALTERNATE COVER BY WILSON TORTOSA

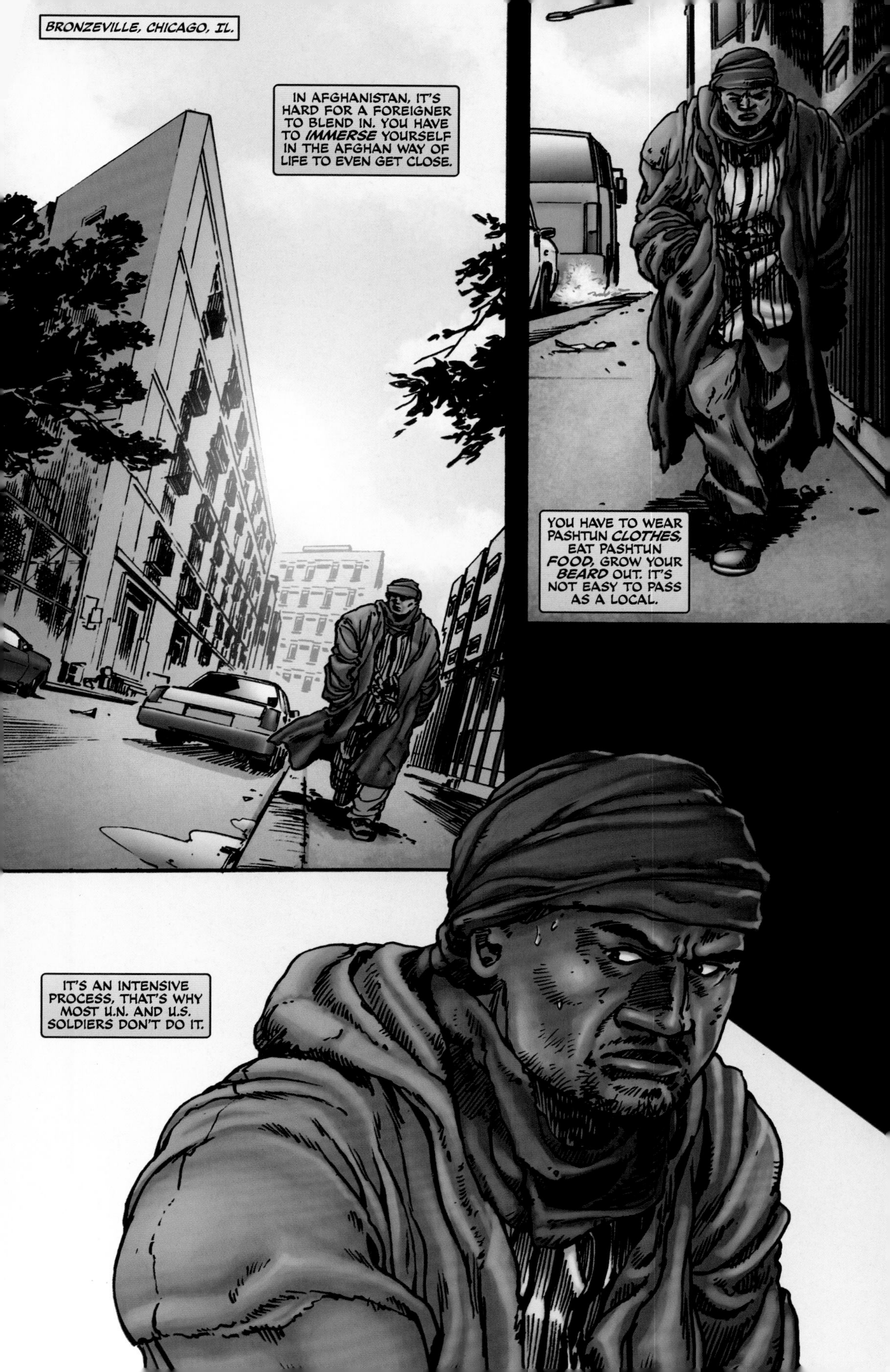
BRONZEVILLE, CHICAGO, IL.
IN AFGHANISTAN, IT'S HARD FOR A FOREIGNER TO BLEND IN. YOU HAVE TO IMMERSE YOURSELF IN THE AFGHAN WAY OF LIFE TO EVEN GET CLOSE.
YOU HAVE TO WEAR PASHTUN CLOTHES, EAT PASHTUN FOOD, GROW YOUR BEARD OUT. IT'S NOT EASY TO PASS AS A LOCAL.
IT'S AN INTENSIVE PROCESS, THAT'S WHY MOST U.N. AND U.S. SOLDIERS DON'T DO IT.

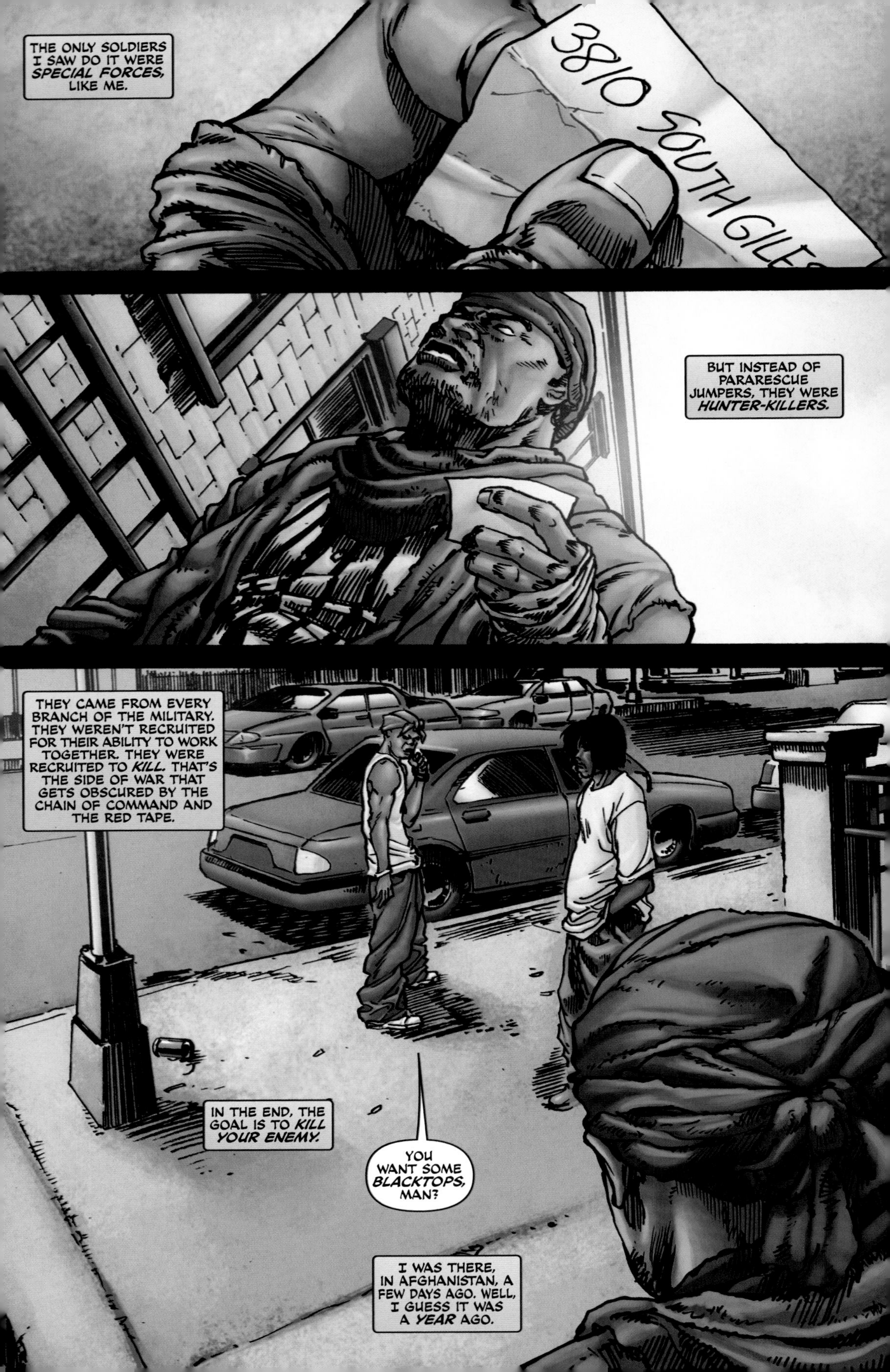

THE ONLY SOLDIERS I SAW DO IT WERE *SPECIAL FORCES,* LIKE ME.
3810 SOUTH GILES
BUT INSTEAD OF PARARESCUE JUMPERS, THEY WERE *HUNTER-KILLERS.*
THEY CAME FROM EVERY BRANCH OF THE MILITARY. THEY WEREN'T RECRUITED FOR THEIR ABILITY TO WORK TOGETHER. THEY WERE RECRUITED TO *KILL.* THAT'S THE SIDE OF WAR THAT GETS OBSCURED BY THE CHAIN OF COMMAND AND THE RED TAPE.
IN THE END, THE GOAL IS TO *KILL YOUR ENEMY.*
YOU WANT SOME *BLACKTOPS,* MAN?
I WAS THERE, IN AFGHANISTAN, A FEW DAYS AGO. WELL, I GUESS IT WAS A *YEAR* AGO.

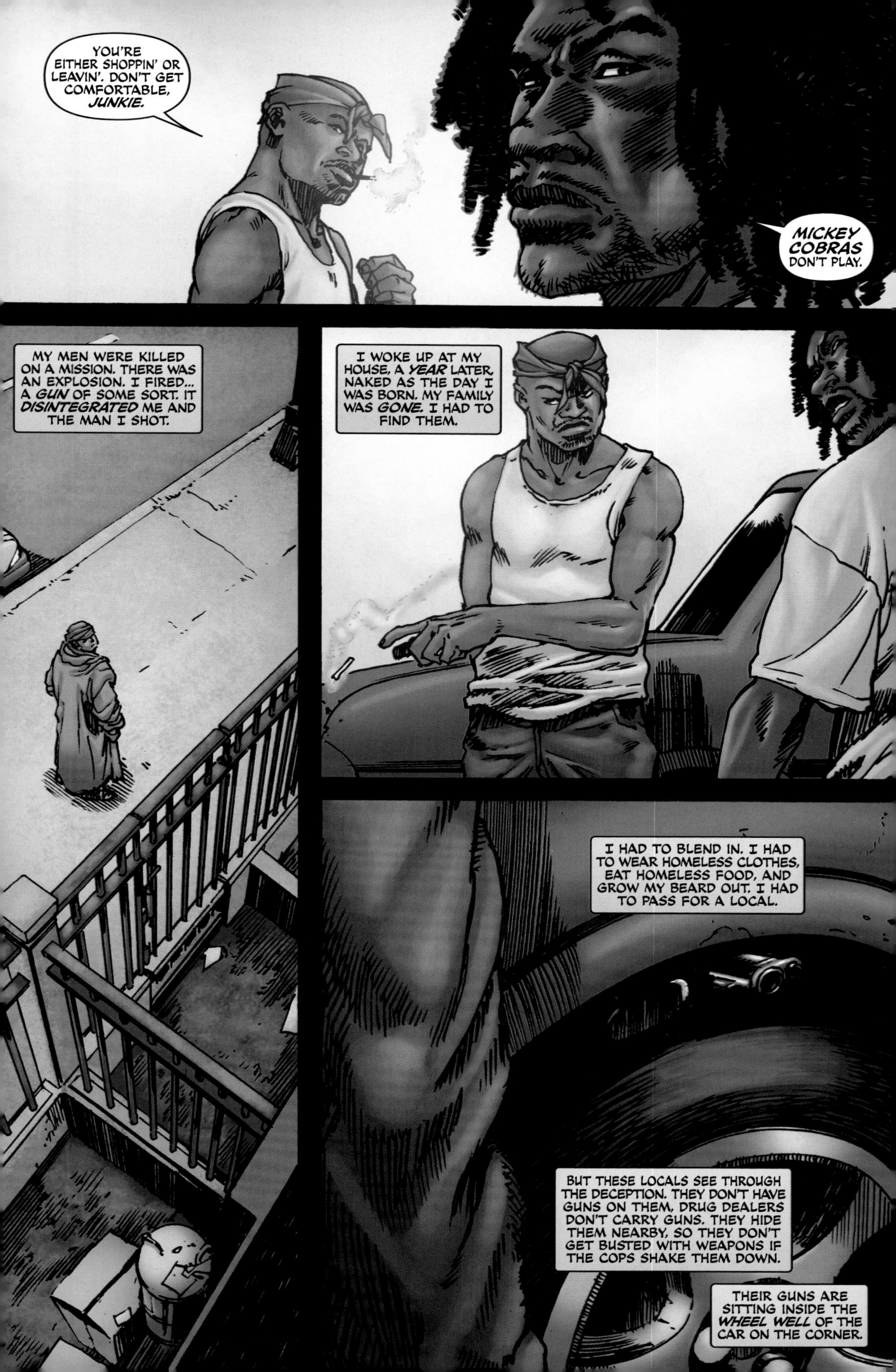
YOU'RE EITHER SHOPPIN' OR LEAVIN'. DON'T GET COMFORTABLE, JUNKIE.
MICKEY COBRAS DON'T PLAY.
MY MEN WERE KILLED ON A MISSION. THERE WAS AN EXPLOSION. I FIRED... A GUN OF SOME SORT. IT DISINTEGRATED ME AND THE MAN I SHOT.
I WOKE UP AT MY HOUSE, A YEAR LATER, NAKED AS THE DAY I WAS BORN. MY FAMILY WAS GONE. I HAD TO FIND THEM.
I HAD TO BLEND IN. I HAD TO WEAR HOMELESS CLOTHES, EAT HOMELESS FOOD, AND GROW MY BEARD OUT. I HAD TO PASS FOR A LOCAL.
BUT THESE LOCALS SEE THROUGH THE DECEPTION. THEY DON'T HAVE GUNS ON THEM, DRUG DEALERS DON'T CARRY GUNS. THEY HIDE THEM NEARBY, SO THEY DON'T GET BUSTED WITH WEAPONS IF THE COPS SHAKE THEM DOWN.
THEIR GUNS ARE SITTING INSIDE THE WHEEL WELL OF THE CAR ON THE CORNER.

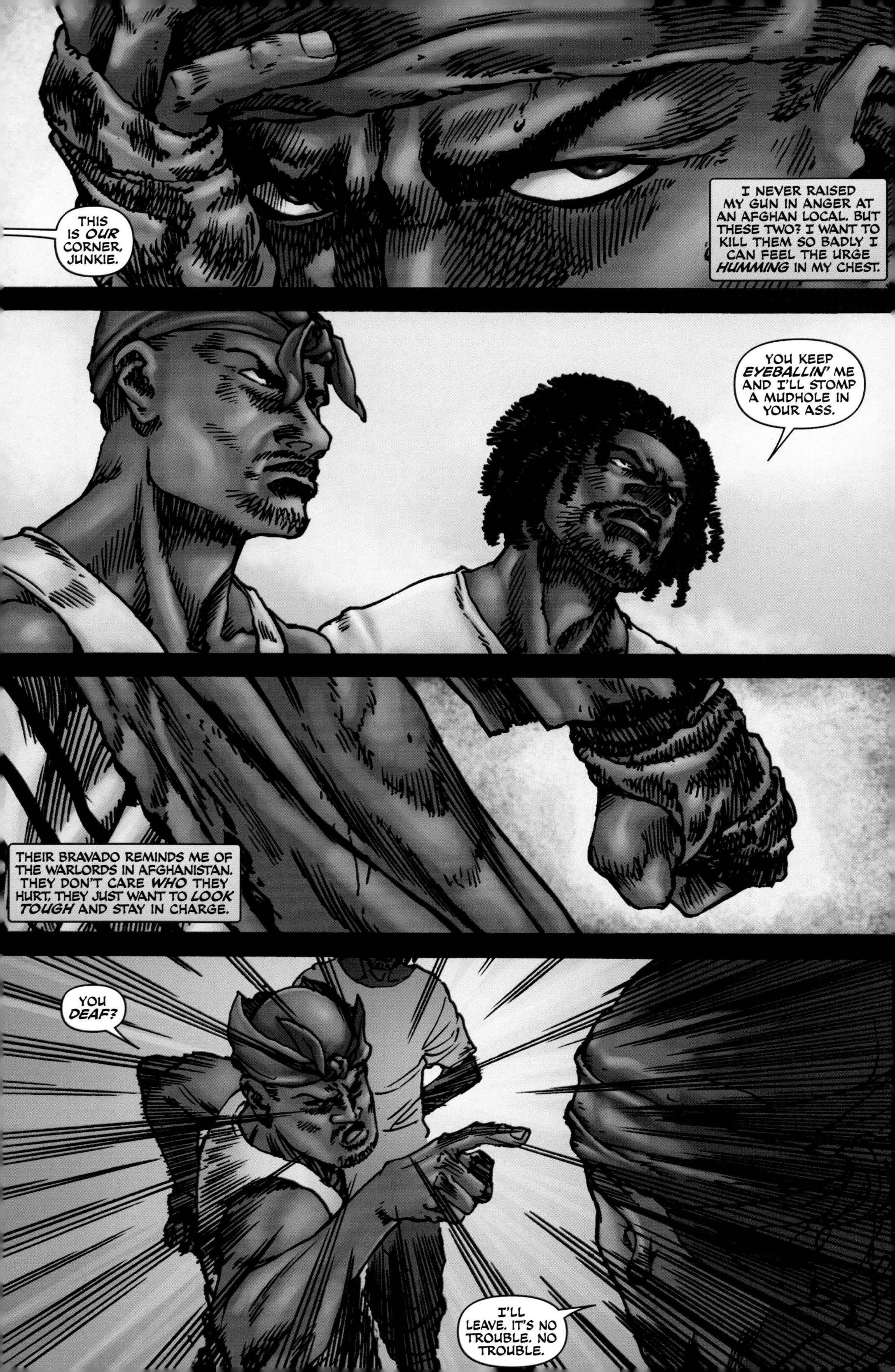
THIS IS OUR CORNER, JUNKIE.
I NEVER RAISED MY GUN IN ANGER AT AN AFGHAN LOCAL. BUT THESE TWO? I WANT TO KILL THEM SO BADLY I CAN FEEL THE URGE HUMMING IN MY CHEST.
YOU KEEP EYEBALLIN' ME AND I'LL STOMP A MUDHOLE IN YOUR ASS.
THEIR BRAVADO REMINDS ME OF THE WARLORDS IN AFGHANISTAN. THEY DON'T CARE WHO THEY HURT, THEY JUST WANT TO LOOK TOUGH AND STAY IN CHARGE.
YOU DEAF?
I'LL LEAVE. IT'S NO TROUBLE. NO TROUBLE.

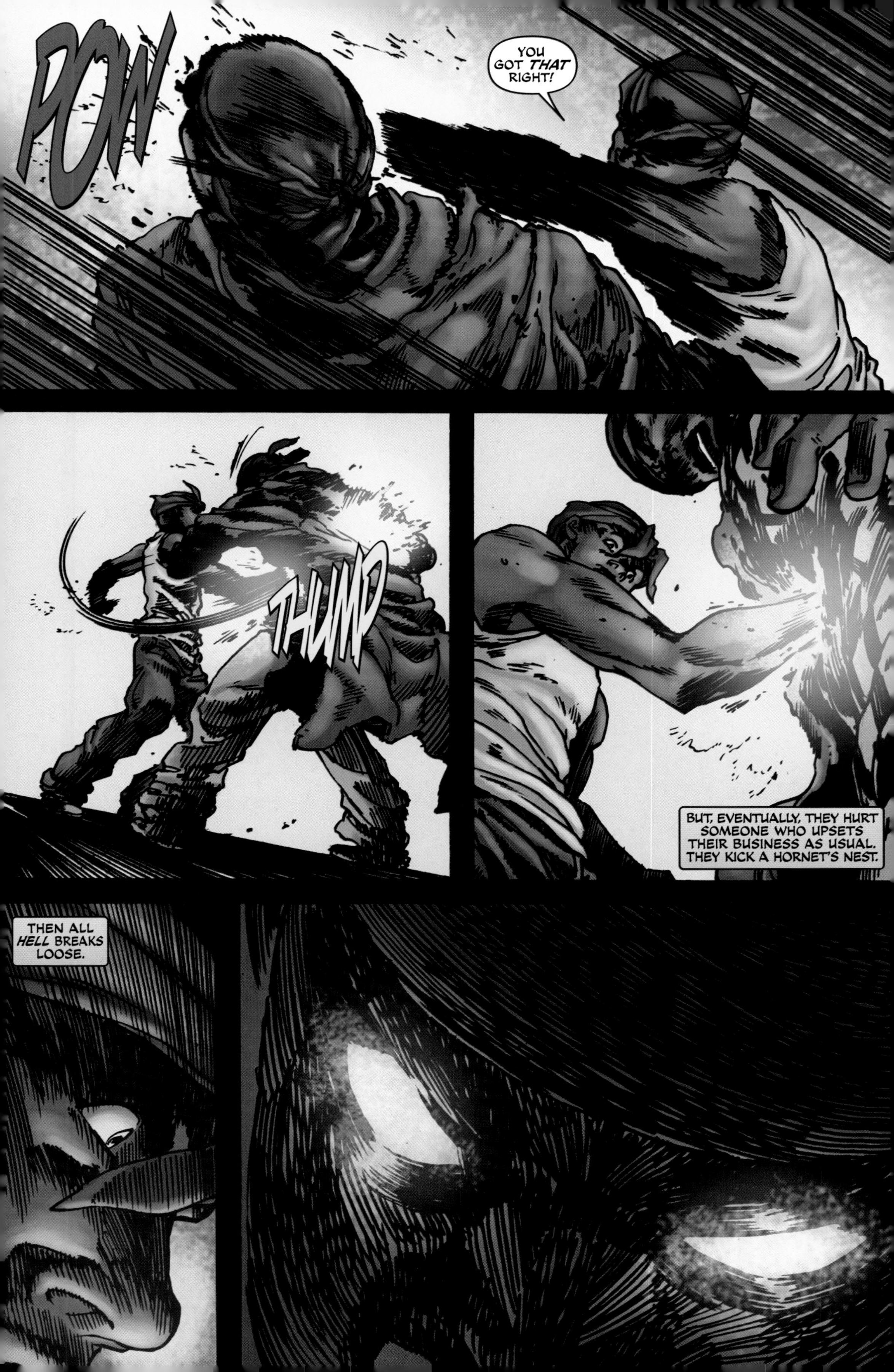
POW
YOU GOT *THAT* RIGHT!
THUMP
BUT, EVENTUALLY, THEY HURT SOMEONE WHO UPSETS THEIR BUSINESS AS USUAL. THEY KICK A HORNET'S NEST.
THEN ALL *HELL* BREAKS LOOSE.

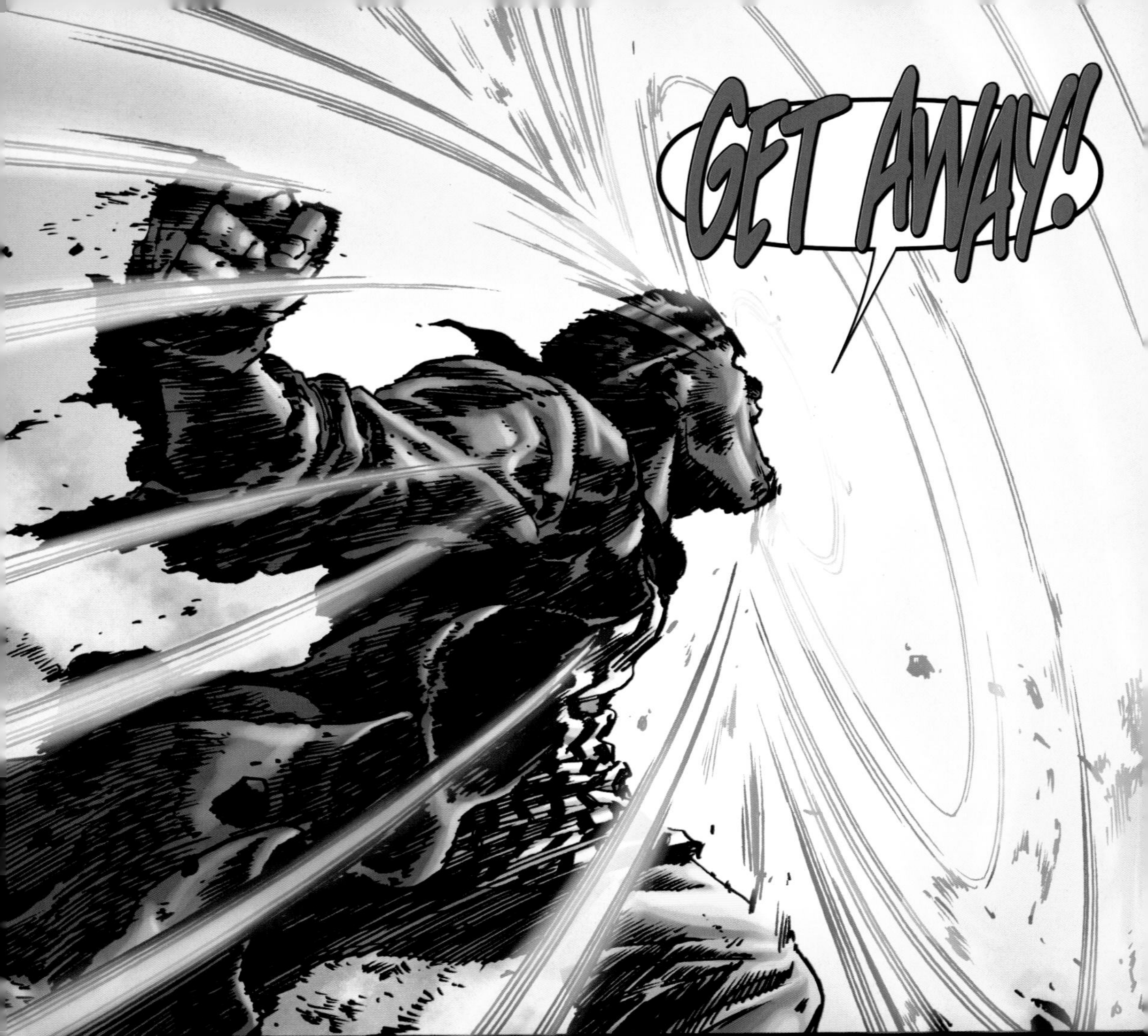
GET AWAY!

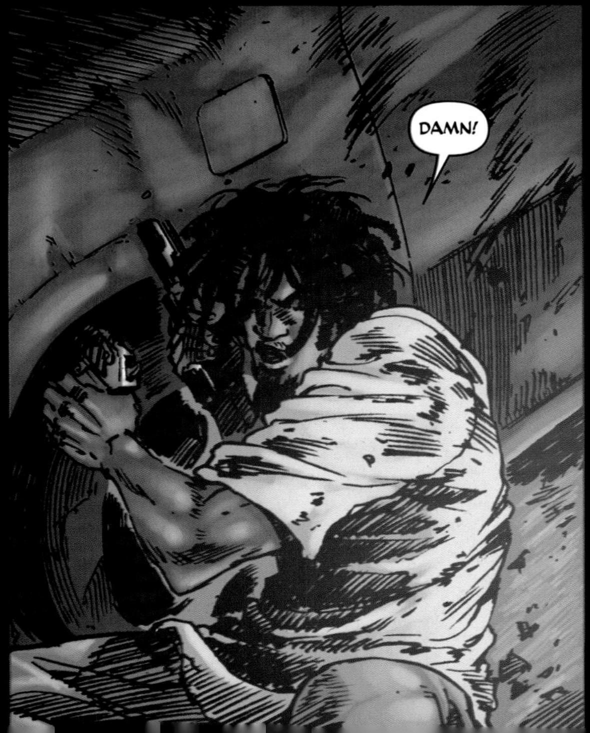
DAMN!

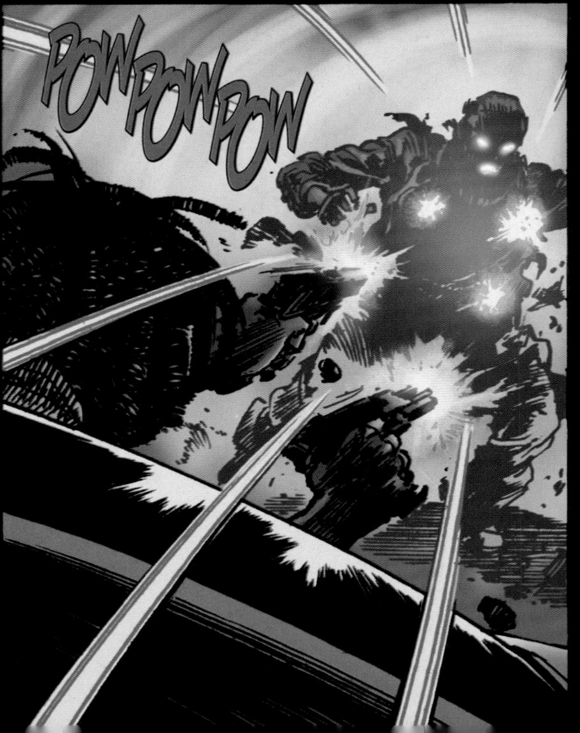
POW POW POW

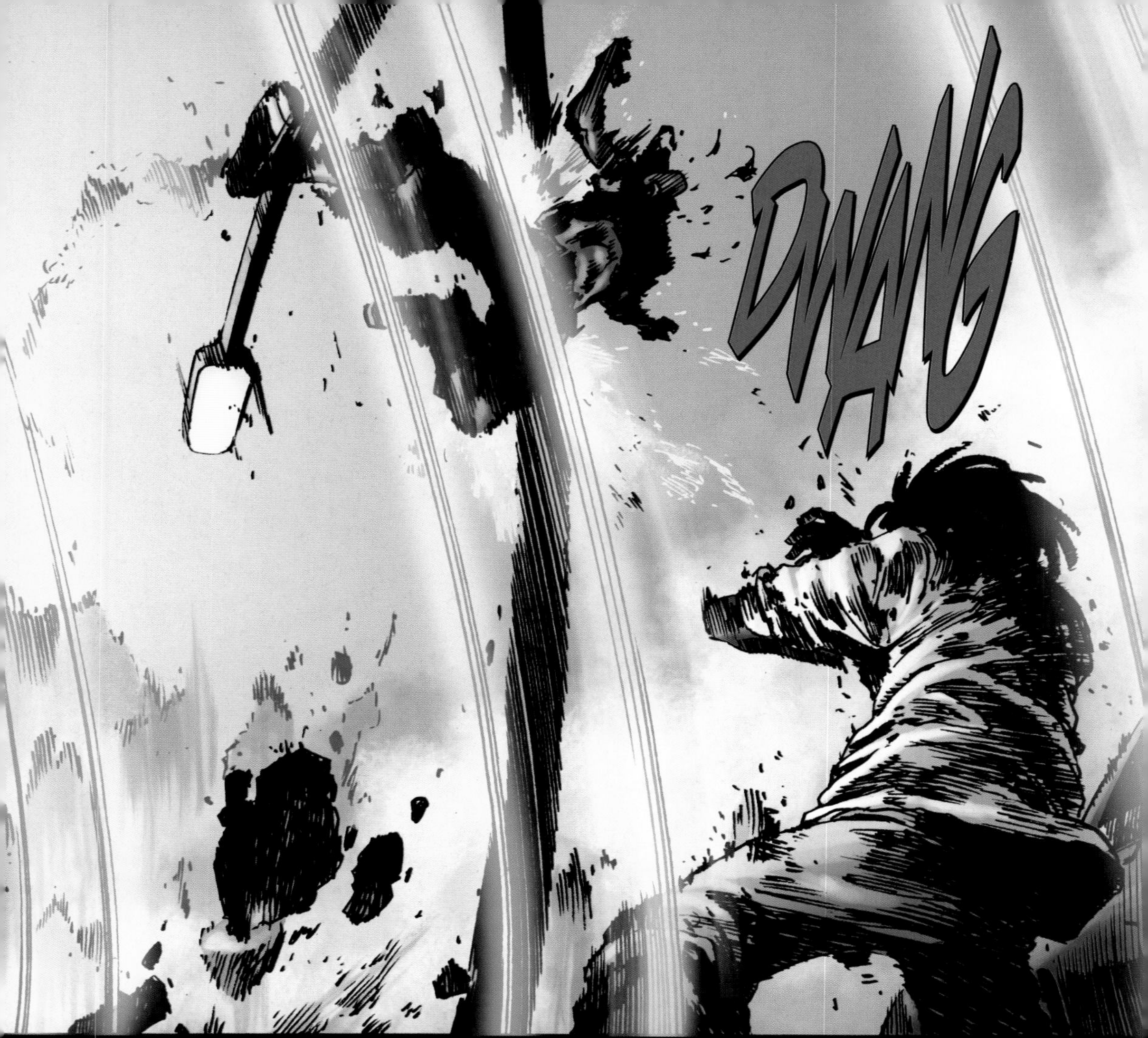
DWANG

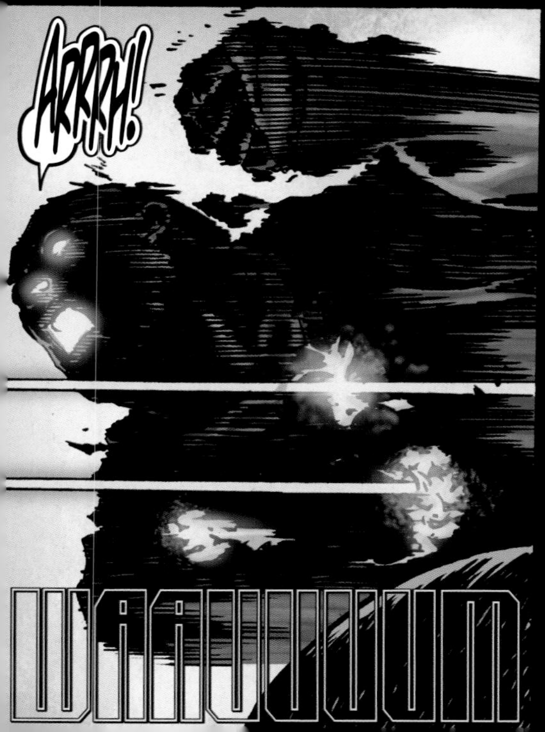
ARRRH!
WAAUUUUUM

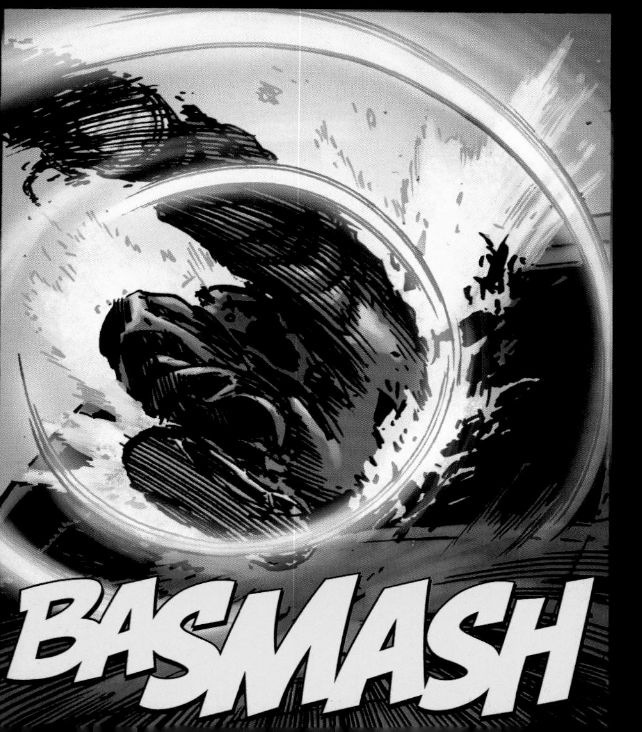
BASMASH

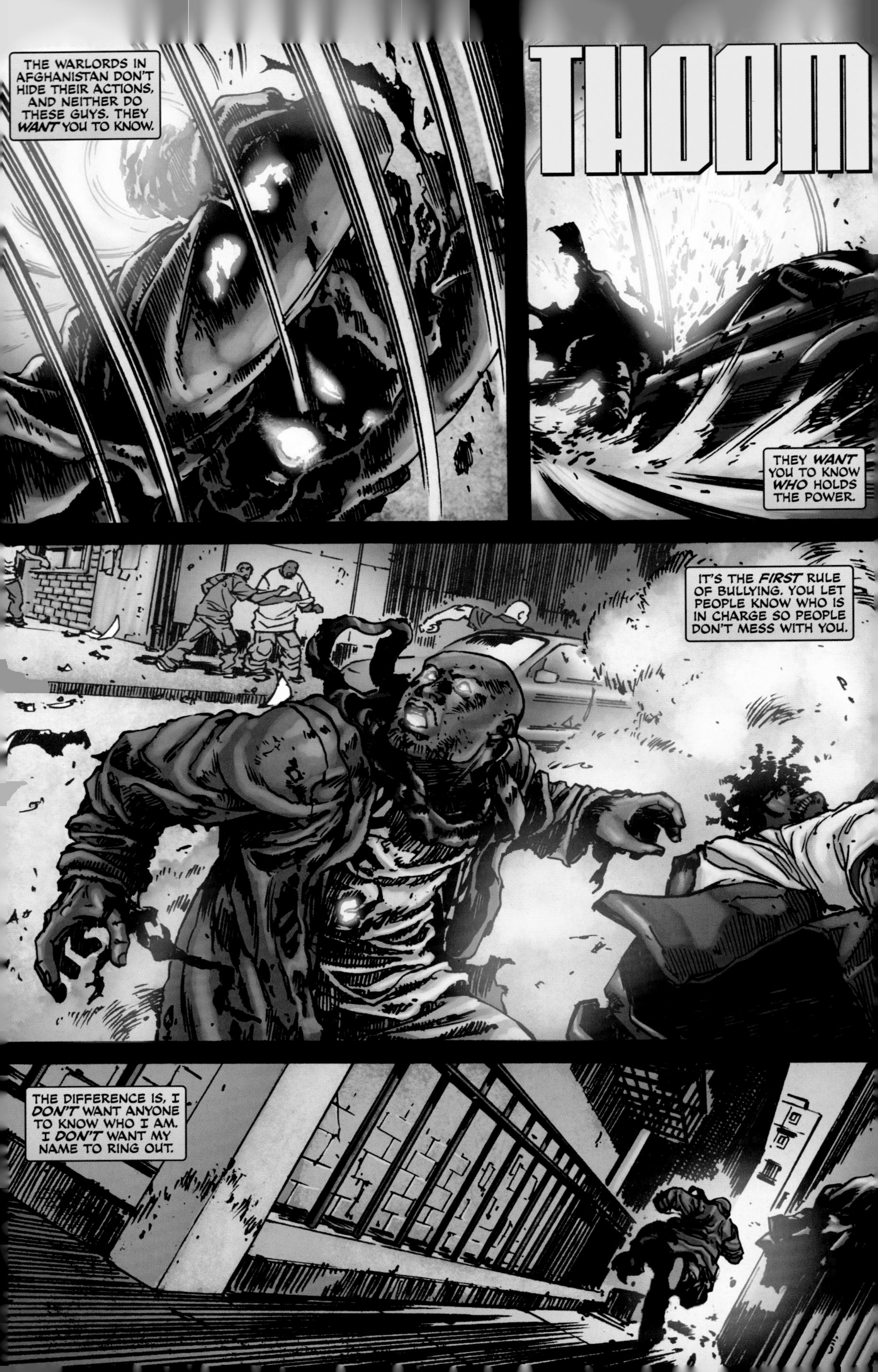
THE WARLORDS IN AFGHANISTAN DON'T HIDE THEIR ACTIONS, AND NEITHER DO THESE GUYS. THEY *WANT* YOU TO KNOW.
THOOM
THEY *WANT* YOU TO KNOW *WHO* HOLDS THE POWER.
IT'S THE *FIRST* RULE OF BULLYING. YOU LET PEOPLE KNOW WHO IS IN CHARGE SO PEOPLE DON'T MESS WITH YOU.
THE DIFFERENCE IS, I *DON'T* WANT ANYONE TO KNOW WHO I AM. I *DON'T* WANT MY NAME TO RING OUT.

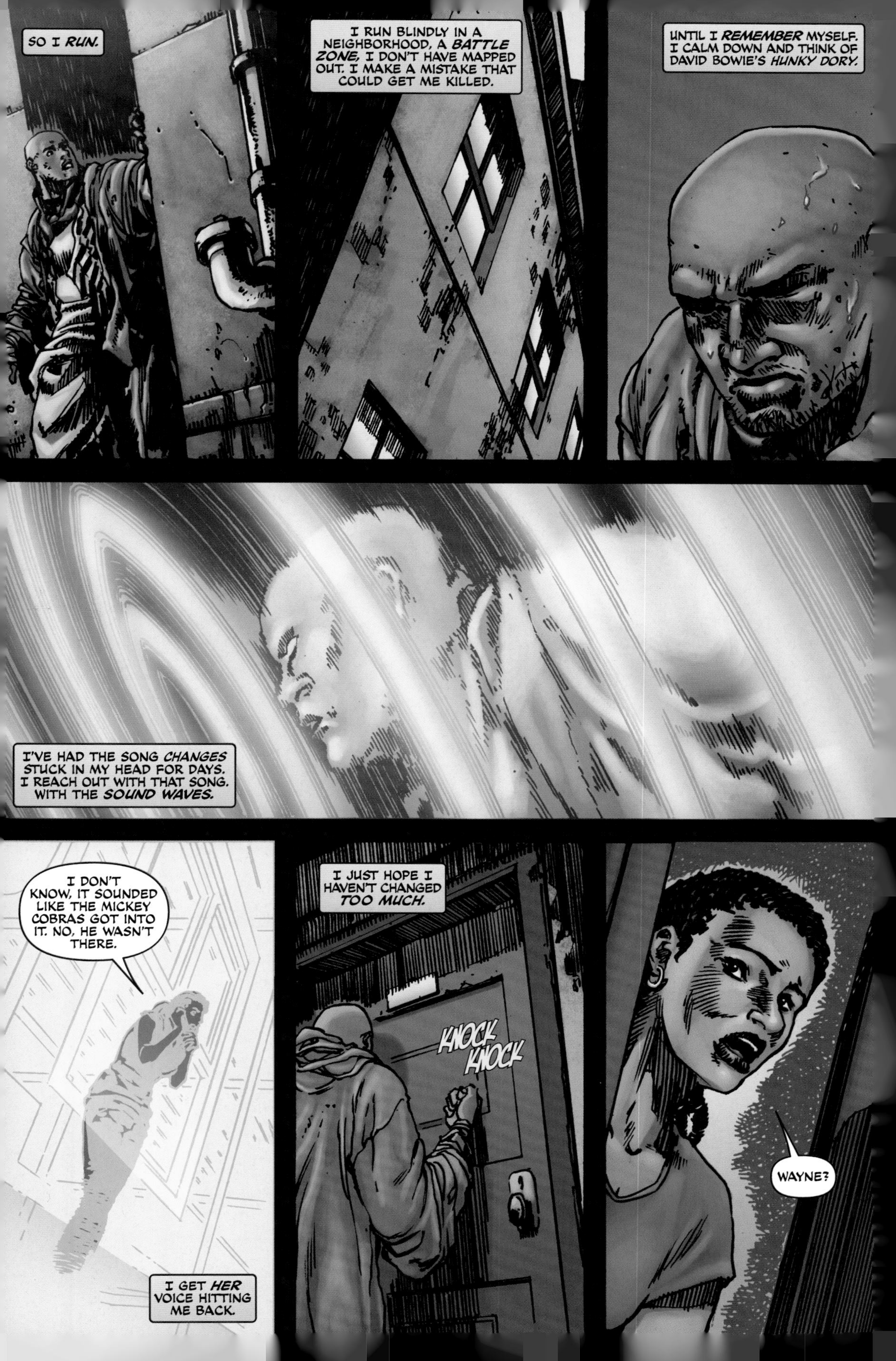
SO I *RUN.*
I RUN BLINDLY IN A NEIGHBORHOOD, A *BATTLE ZONE,* I DON'T HAVE MAPPED OUT. I MAKE A MISTAKE THAT COULD GET ME KILLED.
UNTIL I *REMEMBER* MYSELF. I CALM DOWN AND THINK OF DAVID BOWIE'S *HUNKY DORY.*
I'VE HAD THE SONG *CHANGES* STUCK IN MY HEAD FOR DAYS. I REACH OUT WITH THAT SONG. WITH THE *SOUND WAVES.*
I DON'T KNOW, IT SOUNDED LIKE THE MICKEY COBRAS GOT INTO IT. NO, HE WASN'T THERE.
I GET *HER* VOICE HITTING ME BACK.
I JUST HOPE I HAVEN'T CHANGED *TOO MUCH.*
KNOCK KNOCK
WAYNE?

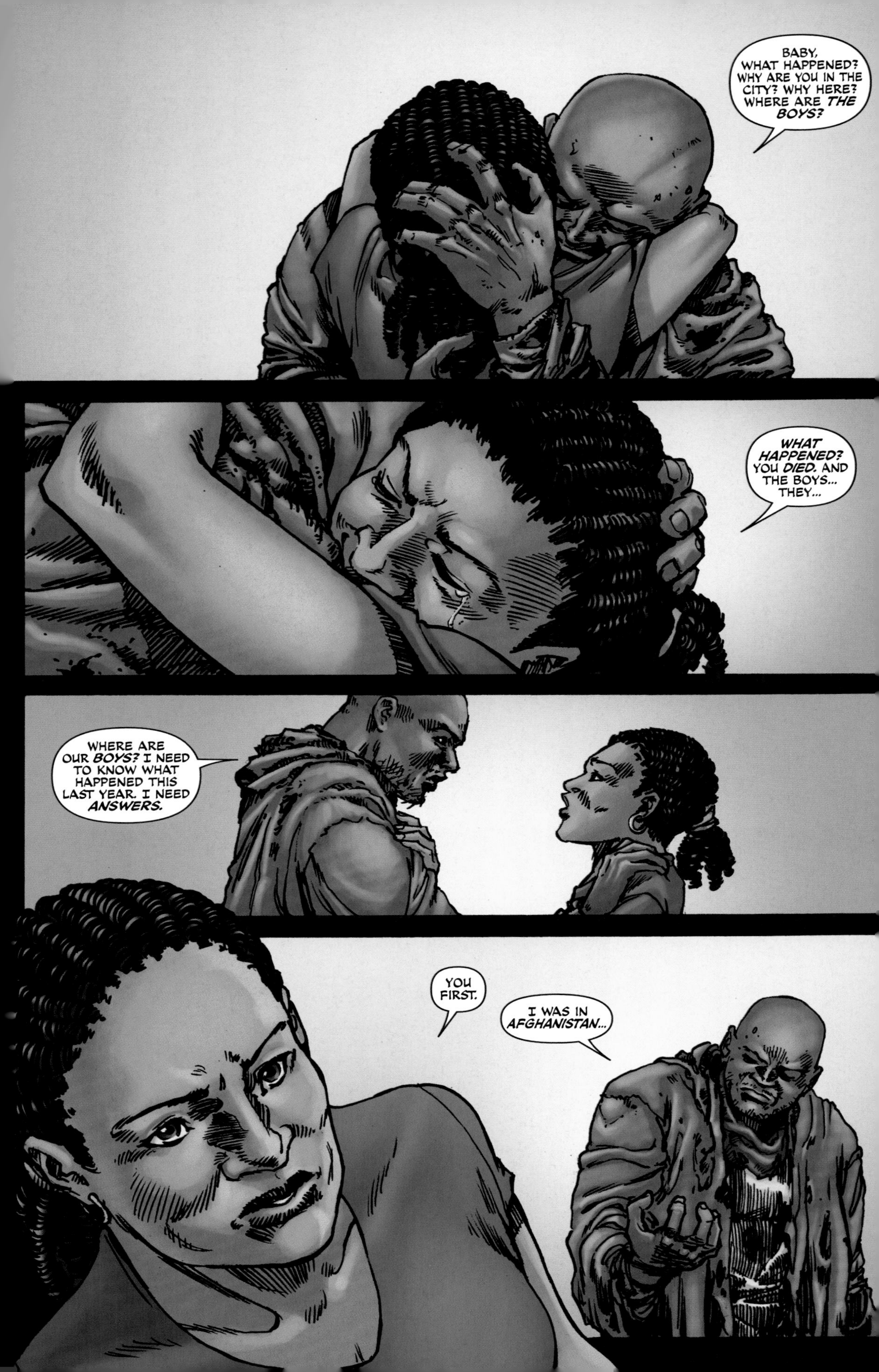
BABY, WHAT HAPPENED? WHY ARE YOU IN THE CITY? WHY HERE? WHERE ARE *THE BOYS?*
WHAT HAPPENED? YOU *DIED.* AND THE BOYS... THEY...
WHERE ARE OUR *BOYS?* I NEED TO KNOW WHAT HAPPENED THIS LAST YEAR. I NEED *ANSWERS.*
YOU FIRST.
I WAS IN *AFGHANISTAN...*

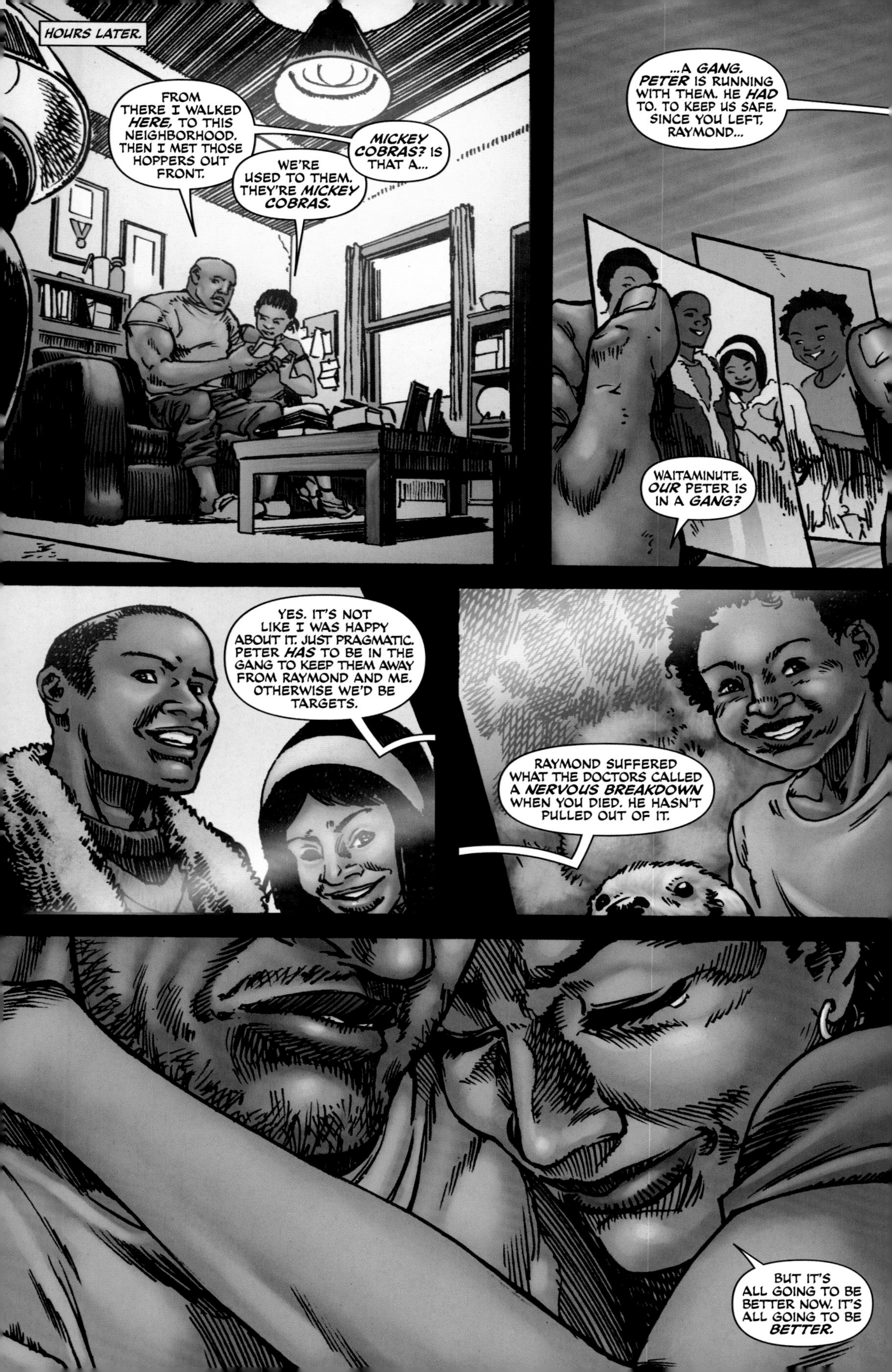
HOURS LATER.
FROM THERE I WALKED *HERE,* TO THIS NEIGHBORHOOD. THEN I MET THOSE HOPPERS OUT FRONT.
WE'RE USED TO THEM. THEY'RE *MICKEY COBRAS.*
MICKEY COBRAS? IS THAT A...
...A *GANG.* *PETER* IS RUNNING WITH THEM. HE *HAD* TO. TO KEEP US SAFE. SINCE YOU LEFT, RAYMOND...
WAITAMINUTE. *OUR* PETER IS IN A *GANG?*
YES. IT'S NOT LIKE I WAS HAPPY ABOUT IT. JUST PRAGMATIC. PETER *HAS* TO BE IN THE GANG TO KEEP THEM AWAY FROM RAYMOND AND ME. OTHERWISE WE'D BE TARGETS.
RAYMOND SUFFERED WHAT THE DOCTORS CALLED A *NERVOUS BREAKDOWN* WHEN YOU DIED. HE HASN'T PULLED OUT OF IT.
BUT IT'S ALL GOING TO BE BETTER NOW. IT'S ALL GOING TO BE *BETTER.*

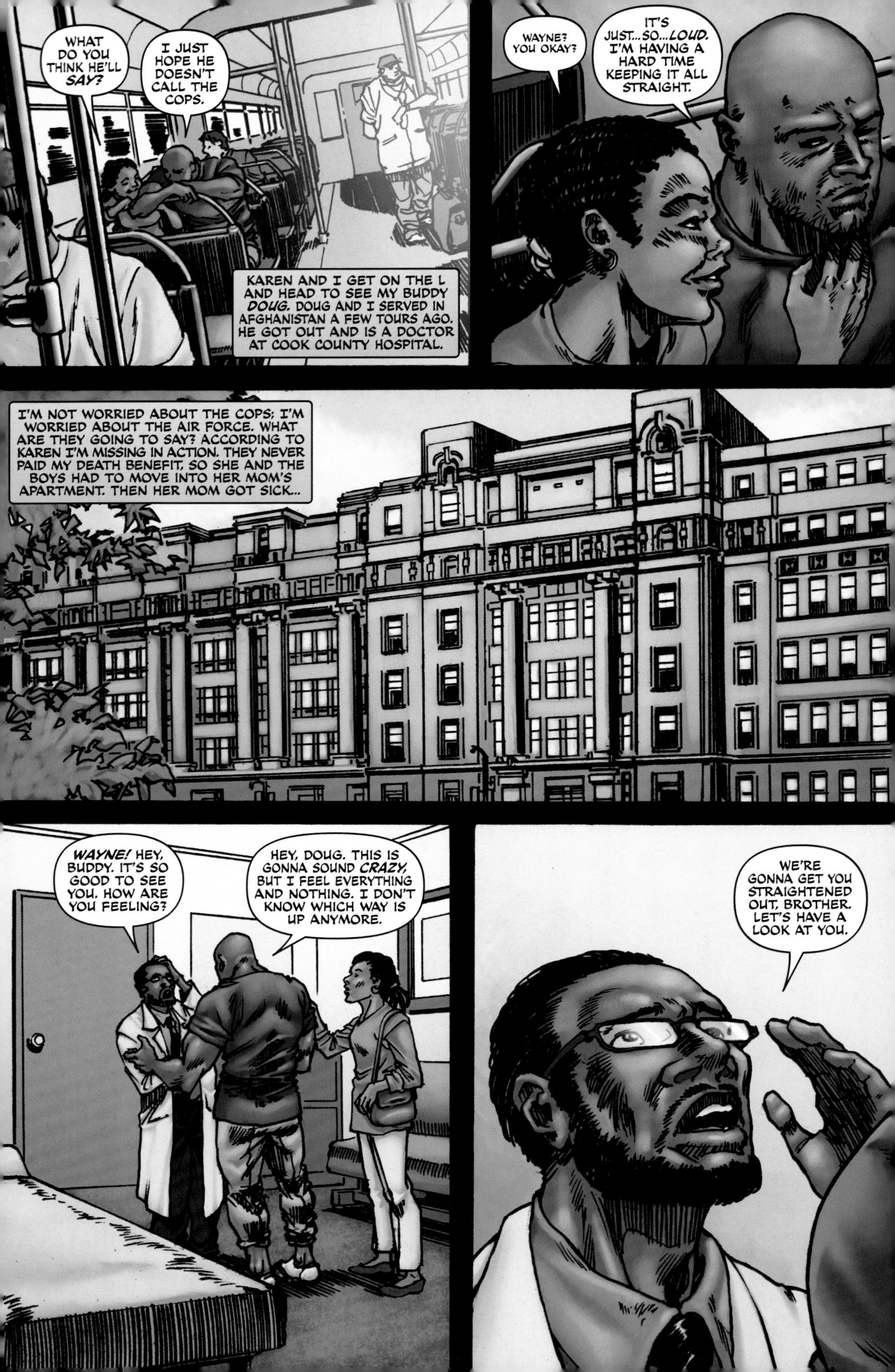
WHAT DO YOU THINK HE'LL *SAY?*
I JUST HOPE HE DOESN'T CALL THE COPS.
KAREN AND I GET ON THE L AND HEAD TO SEE MY BUDDY *DOUG.* DOUG AND I SERVED IN AFGHANISTAN A FEW TOURS AGO. HE GOT OUT AND IS A DOCTOR AT COOK COUNTY HOSPITAL.
WAYNE? YOU OKAY?
IT'S JUST...SO...*LOUD.* I'M HAVING A HARD TIME KEEPING IT ALL STRAIGHT.
I'M NOT WORRIED ABOUT THE COPS; I'M WORRIED ABOUT THE AIR FORCE. WHAT ARE THEY GOING TO SAY? ACCORDING TO KAREN I'M MISSING IN ACTION. THEY NEVER PAID MY DEATH BENEFIT, SO SHE AND THE BOYS HAD TO MOVE INTO HER MOM'S APARTMENT. THEN HER MOM GOT SICK...
WAYNE! HEY, BUDDY. IT'S SO GOOD TO SEE YOU. HOW ARE YOU FEELING?
HEY, DOUG. THIS IS GONNA SOUND *CRAZY,* BUT I FEEL EVERYTHING AND NOTHING. I DON'T KNOW WHICH WAY IS UP ANYMORE.
WE'RE GONNA GET YOU STRAIGHTENED OUT, BROTHER. LET'S HAVE A LOOK AT YOU.

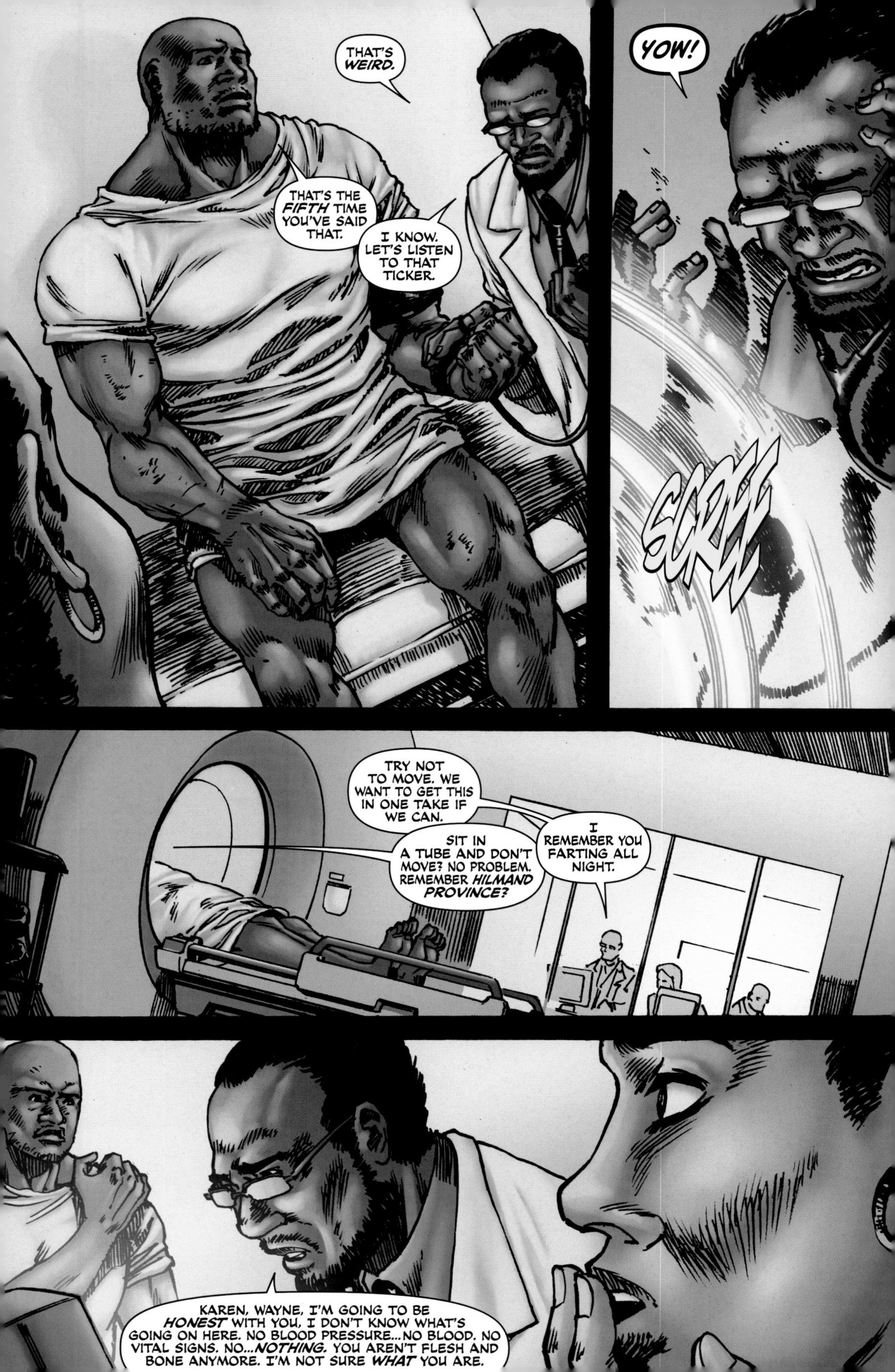
THAT'S WEIRD.
THAT'S THE FIFTH TIME YOU'VE SAID THAT.
I KNOW. LET'S LISTEN TO THAT TICKER.
YOW!
SCREE
TRY NOT TO MOVE. WE WANT TO GET THIS IN ONE TAKE IF WE CAN.
SIT IN A TUBE AND DON'T MOVE? NO PROBLEM. REMEMBER HILMAND PROVINCE?
I REMEMBER YOU FARTING ALL NIGHT.
KAREN, WAYNE, I'M GOING TO BE HONEST WITH YOU, I DON'T KNOW WHAT'S GOING ON HERE. NO BLOOD PRESSURE...NO BLOOD. NO VITAL SIGNS. NO...NOTHING. YOU AREN'T FLESH AND BONE ANYMORE. I'M NOT SURE WHAT YOU ARE.

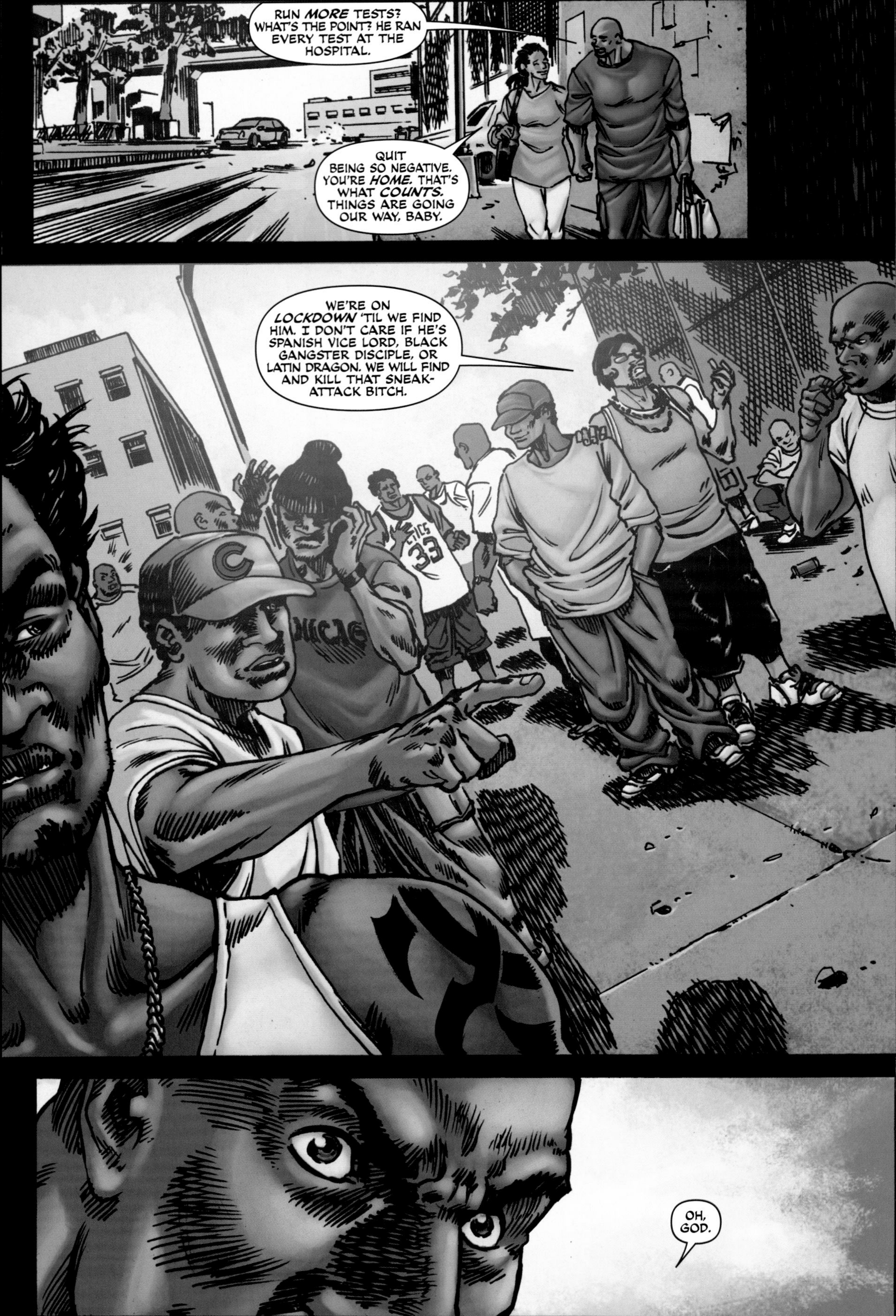
RUN MORE TESTS? WHAT'S THE POINT? HE RAN EVERY TEST AT THE HOSPITAL.
QUIT BEING SO NEGATIVE. YOU'RE HOME. THAT'S WHAT COUNTS. THINGS ARE GOING OUR WAY, BABY.
WE'RE ON LOCKDOWN 'TIL WE FIND HIM. I DON'T CARE IF HE'S SPANISH VICE LORD, BLACK GANGSTER DISCIPLE, OR LATIN DRAGON. WE WILL FIND AND KILL THAT SNEAK-ATTACK BITCH.
OH, GOD.

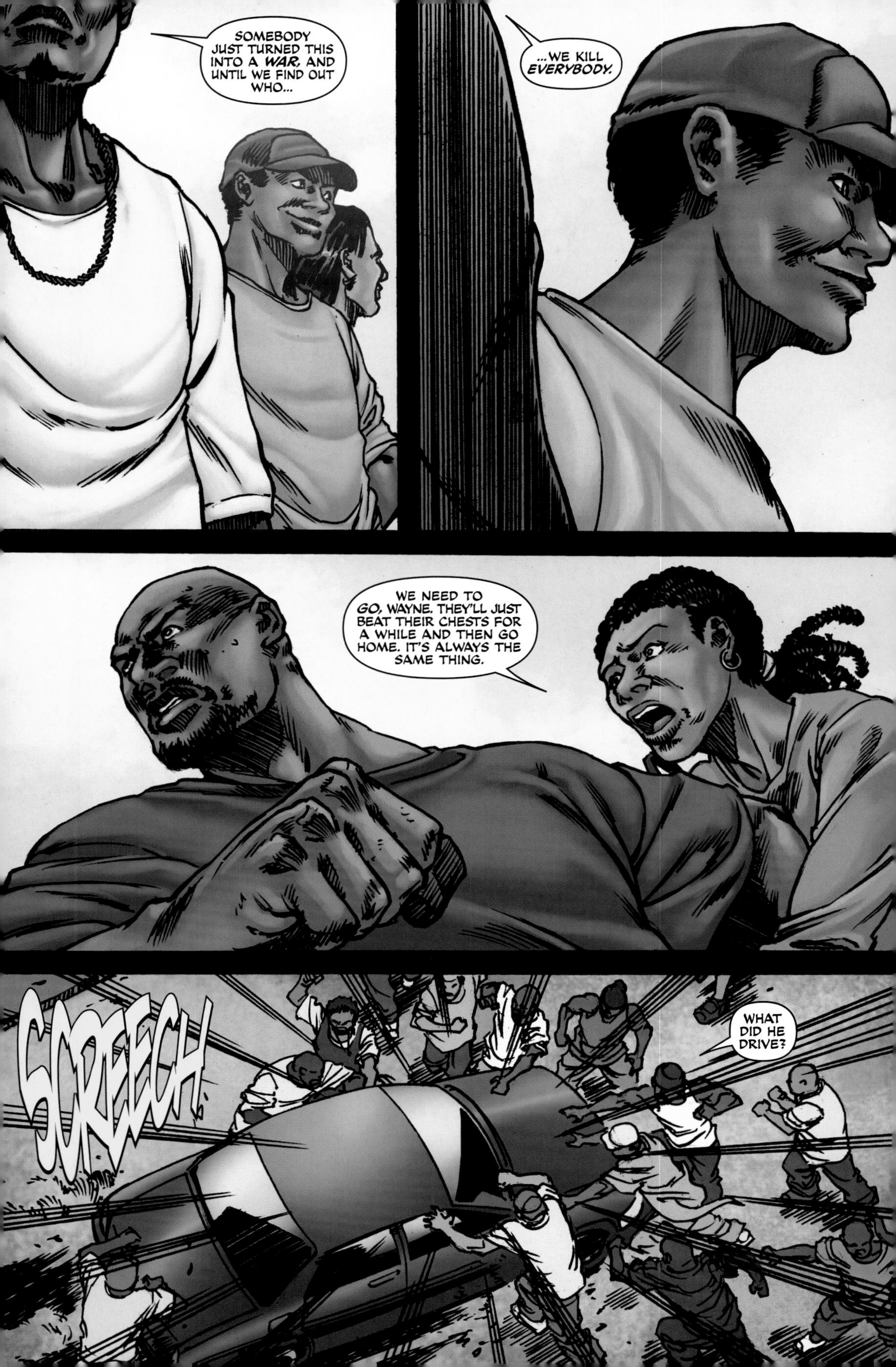
SOMEBODY JUST TURNED THIS INTO A *WAR*, AND UNTIL WE FIND OUT WHO...
...WE KILL *EVERYBODY*.
WE NEED TO GO, WAYNE. THEY'LL JUST BEAT THEIR CHESTS FOR A WHILE AND THEN GO HOME. IT'S ALWAYS THE SAME THING.
SCREECH!
WHAT DID HE DRIVE?

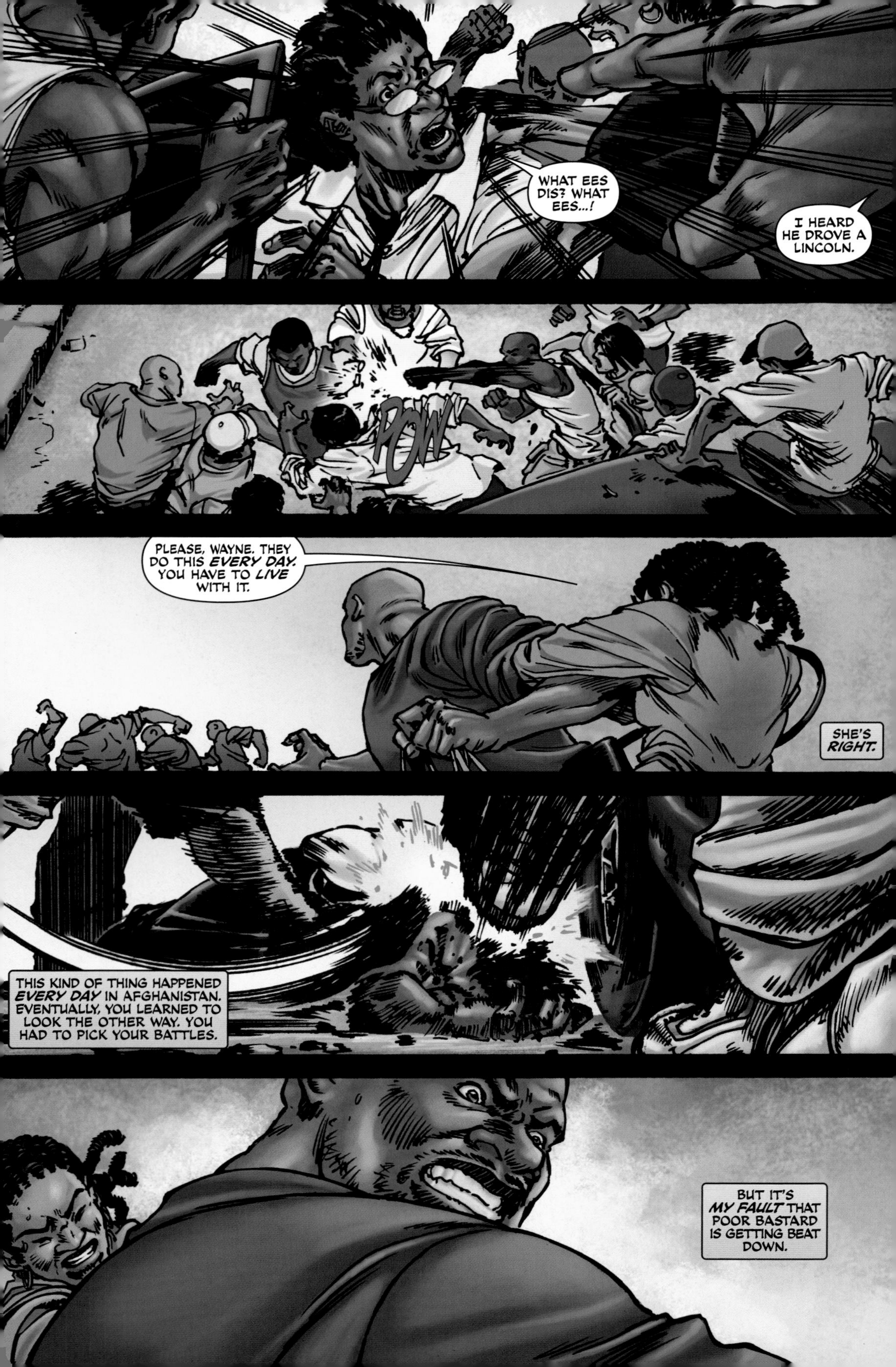

WHAT EES DIS? WHAT EES...!
I HEARD HE DROVE A LINCOLN.
POW
PLEASE, WAYNE. THEY DO THIS EVERY DAY. YOU HAVE TO LIVE WITH IT.
SHE'S RIGHT.
THIS KIND OF THING HAPPENED EVERY DAY IN AFGHANISTAN. EVENTUALLY, YOU LEARNED TO LOOK THE OTHER WAY. YOU HAD TO PICK YOUR BATTLES.
BUT IT'S MY FAULT THAT POOR BASTARD IS GETTING BEAT DOWN.

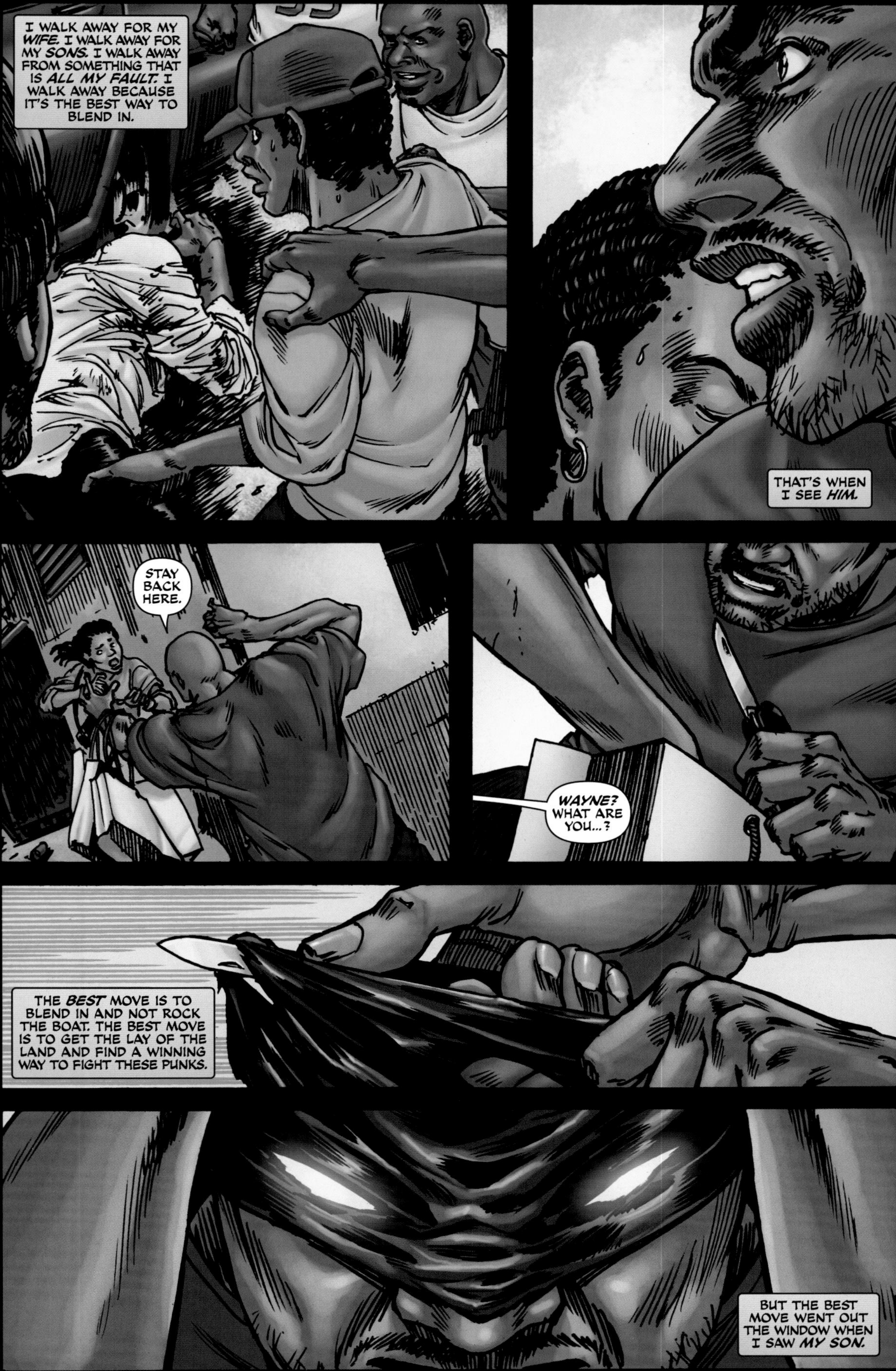
I WALK AWAY FOR MY WIFE. I WALK AWAY FOR MY SONS. I WALK AWAY FROM SOMETHING THAT IS ALL MY FAULT. I WALK AWAY BECAUSE IT'S THE BEST WAY TO BLEND IN.
THAT'S WHEN I SEE HIM.
STAY BACK HERE.
WAYNE? WHAT ARE YOU...?
THE BEST MOVE IS TO BLEND IN AND NOT ROCK THE BOAT. THE BEST MOVE IS TO GET THE LAY OF THE LAND AND FIND A WINNING WAY TO FIGHT THESE PUNKS.
BUT THE BEST MOVE WENT OUT THE WINDOW WHEN I SAW MY SON.

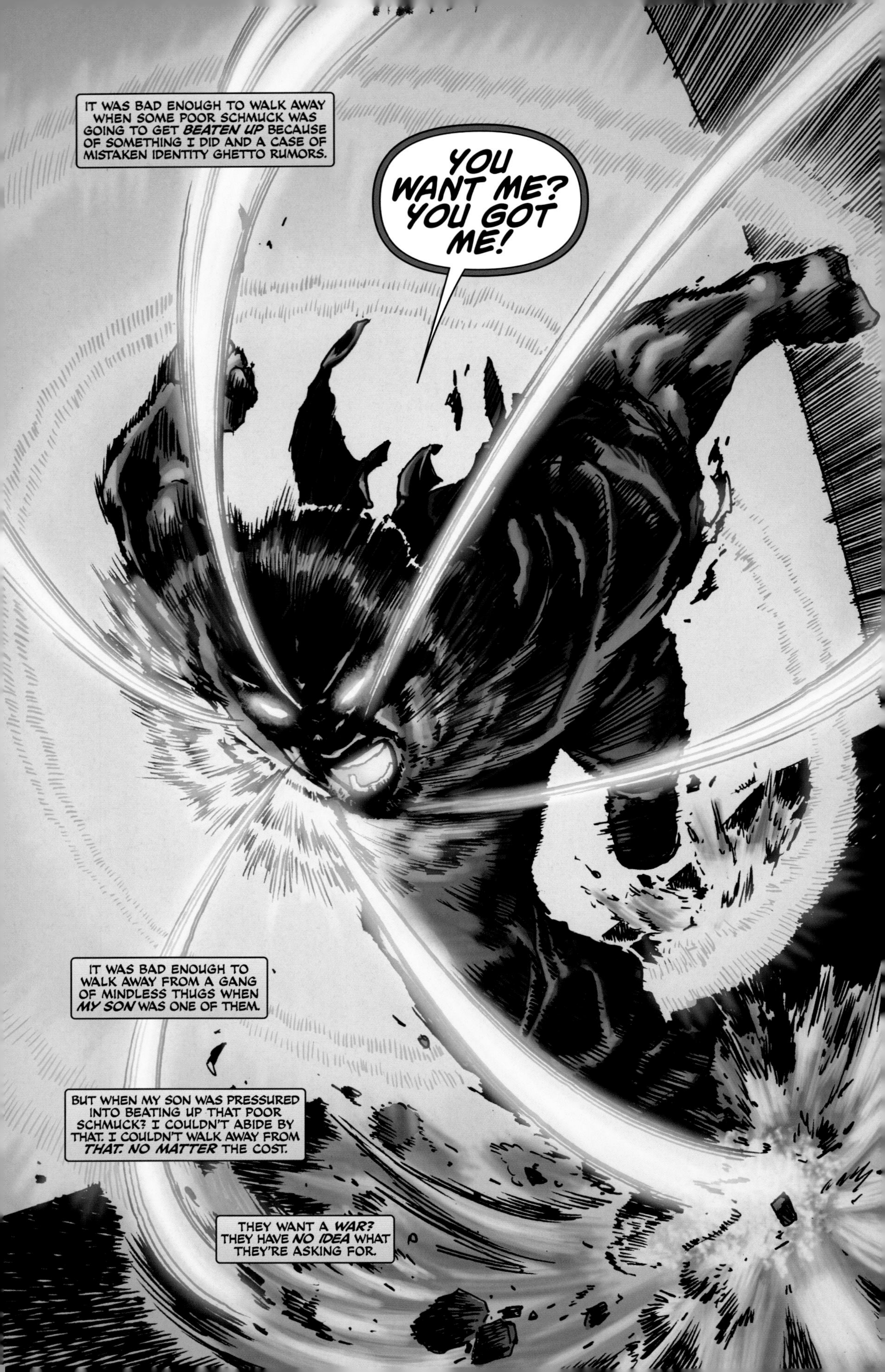
IT WAS BAD ENOUGH TO WALK AWAY WHEN SOME POOR SCHMUCK WAS GOING TO GET BEATEN UP BECAUSE OF SOMETHING I DID AND A CASE OF MISTAKEN IDENTITY GHETTO RUMORS.
YOU WANT ME? YOU GOT ME!
IT WAS BAD ENOUGH TO WALK AWAY FROM A GANG OF MINDLESS THUGS WHEN MY SON WAS ONE OF THEM.
BUT WHEN MY SON WAS PRESSURED INTO BEATING UP THAT POOR SCHMUCK? I COULDN'T ABIDE BY THAT. I COULDN'T WALK AWAY FROM THAT. NO MATTER THE COST.
THEY WANT A WAR? THEY HAVE NO IDEA WHAT THEY'RE ASKING FOR.

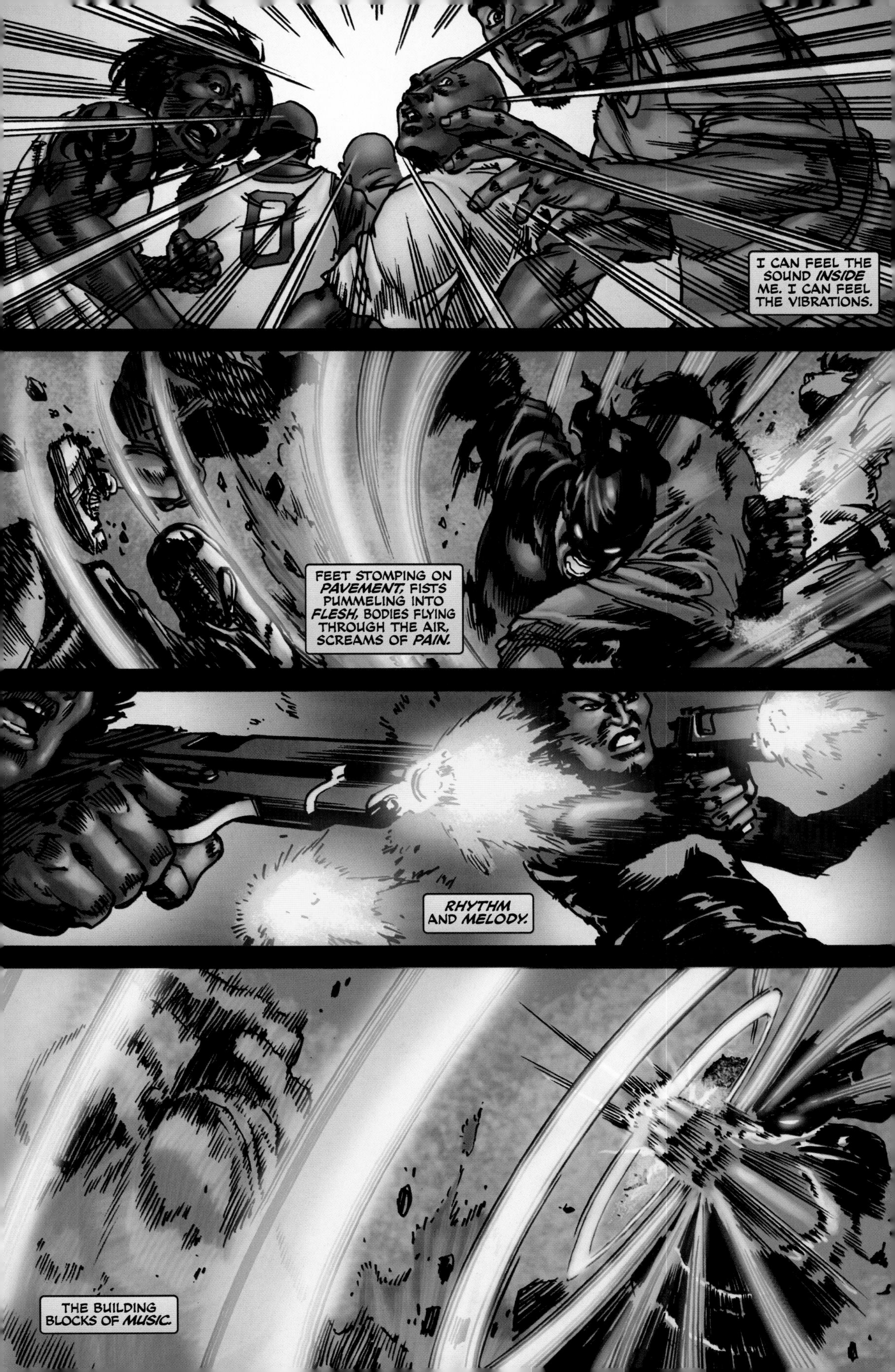
I CAN FEEL THE SOUND *INSIDE* ME. I CAN FEEL THE VIBRATIONS.
FEET STOMPING ON *PAVEMENT,* FISTS PUMMELING INTO *FLESH,* BODIES FLYING THROUGH THE AIR, SCREAMS OF *PAIN.*
RHYTHM AND *MELODY.*
THE BUILDING BLOCKS OF *MUSIC.*

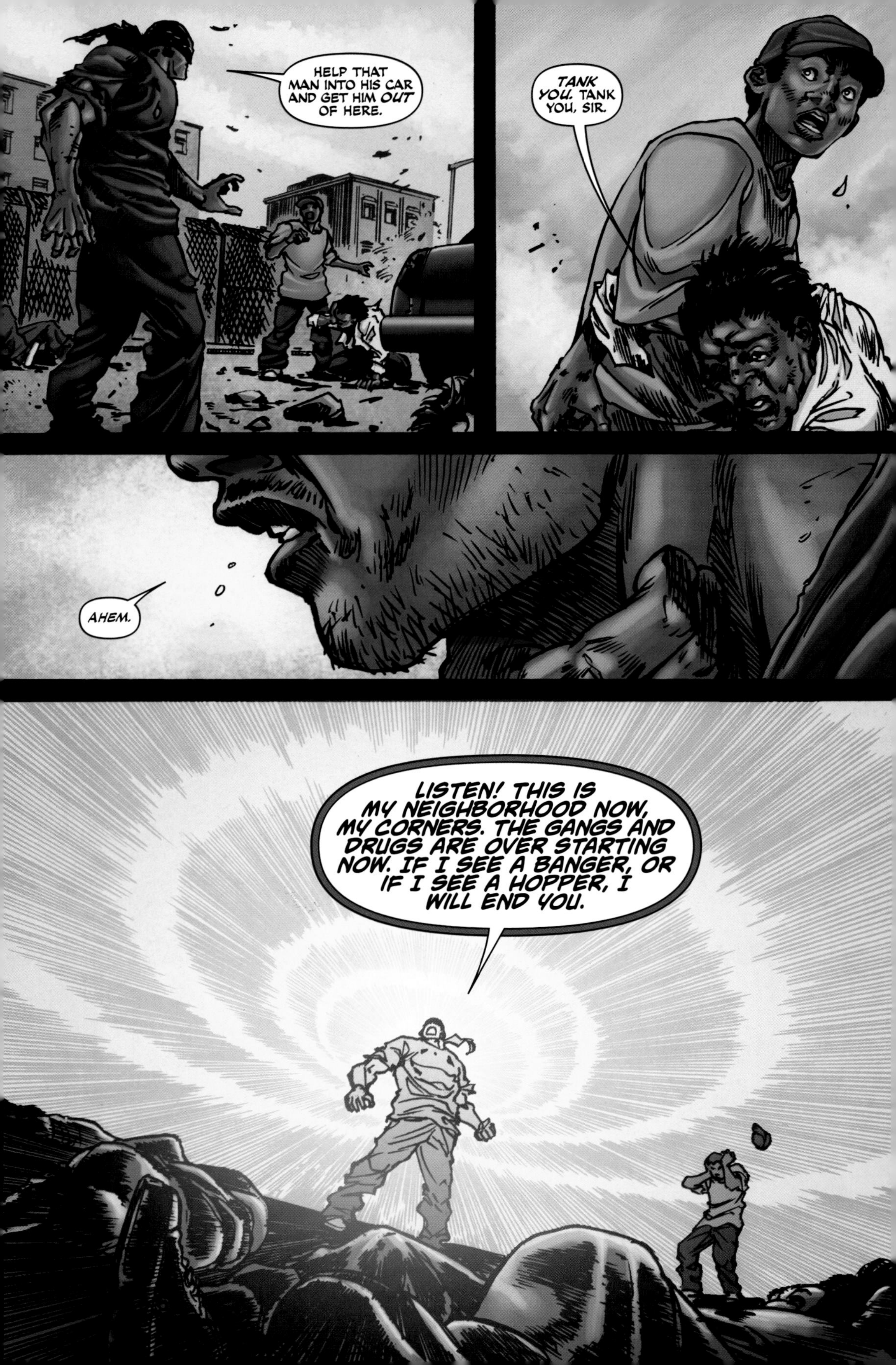
HELP THAT MAN INTO HIS CAR AND GET HIM OUT OF HERE.
TANK YOU. TANK YOU, SIR.
AHEM.
LISTEN! THIS IS MY NEIGHBORHOOD NOW, MY CORNERS. THE GANGS AND DRUGS ARE OVER STARTING NOW. IF I SEE A BANGER, OR IF I SEE A HOPPER, I WILL END YOU.

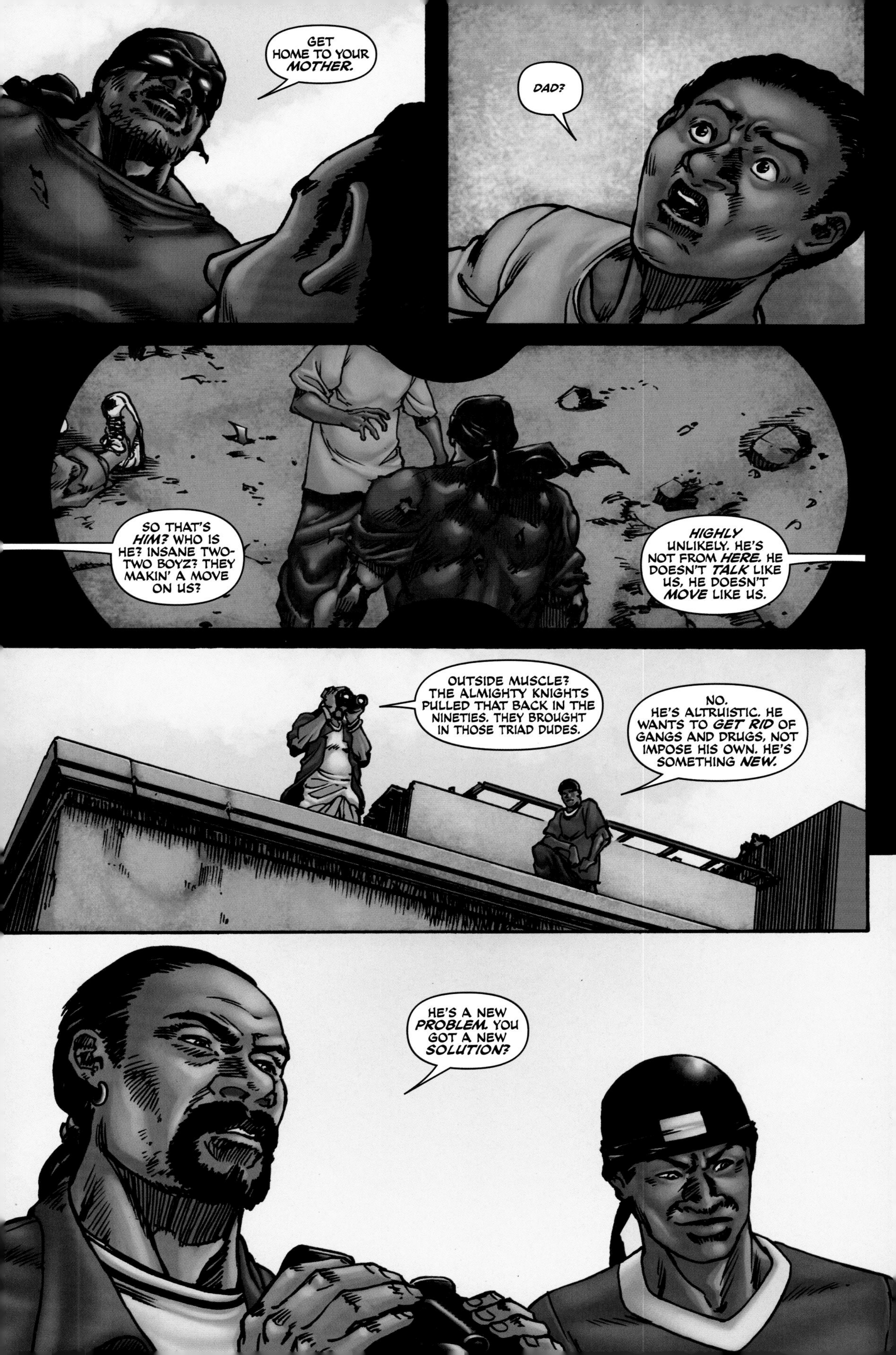
GET HOME TO YOUR MOTHER.
DAD?
SO THAT'S HIM? WHO IS HE? INSANE TWO-TWO BOYZ? THEY MAKIN' A MOVE ON US?
HIGHLY UNLIKELY. HE'S NOT FROM HERE. HE DOESN'T TALK LIKE US, HE DOESN'T MOVE LIKE US.
OUTSIDE MUSCLE? THE ALMIGHTY KNIGHTS PULLED THAT BACK IN THE NINETIES. THEY BROUGHT IN THOSE TRIAD DUDES.
NO. HE'S ALTRUISTIC. HE WANTS TO GET RID OF GANGS AND DRUGS, NOT IMPOSE HIS OWN. HE'S SOMETHING NEW.
HE'S A NEW PROBLEM. YOU GOT A NEW SOLUTION?

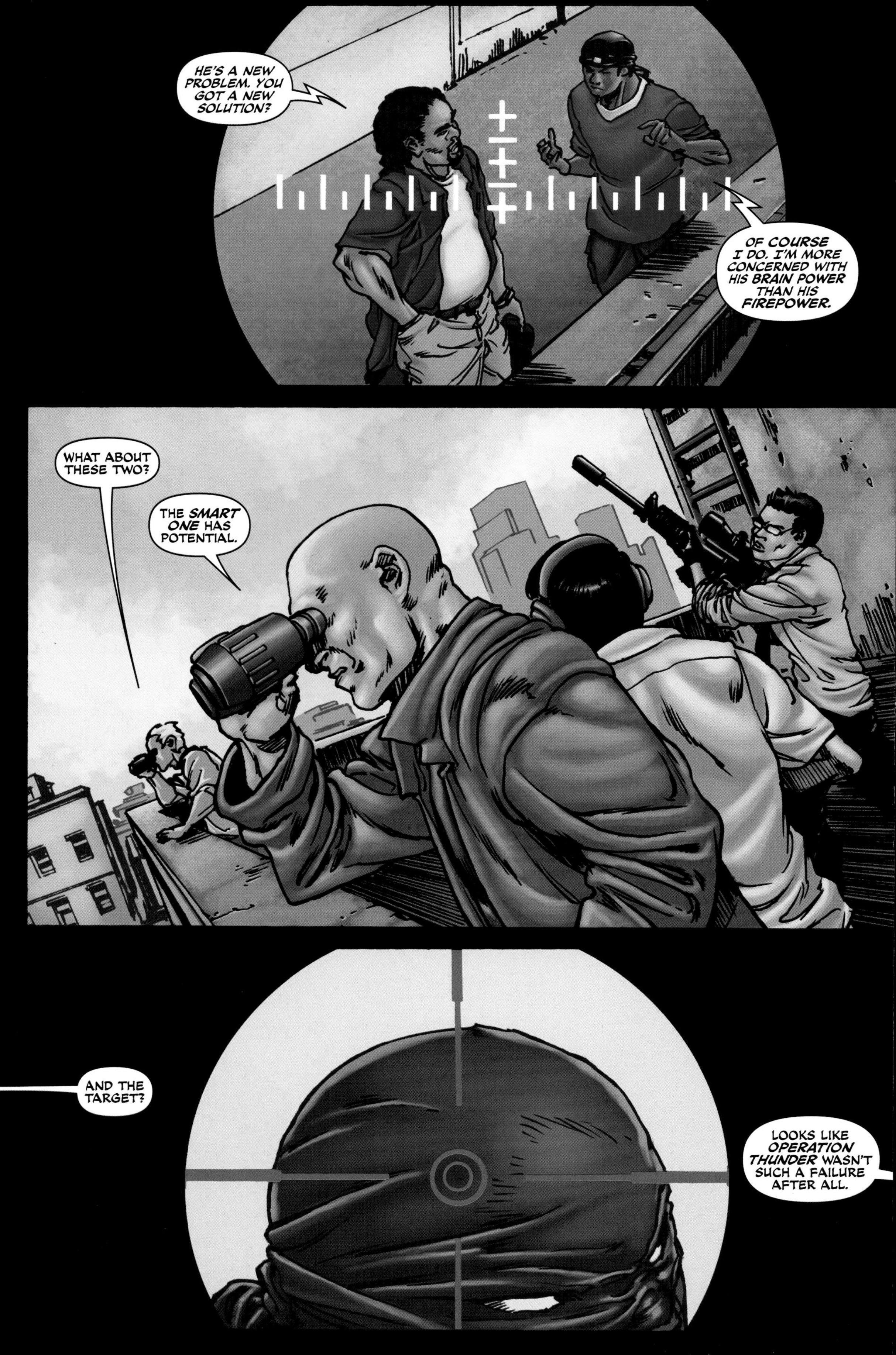
HE'S A NEW PROBLEM. YOU GOT A NEW SOLUTION?
OF COURSE I DO. I'M MORE CONCERNED WITH HIS BRAIN POWER THAN HIS FIREPOWER.
WHAT ABOUT THESE TWO?
THE SMART ONE HAS POTENTIAL.
AND THE TARGET?
LOOKS LIKE OPERATION THUNDER WASN'T SUCH A FAILURE AFTER ALL.

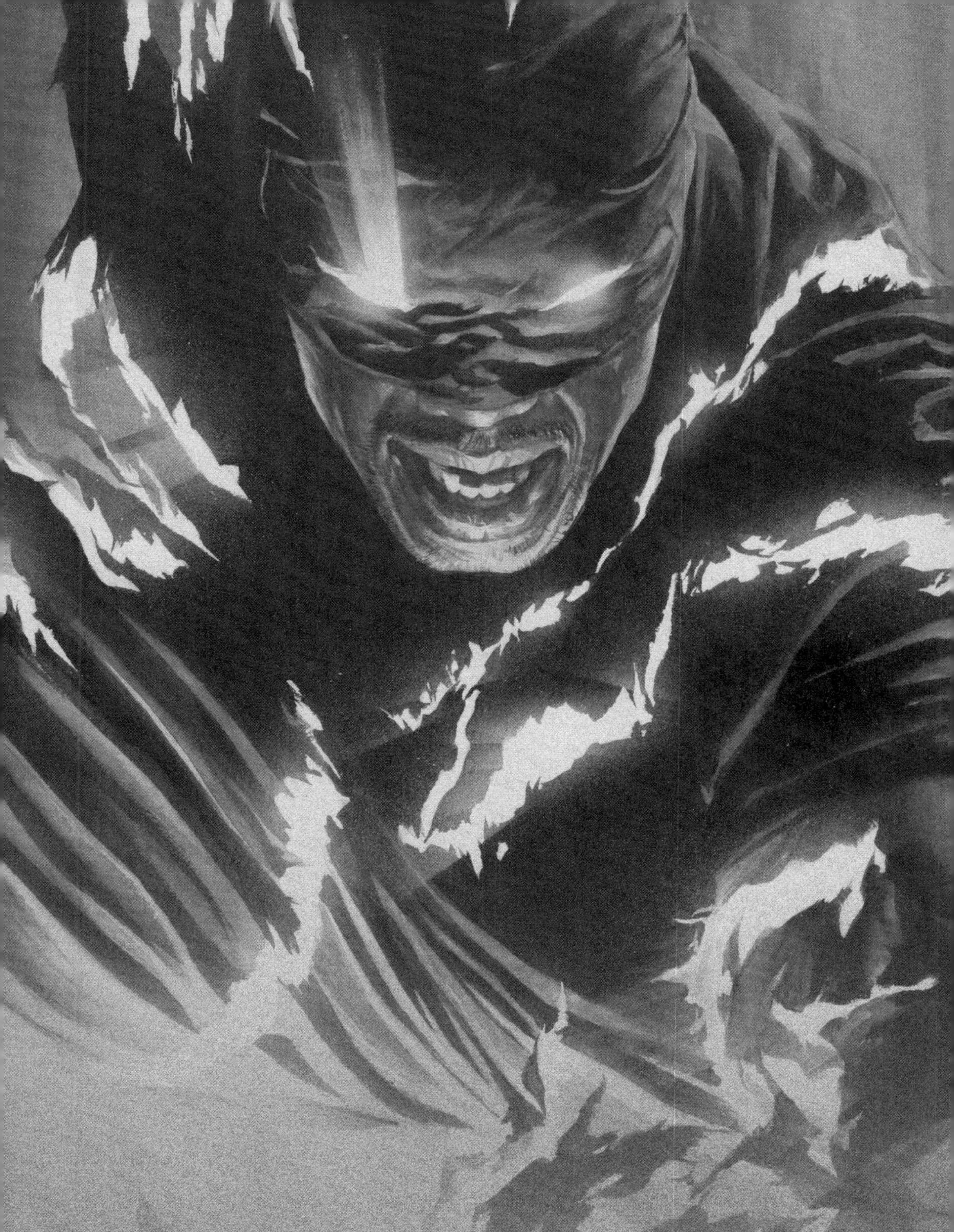

THREE

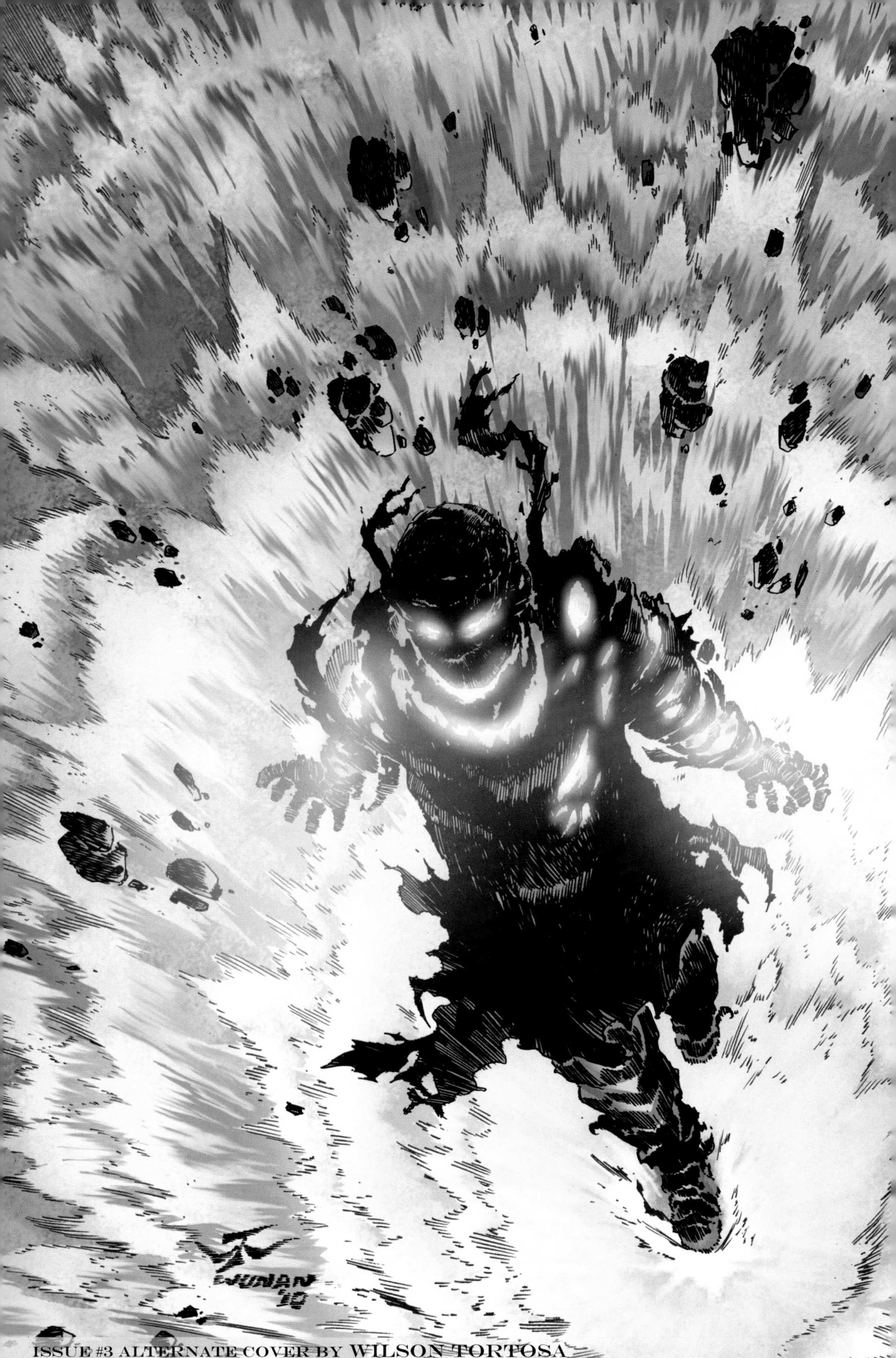
WUNAN '10

ISSUE #3 ALTERNATE COVER BY WILSON TORTOSA

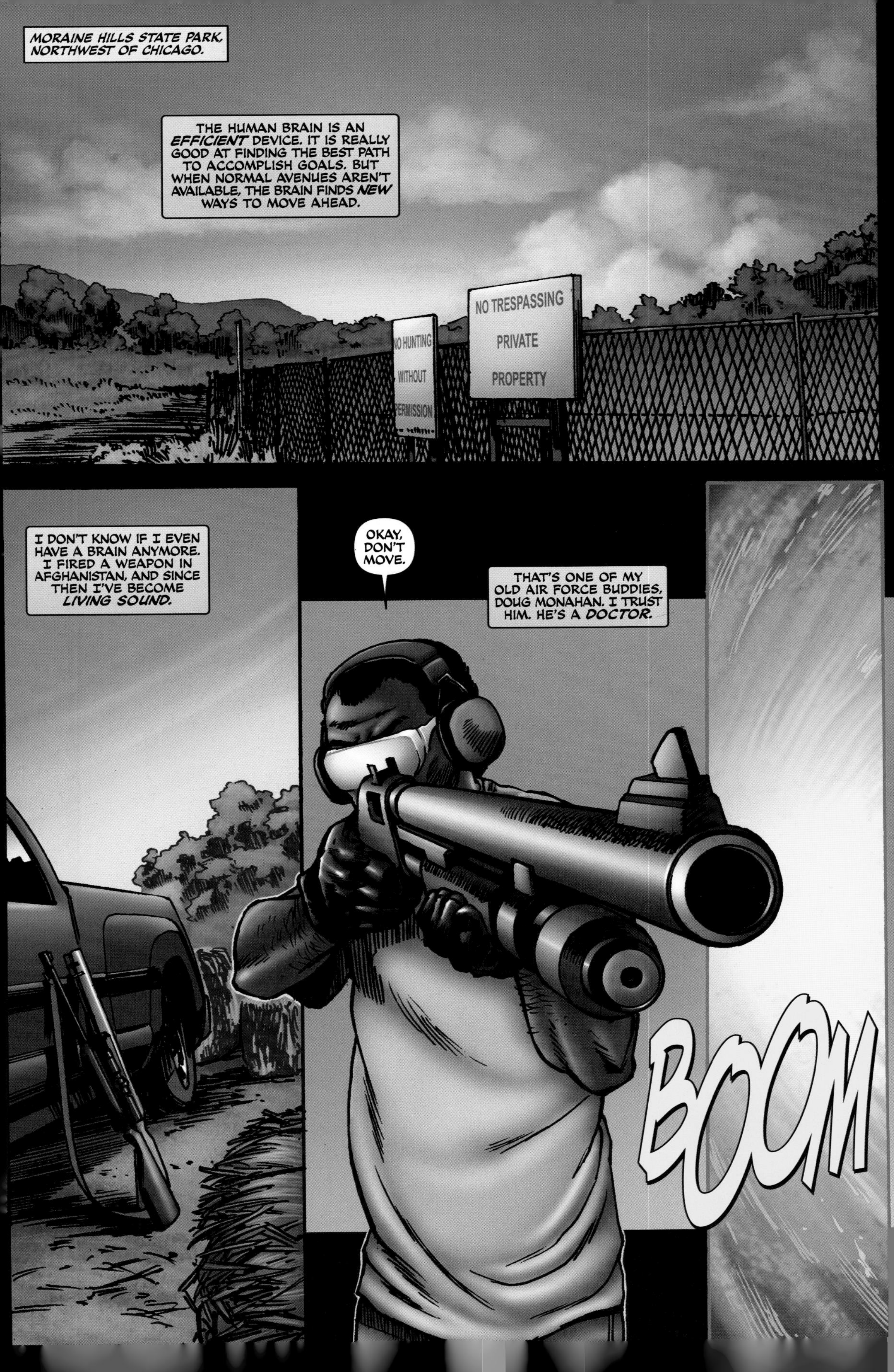
MORAINE HILLS STATE PARK, NORTHWEST OF CHICAGO.
THE HUMAN BRAIN IS AN *EFFICIENT* DEVICE. IT IS REALLY GOOD AT FINDING THE BEST PATH TO ACCOMPLISH GOALS. BUT WHEN NORMAL AVENUES AREN'T AVAILABLE, THE BRAIN FINDS *NEW* WAYS TO MOVE AHEAD.
NO HUNTING WITHOUT PERMISSION
NO TRESPASSING PRIVATE PROPERTY
I DON'T KNOW IF I EVEN HAVE A BRAIN ANYMORE. I FIRED A WEAPON IN AFGHANISTAN, AND SINCE THEN I'VE BECOME *LIVING SOUND.*
OKAY, DON'T MOVE.
THAT'S ONE OF MY OLD AIR FORCE BUDDIES, DOUG MONAHAN. I TRUST HIM. HE'S A *DOCTOR.*
BOOM

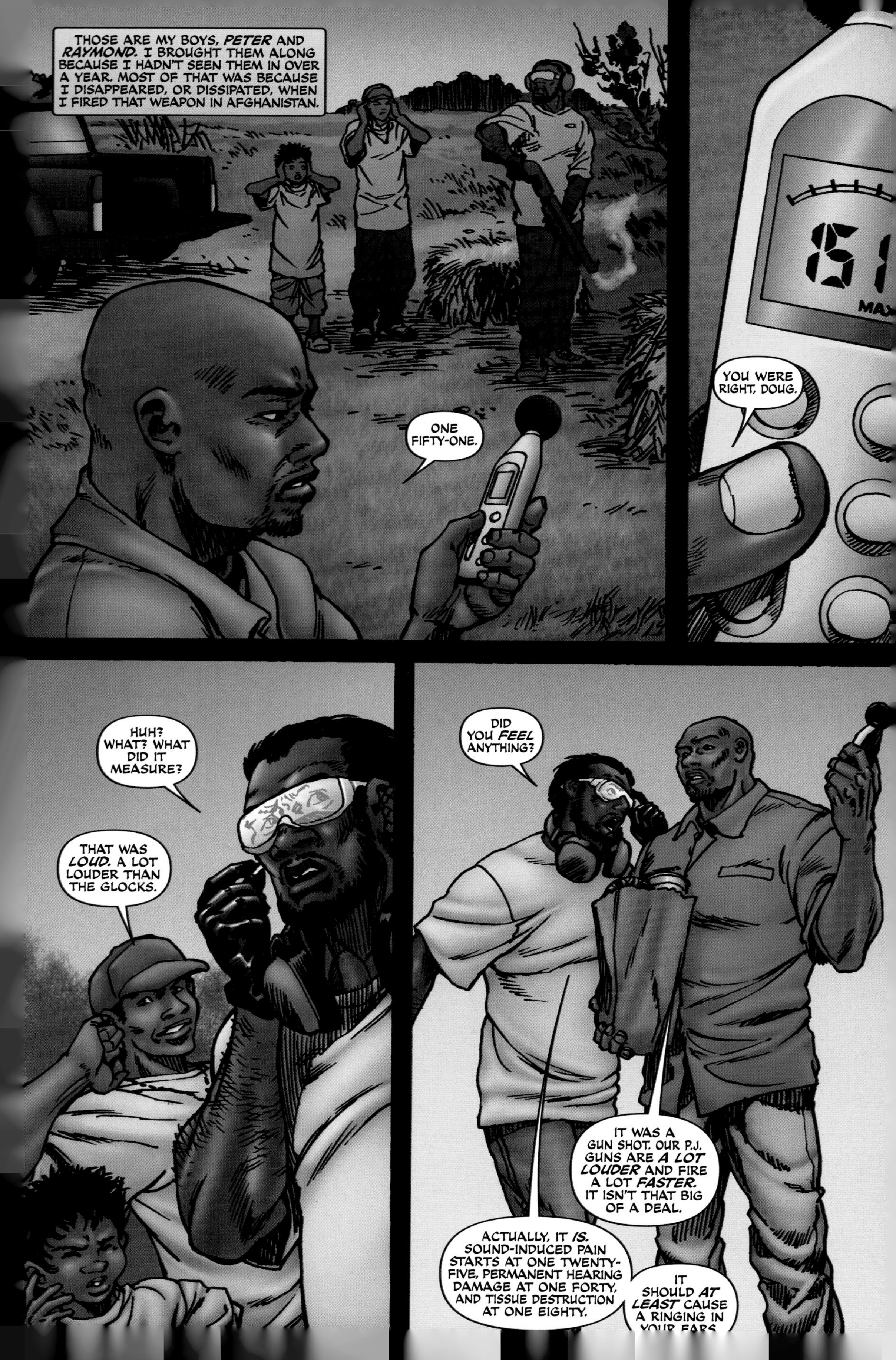

THOSE ARE MY BOYS, *PETER* AND *RAYMOND.* I BROUGHT THEM ALONG BECAUSE I HADN'T SEEN THEM IN OVER A YEAR. MOST OF THAT WAS BECAUSE I DISAPPEARED, OR DISSIPATED, WHEN I FIRED THAT WEAPON IN AFGHANISTAN.
ONE FIFTY-ONE.
YOU WERE RIGHT, DOUG.
HUH? WHAT? WHAT DID IT MEASURE?
THAT WAS *LOUD.* A LOT LOUDER THAN THE GLOCKS.
DID YOU *FEEL* ANYTHING?
IT WAS A GUN SHOT. OUR P.J. GUNS ARE *A LOT LOUDER* AND FIRE A LOT *FASTER.* IT ISN'T THAT BIG OF A DEAL.
ACTUALLY, IT *IS.* SOUND-INDUCED PAIN STARTS AT ONE TWENTY-FIVE, PERMANENT HEARING DAMAGE AT ONE FORTY, AND TISSUE DESTRUCTION AT ONE EIGHTY.
IT SHOULD *AT LEAST* CAUSE A RINGING IN

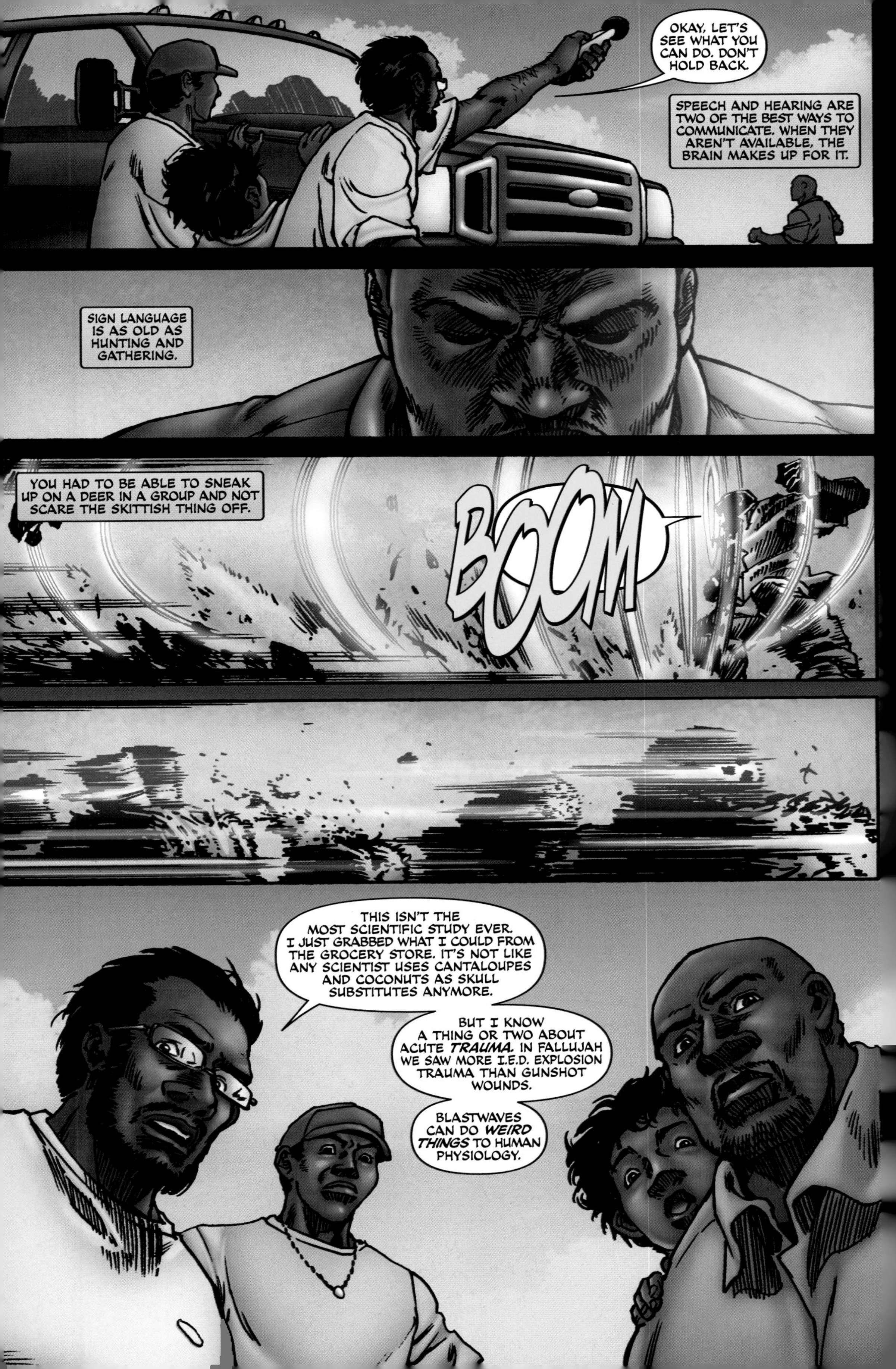
OKAY, LET'S SEE WHAT YOU CAN DO. DON'T HOLD BACK.
SPEECH AND HEARING ARE TWO OF THE BEST WAYS TO COMMUNICATE. WHEN THEY AREN'T AVAILABLE, THE BRAIN MAKES UP FOR IT.
SIGN LANGUAGE IS AS OLD AS HUNTING AND GATHERING.
YOU HAD TO BE ABLE TO SNEAK UP ON A DEER IN A GROUP AND NOT SCARE THE SKITTISH THING OFF.
BOOM
THIS ISN'T THE MOST SCIENTIFIC STUDY EVER. I JUST GRABBED WHAT I COULD FROM THE GROCERY STORE. IT'S NOT LIKE ANY SCIENTIST USES CANTALOUPES AND COCONUTS AS SKULL SUBSTITUTES ANYMORE.
BUT I KNOW A THING OR TWO ABOUT ACUTE *TRAUMA.* IN FALLUJAH WE SAW MORE I.E.D. EXPLOSION TRAUMA THAN GUNSHOT WOUNDS.
BLASTWAVES CAN DO *WEIRD THINGS* TO HUMAN PHYSIOLOGY.

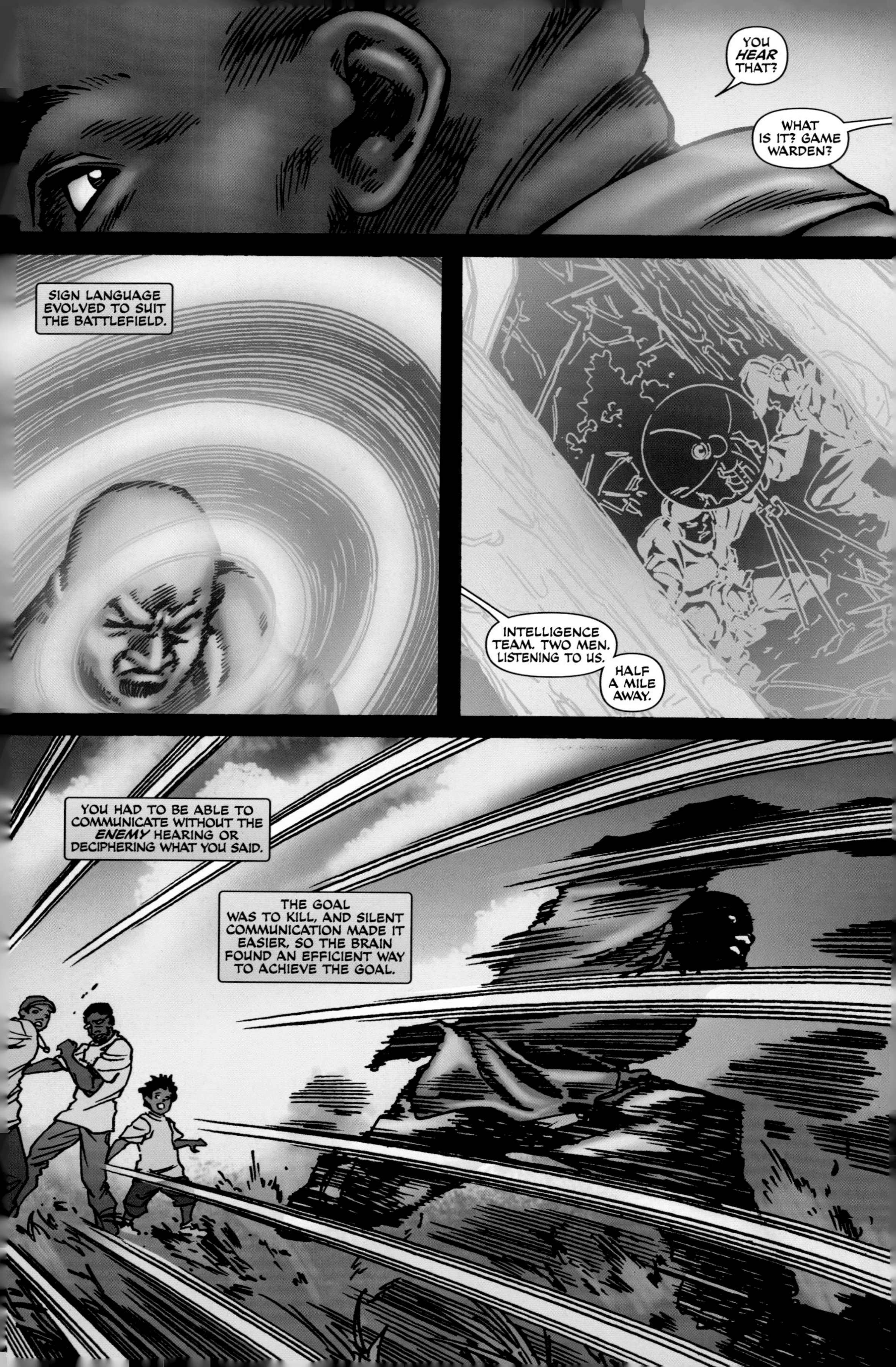
YOU HEAR THAT?
WHAT IS IT? GAME WARDEN?
SIGN LANGUAGE EVOLVED TO SUIT THE BATTLEFIELD.
INTELLIGENCE TEAM. TWO MEN. LISTENING TO US.
HALF A MILE AWAY.
YOU HAD TO BE ABLE TO COMMUNICATE WITHOUT THE ENEMY HEARING OR DECIPHERING WHAT YOU SAID.
THE GOAL WAS TO KILL, AND SILENT COMMUNICATION MADE IT EASIER, SO THE BRAIN FOUND AN EFFICIENT WAY TO ACHIEVE THE GOAL.

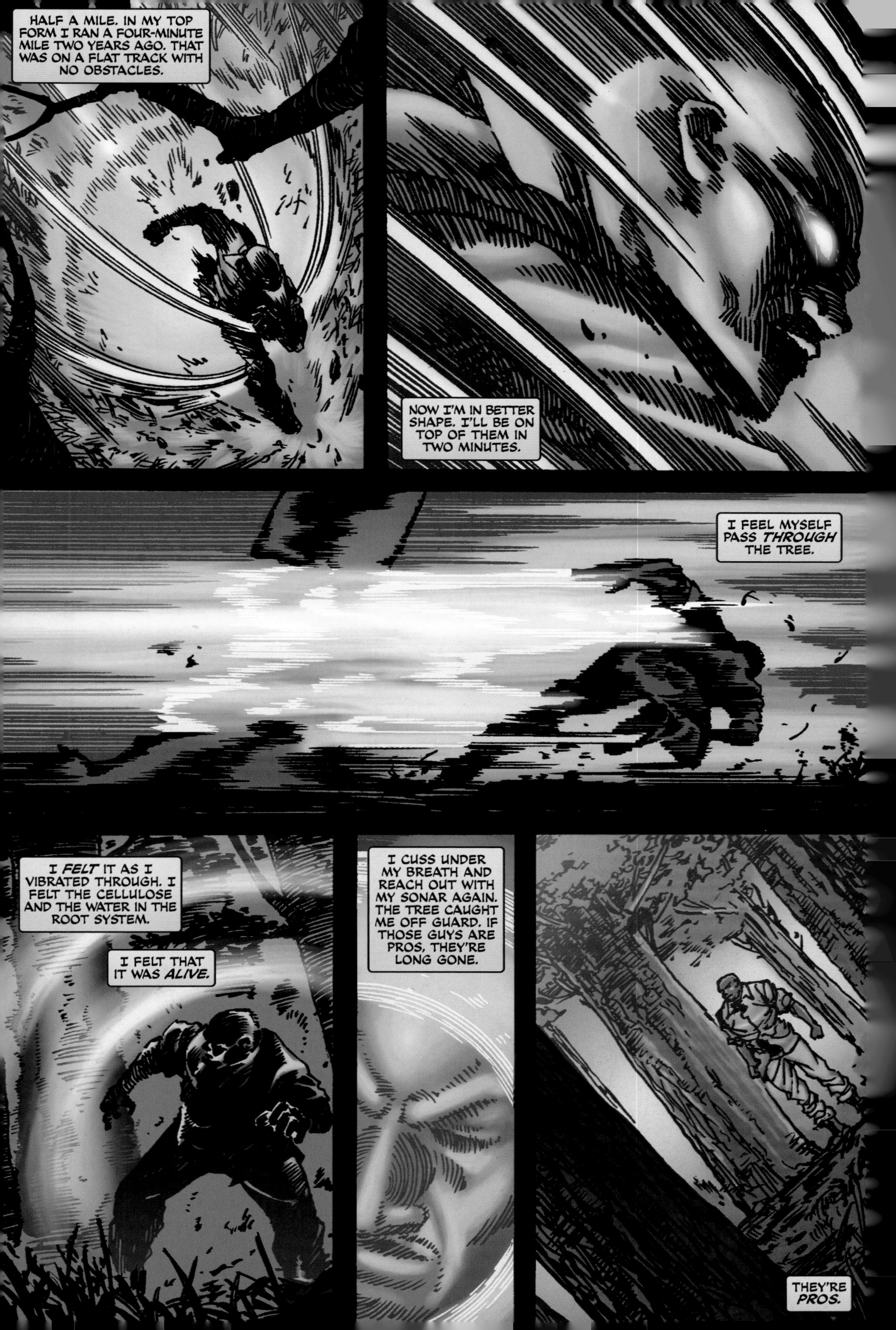
HALF A MILE. IN MY TOP FORM I RAN A FOUR-MINUTE MILE TWO YEARS AGO. THAT WAS ON A FLAT TRACK WITH NO OBSTACLES.
NOW I'M IN BETTER SHAPE. I'LL BE ON TOP OF THEM IN TWO MINUTES.
I FEEL MYSELF PASS *THROUGH* THE TREE.
I *FELT* IT AS I VIBRATED THROUGH. I FELT THE CELLULOSE AND THE WATER IN THE ROOT SYSTEM.
I FELT THAT IT WAS *ALIVE*.
I CUSS UNDER MY BREATH AND REACH OUT WITH MY SONAR AGAIN. THE TREE CAUGHT ME OFF GUARD. IF THOSE GUYS ARE PROS, THEY'RE LONG GONE.
THEY'RE *PROS*.

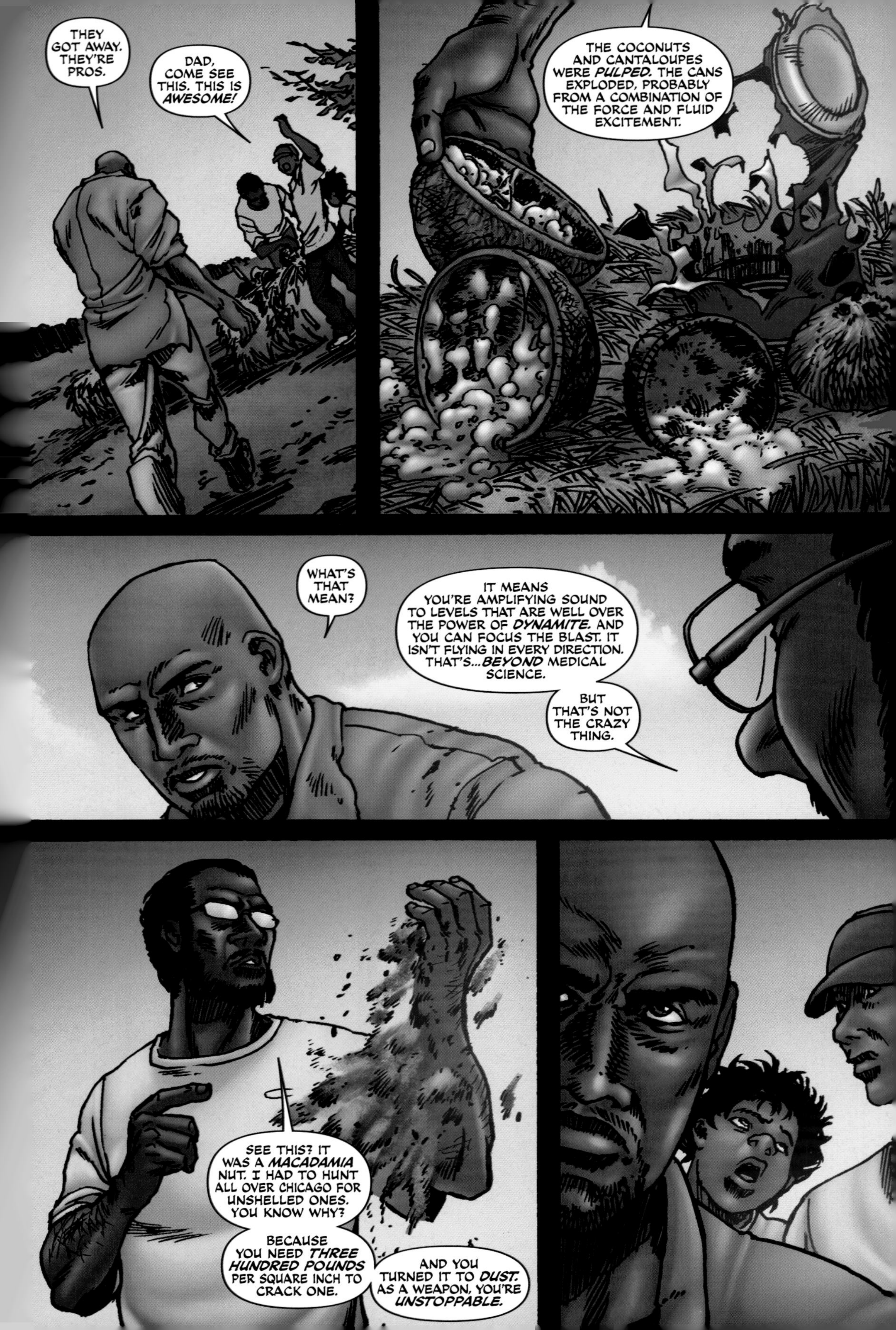
THEY GOT AWAY. THEY'RE PROS.
DAD, COME SEE THIS. THIS IS AWESOME!
THE COCONUTS AND CANTALOUPES WERE PULPED. THE CANS EXPLODED, PROBABLY FROM A COMBINATION OF THE FORCE AND FLUID EXCITEMENT.
WHAT'S THAT MEAN?
IT MEANS YOU'RE AMPLIFYING SOUND TO LEVELS THAT ARE WELL OVER THE POWER OF DYNAMITE. AND YOU CAN FOCUS THE BLAST. IT ISN'T FLYING IN EVERY DIRECTION. THAT'S...BEYOND MEDICAL SCIENCE.
BUT THAT'S NOT THE CRAZY THING.
SEE THIS? IT WAS A MACADAMIA NUT. I HAD TO HUNT ALL OVER CHICAGO FOR UNSHELLED ONES. YOU KNOW WHY?
BECAUSE YOU NEED THREE HUNDRED POUNDS PER SQUARE INCH TO CRACK ONE.
AND YOU TURNED IT TO DUST. AS A WEAPON, YOU'RE UNSTOPPABLE.

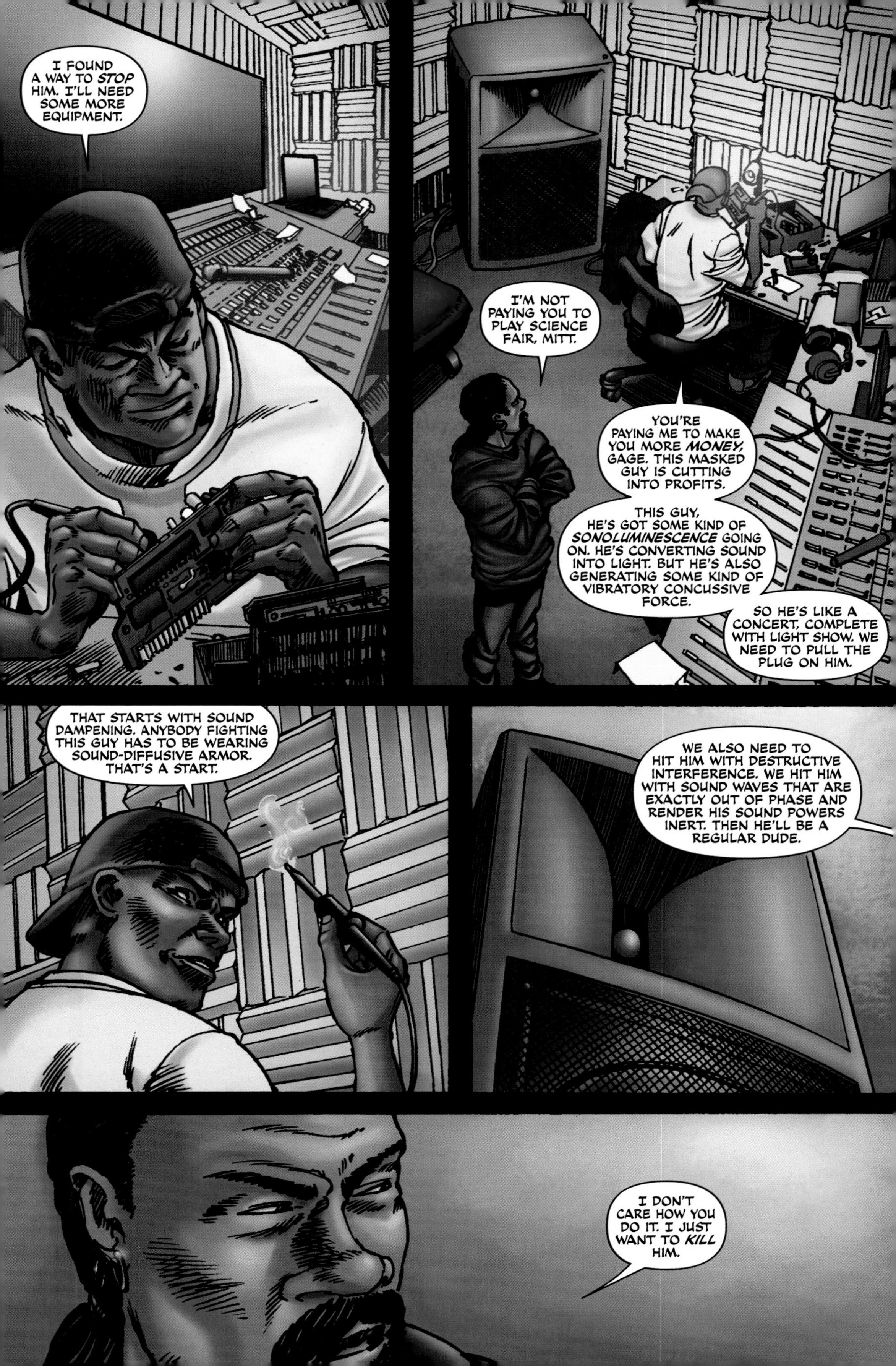
I FOUND A WAY TO *STOP* HIM. I'LL NEED SOME MORE EQUIPMENT.
I'M NOT PAYING YOU TO PLAY SCIENCE FAIR, MITT.
YOU'RE PAYING ME TO MAKE YOU MORE *MONEY*, GAGE. THIS MASKED GUY IS CUTTING INTO PROFITS.
THIS GUY, HE'S GOT SOME KIND OF *SONOLUMINESCENCE* GOING ON. HE'S CONVERTING SOUND INTO LIGHT. BUT HE'S ALSO GENERATING SOME KIND OF VIBRATORY CONCUSSIVE FORCE.
SO HE'S LIKE A CONCERT, COMPLETE WITH LIGHT SHOW. WE NEED TO PULL THE PLUG ON HIM.
THAT STARTS WITH SOUND DAMPENING. ANYBODY FIGHTING THIS GUY HAS TO BE WEARING SOUND-DIFFUSIVE ARMOR. THAT'S A START.
WE ALSO NEED TO HIT HIM WITH DESTRUCTIVE INTERFERENCE. WE HIT HIM WITH SOUND WAVES THAT ARE EXACTLY OUT OF PHASE AND RENDER HIS SOUND POWERS INERT. THEN HE'LL BE A REGULAR DUDE.
I DON'T CARE HOW YOU DO IT. I JUST WANT TO *KILL* HIM.

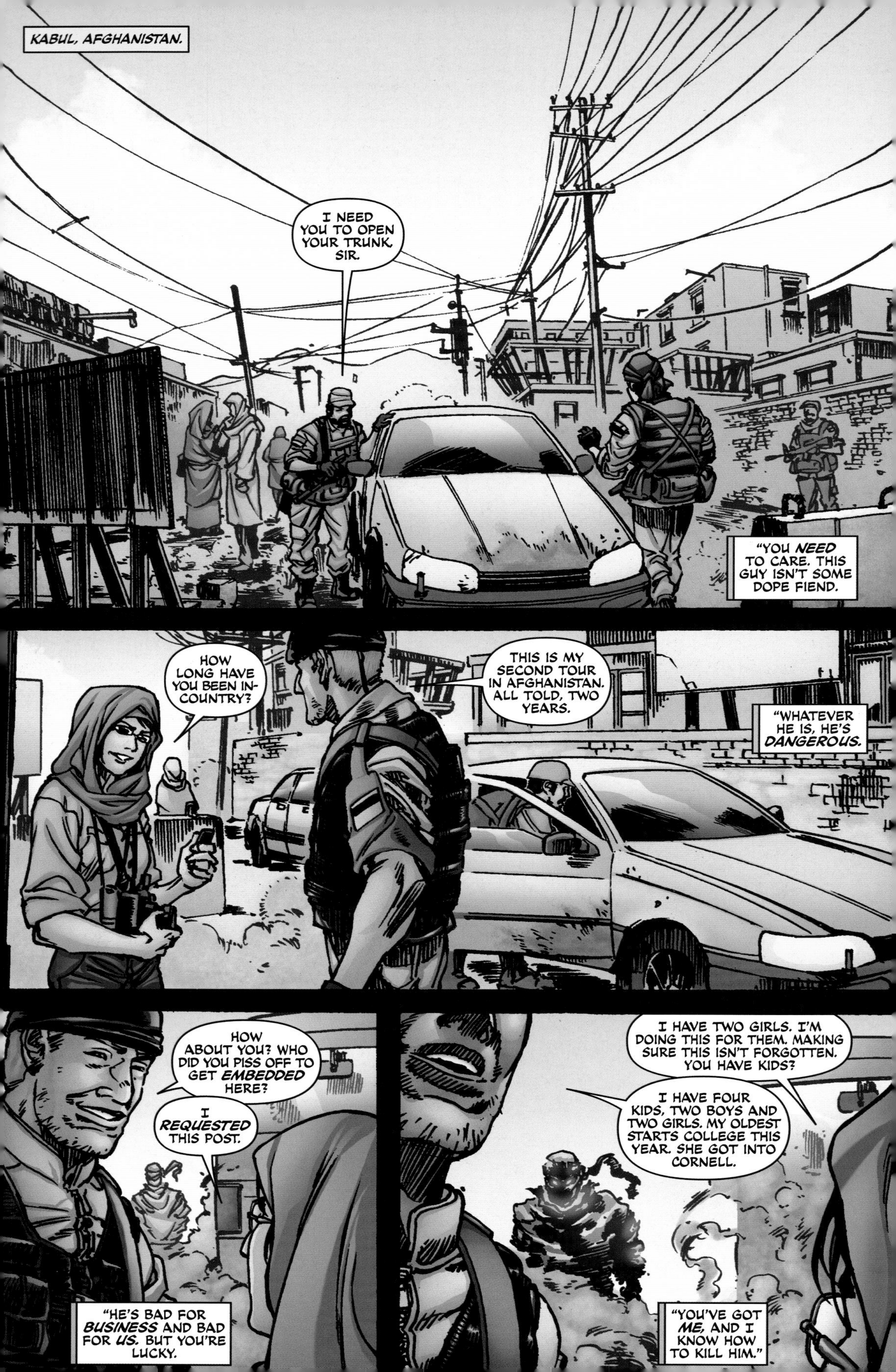
KABUL, AFGHANISTAN.
I NEED YOU TO OPEN YOUR TRUNK, SIR.
"YOU NEED TO CARE. THIS GUY ISN'T SOME DOPE FIEND.
HOW LONG HAVE YOU BEEN IN-COUNTRY?
THIS IS MY SECOND TOUR IN AFGHANISTAN. ALL TOLD, TWO YEARS.
"WHATEVER HE IS, HE'S DANGEROUS.
HOW ABOUT YOU? WHO DID YOU PISS OFF TO GET EMBEDDED HERE?
I REQUESTED THIS POST.
"HE'S BAD FOR BUSINESS AND BAD FOR US. BUT YOU'RE LUCKY.
I HAVE TWO GIRLS. I'M DOING THIS FOR THEM. MAKING SURE THIS ISN'T FORGOTTEN. YOU HAVE KIDS?
I HAVE FOUR KIDS, TWO BOYS AND TWO GIRLS. MY OLDEST STARTS COLLEGE THIS YEAR. SHE GOT INTO CORNELL.
"YOU'VE GOT ME, AND I KNOW HOW TO KILL HIM."

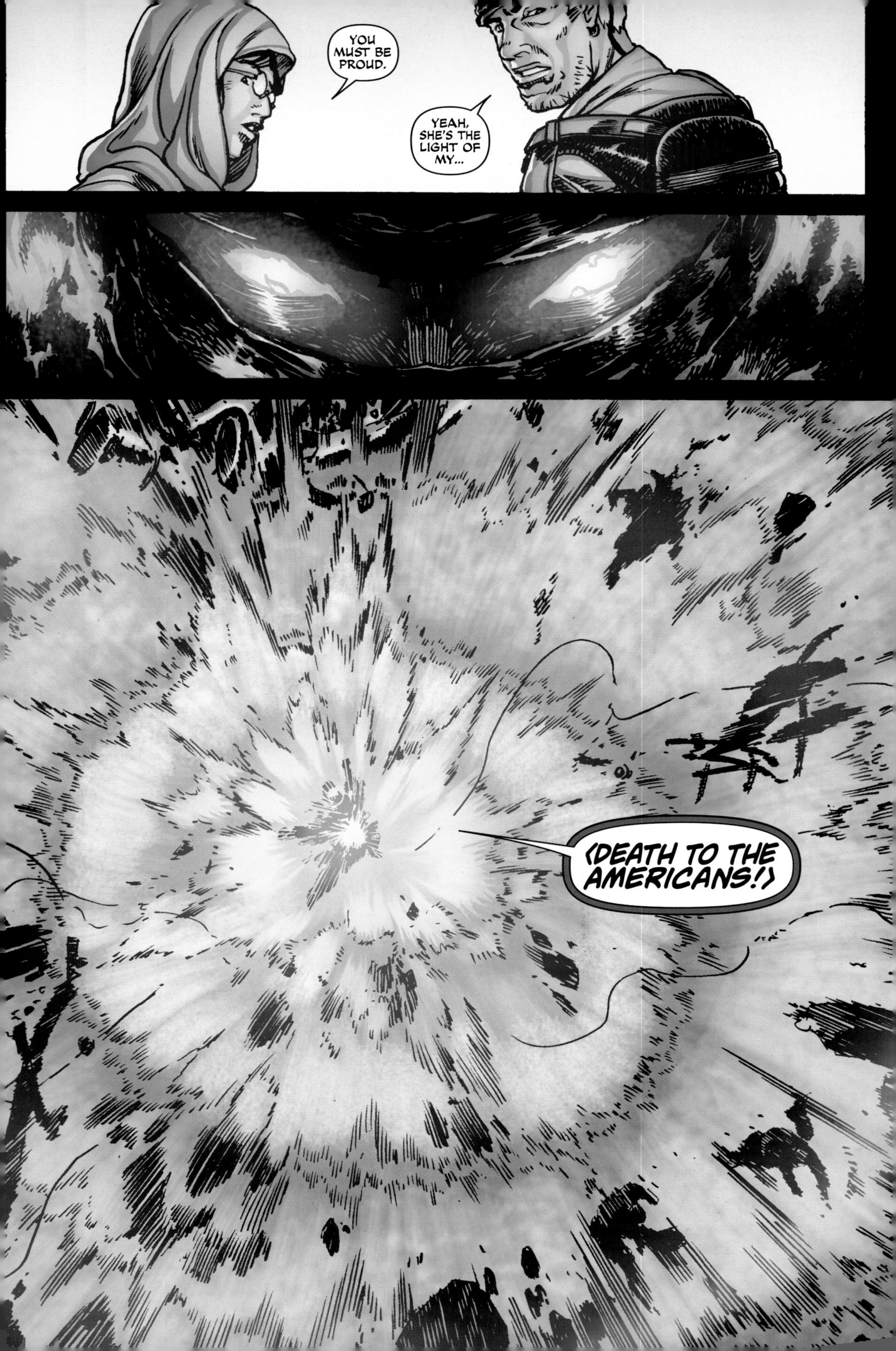
YOU MUST BE PROUD.
YEAH, SHE'S THE LIGHT OF MY...
‹DEATH TO THE AMERICANS!›

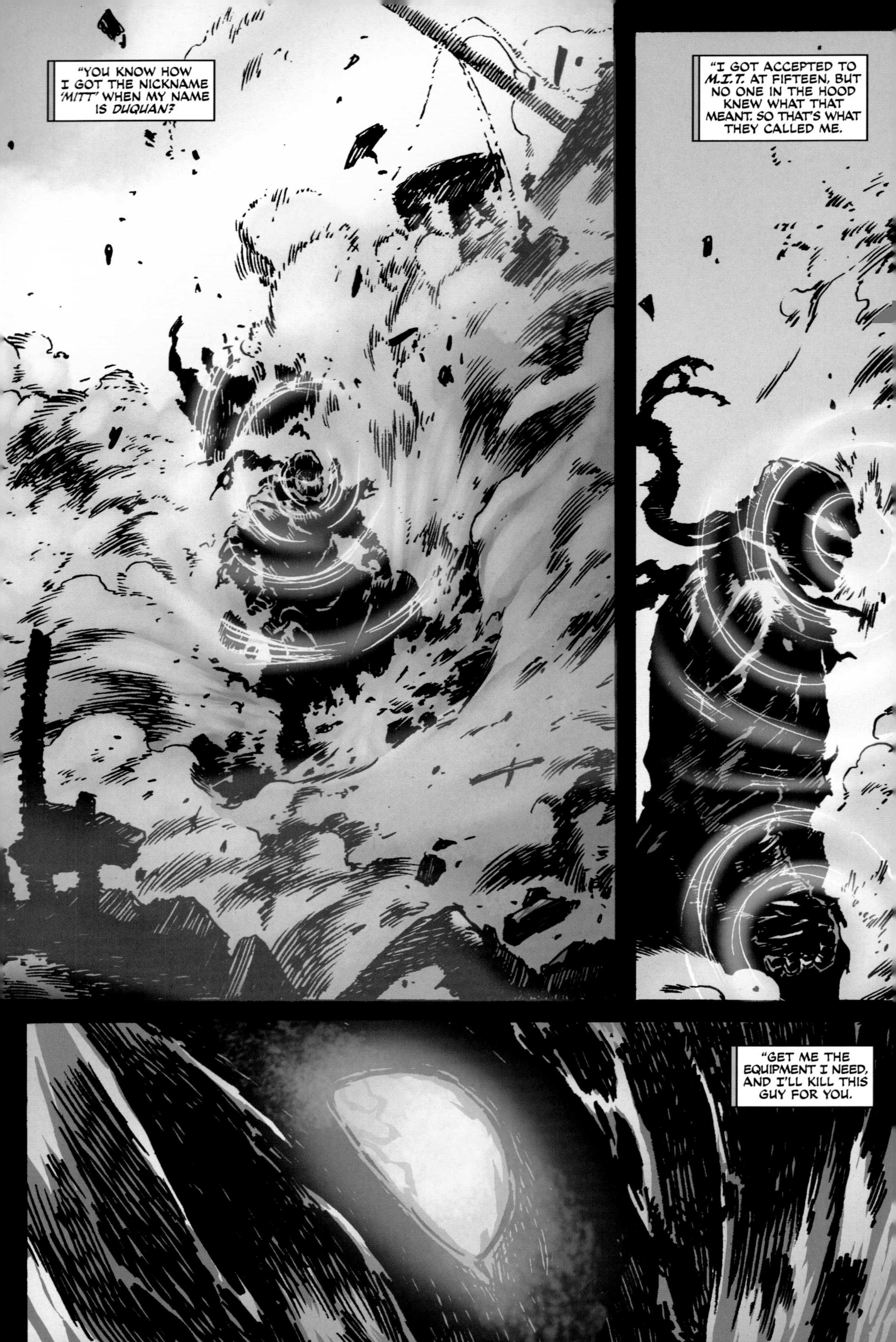
"YOU KNOW HOW I GOT THE NICKNAME 'MITT' WHEN MY NAME IS DUQUAN?
"I GOT ACCEPTED TO M.I.T. AT FIFTEEN, BUT NO ONE IN THE HOOD KNEW WHAT THAT MEANT. SO THAT'S WHAT THEY CALLED ME.
"GET ME THE EQUIPMENT I NEED, AND I'LL KILL THIS GUY FOR YOU.

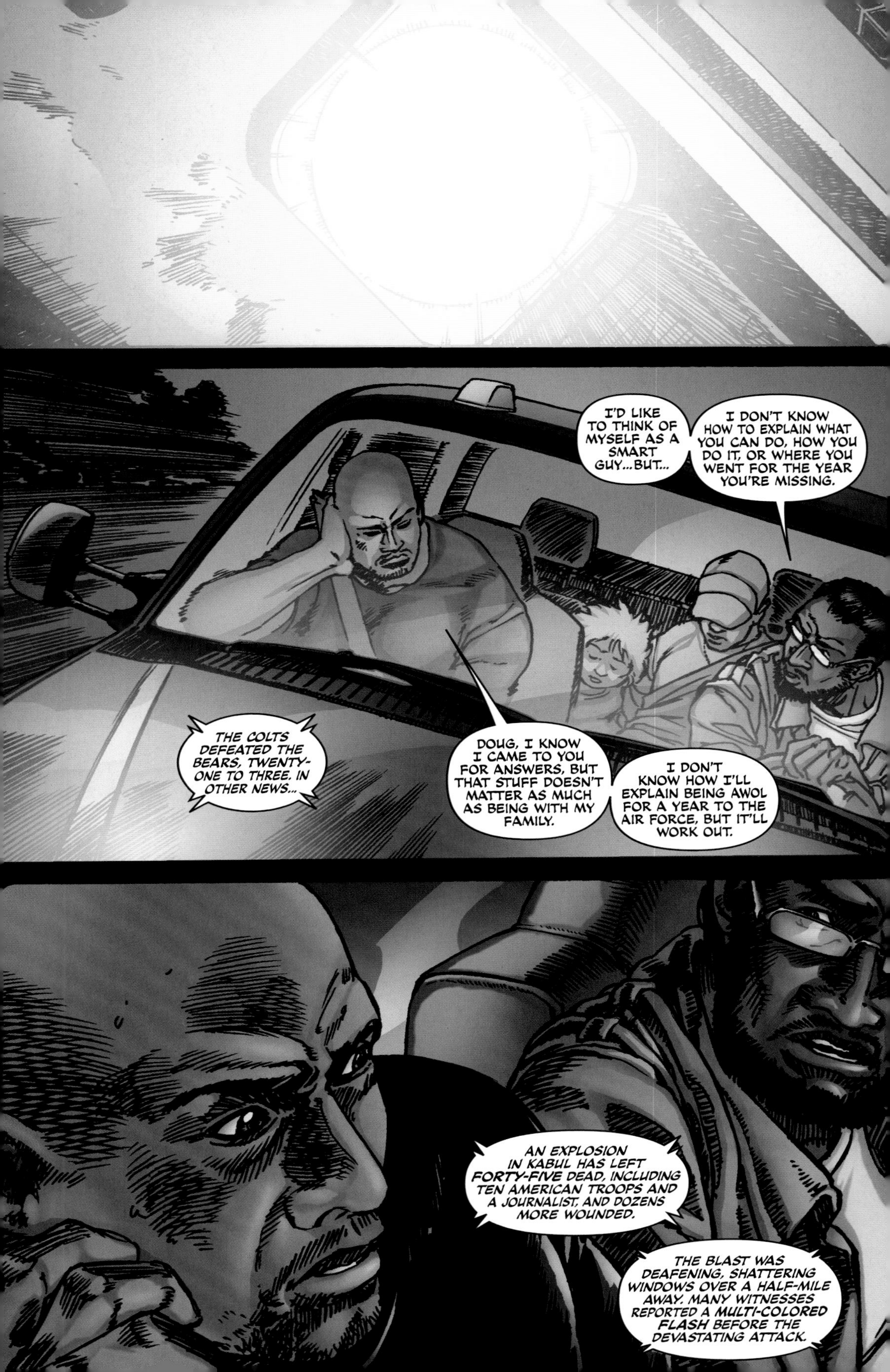
I'D LIKE TO THINK OF MYSELF AS A SMART GUY...BUT...
I DON'T KNOW HOW TO EXPLAIN WHAT YOU CAN DO, HOW YOU DO IT, OR WHERE YOU WENT FOR THE YEAR YOU'RE MISSING.
THE COLTS DEFEATED THE BEARS, TWENTY-ONE TO THREE. IN OTHER NEWS...
DOUG, I KNOW I CAME TO YOU FOR ANSWERS, BUT THAT STUFF DOESN'T MATTER AS MUCH AS BEING WITH MY FAMILY.
I DON'T KNOW HOW I'LL EXPLAIN BEING AWOL FOR A YEAR TO THE AIR FORCE, BUT IT'LL WORK OUT.
AN EXPLOSION IN KABUL HAS LEFT FORTY-FIVE DEAD, INCLUDING TEN AMERICAN TROOPS AND A JOURNALIST, AND DOZENS MORE WOUNDED.
THE BLAST WAS DEAFENING, SHATTERING WINDOWS OVER A HALF-MILE AWAY. MANY WITNESSES REPORTED A MULTI-COLORED FLASH BEFORE THE DEVASTATING ATTACK.

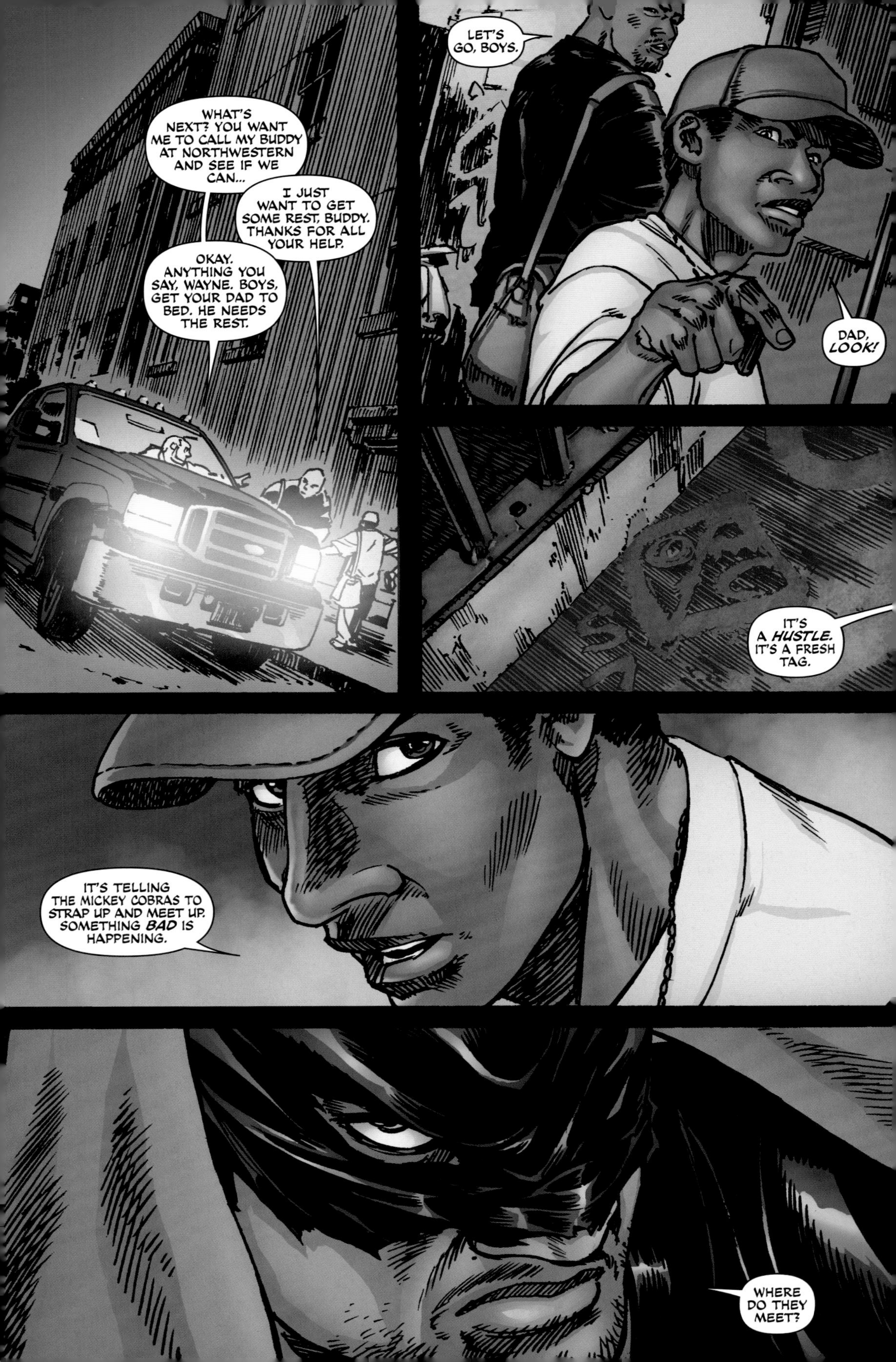
WHAT'S NEXT? YOU WANT ME TO CALL MY BUDDY AT NORTHWESTERN AND SEE IF WE CAN...
I JUST WANT TO GET SOME REST, BUDDY. THANKS FOR ALL YOUR HELP.
OKAY. ANYTHING YOU SAY, WAYNE. BOYS, GET YOUR DAD TO BED. HE NEEDS THE REST.
LET'S GO, BOYS.
DAD, LOOK!
IT'S A HUSTLE. IT'S A FRESH TAG.
IT'S TELLING THE MICKEY COBRAS TO STRAP UP AND MEET UP. SOMETHING BAD IS HAPPENING.
WHERE DO THEY MEET?

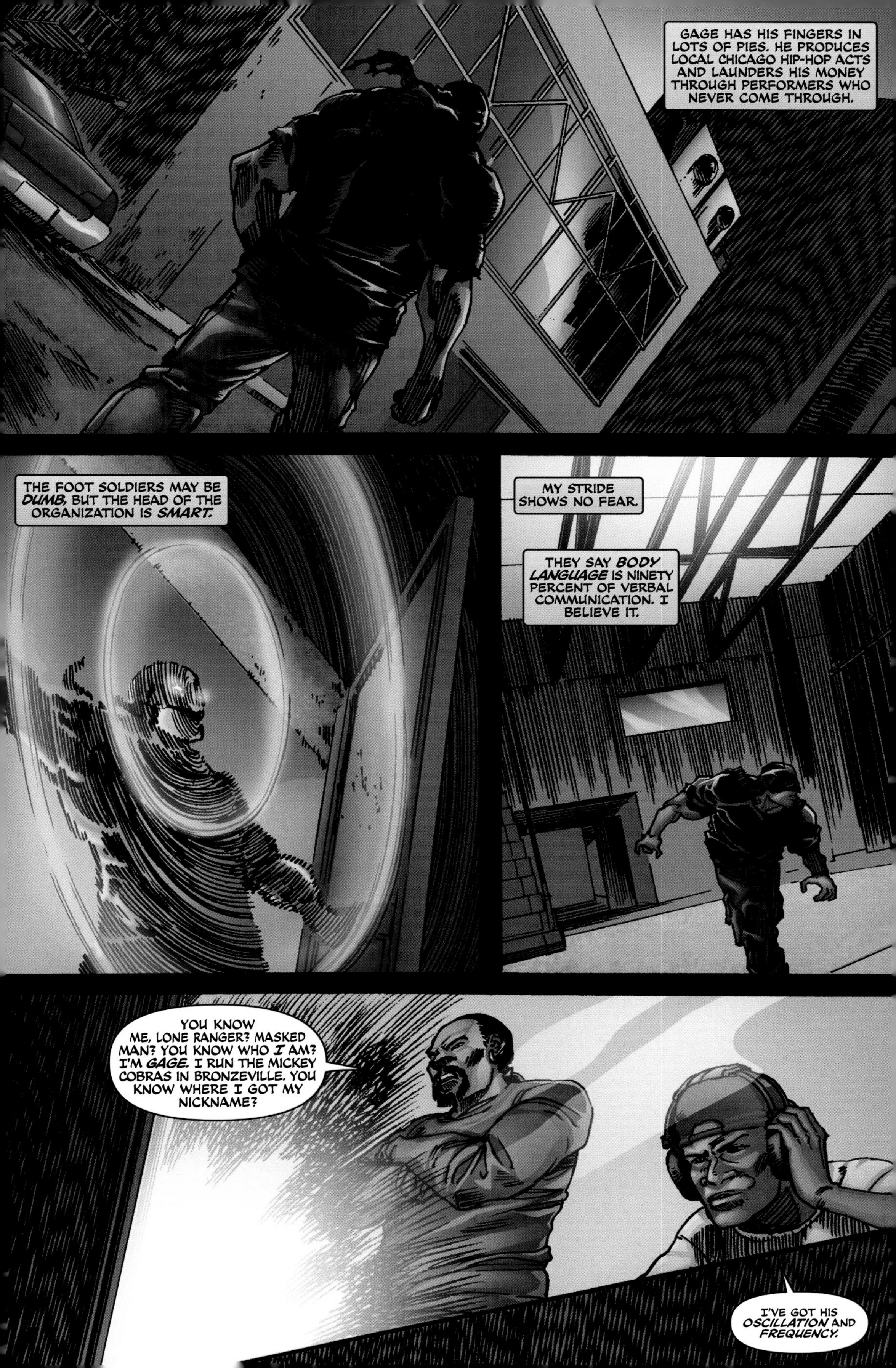
GAGE HAS HIS FINGERS IN LOTS OF PIES. HE PRODUCES LOCAL CHICAGO HIP-HOP ACTS AND LAUNDERS HIS MONEY THROUGH PERFORMERS WHO NEVER COME THROUGH.
THE FOOT SOLDIERS MAY BE *DUMB,* BUT THE HEAD OF THE ORGANIZATION IS *SMART.*
MY STRIDE SHOWS NO FEAR.
THEY SAY *BODY LANGUAGE* IS NINETY PERCENT OF VERBAL COMMUNICATION. I BELIEVE IT.
YOU KNOW ME, LONE RANGER? MASKED MAN? YOU KNOW WHO *I* AM? I'M *GAGE.* I RUN THE MICKEY COBRAS IN BRONZEVILLE. YOU KNOW WHERE I GOT MY NICKNAME?
I'VE GOT HIS *OSCILLATION* AND *FREQUENCY.*

I BROUGHT A *SHOTGUN* TO A *KNIFE FIGHT.*

DID YOU BRING A PILLOW AND JAMMIES TO THIS SLUMBER PARTY? 'CAUSE YOU'RE PUTTING ME TO SLEEP.

HIT THE SPEAKERS.

WE'RE SET.

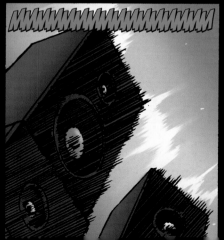

MMMMMMMMMMMMMMMM

MY STOMACH FLIPS OVER AND I FEEL LIKE I'M GOING TO THROW UP.

IT'S THE FIRST TIME I'VE FELT LIKE I *HAD* A STOMACH SINCE AFGHANISTAN.

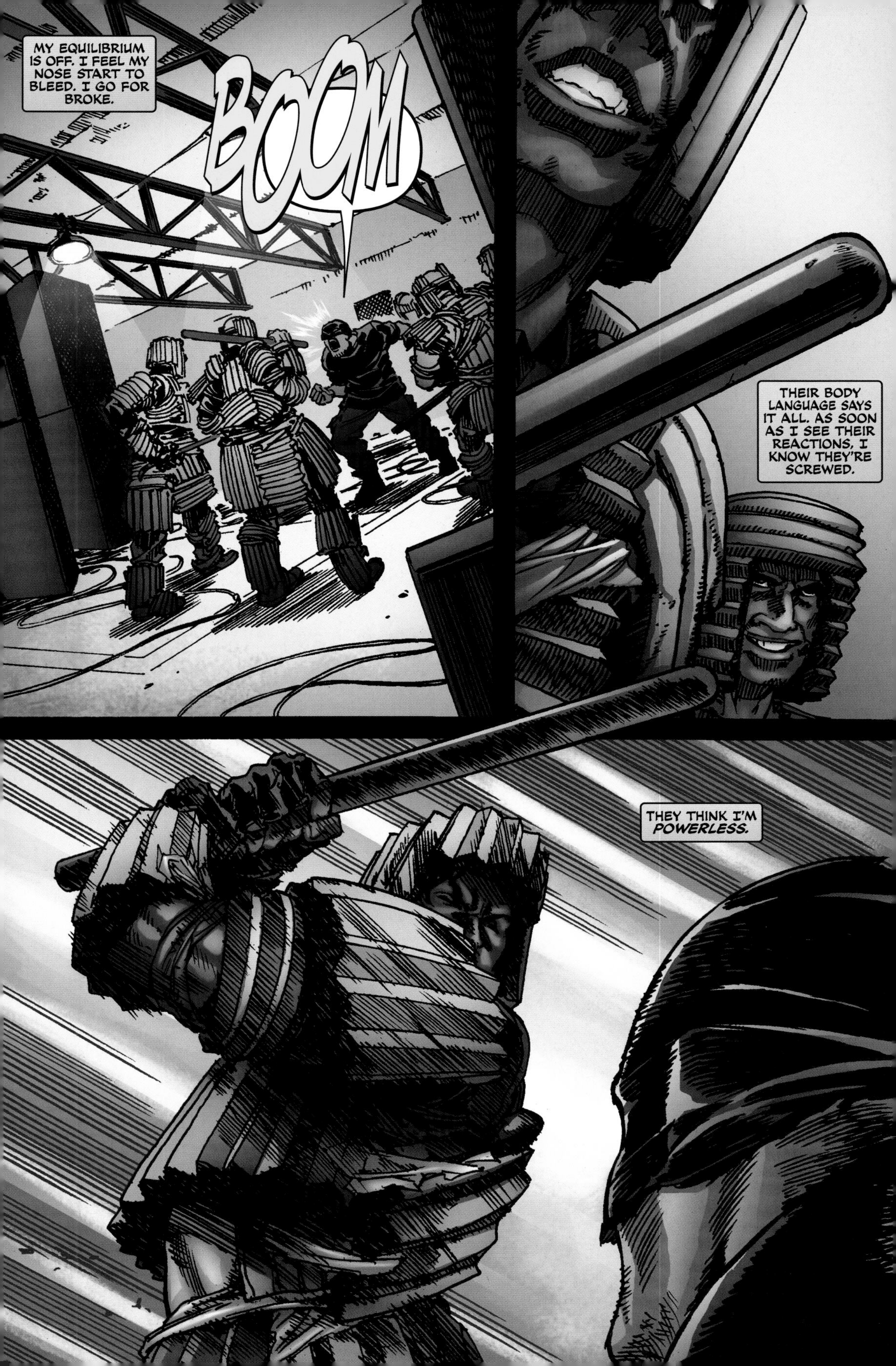
MY EQUILIBRIUM IS OFF. I FEEL MY NOSE START TO BLEED. I GO FOR BROKE.
BOOM
THEIR BODY LANGUAGE SAYS IT ALL. AS SOON AS I SEE THEIR REACTIONS, I KNOW THEY'RE SCREWED.
THEY THINK I'M *POWERLESS.*

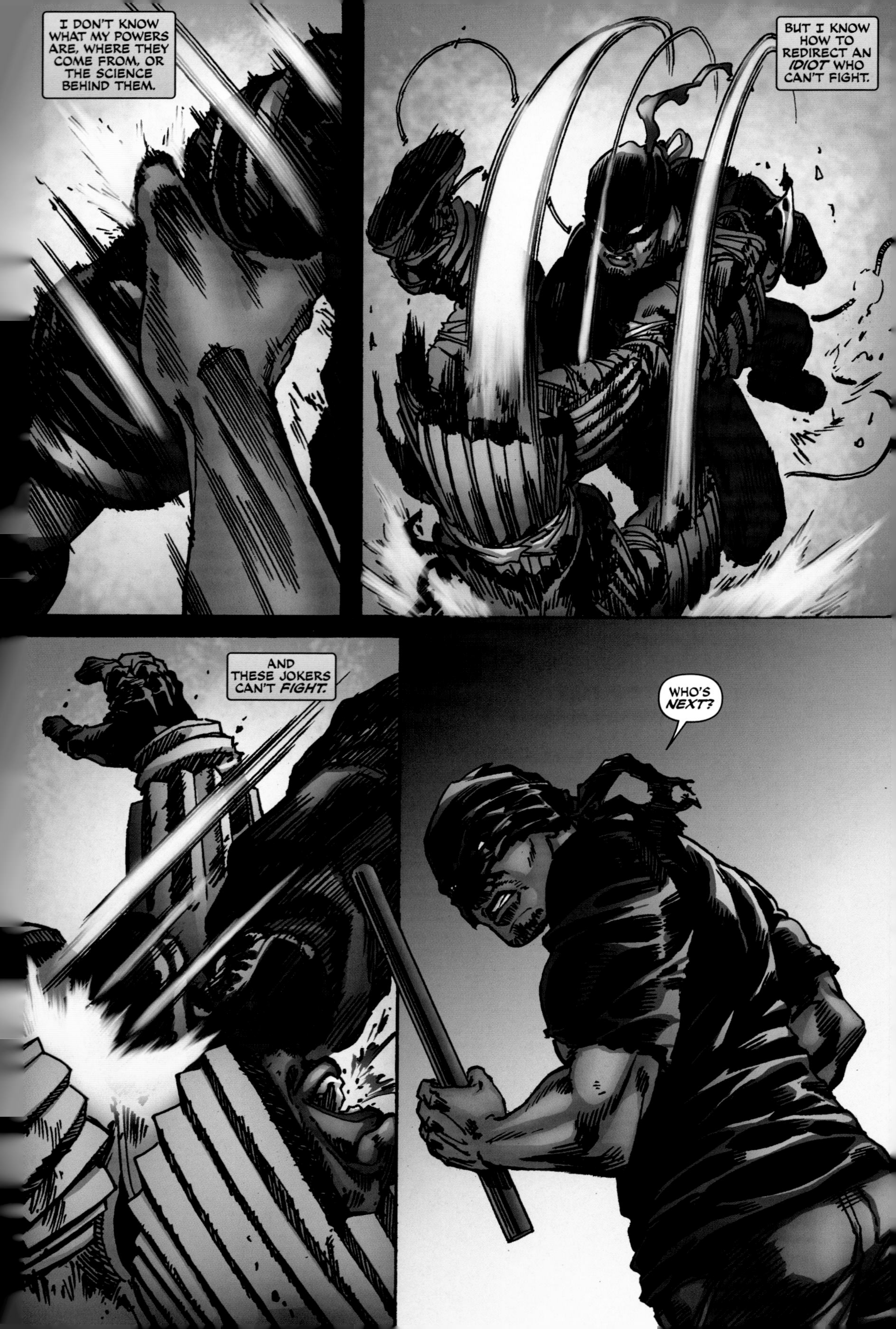
I DON'T KNOW WHAT MY POWERS ARE, WHERE THEY COME FROM, OR THE SCIENCE BEHIND THEM.
BUT I KNOW HOW TO REDIRECT AN *IDIOT* WHO CAN'T FIGHT.
AND THESE JOKERS CAN'T *FIGHT.*
WHO'S *NEXT?*

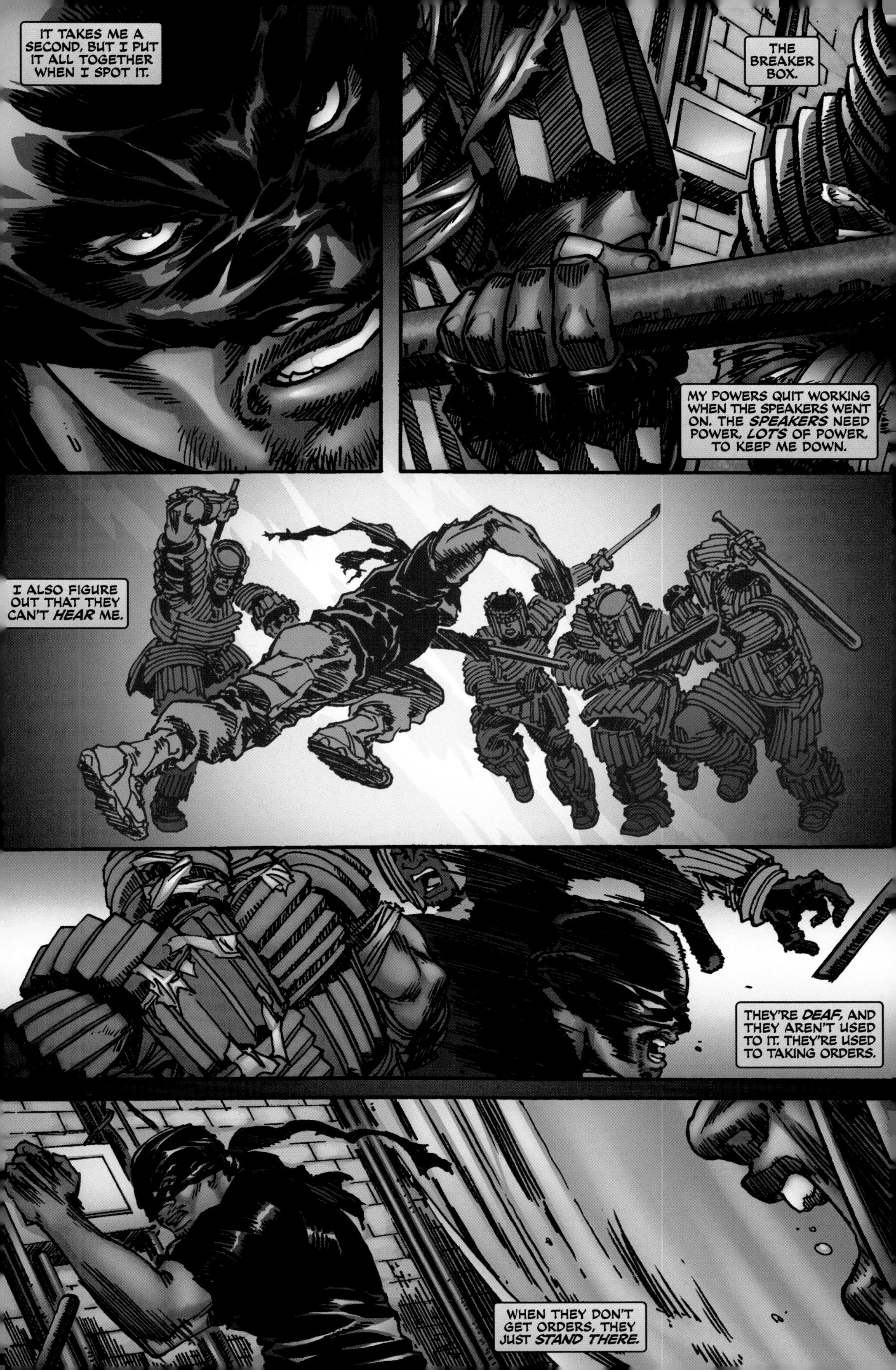
IT TAKES ME A SECOND, BUT I PUT IT ALL TOGETHER WHEN I SPOT IT.
THE BREAKER BOX.
MY POWERS QUIT WORKING WHEN THE SPEAKERS WENT ON. THE *SPEAKERS* NEED POWER, *LOTS* OF POWER, TO KEEP ME DOWN.
I ALSO FIGURE OUT THAT THEY CAN'T *HEAR* ME.
THEY'RE *DEAF,* AND THEY AREN'T USED TO IT. THEY'RE USED TO TAKING ORDERS.
WHEN THEY DON'T GET ORDERS, THEY JUST *STAND THERE.*

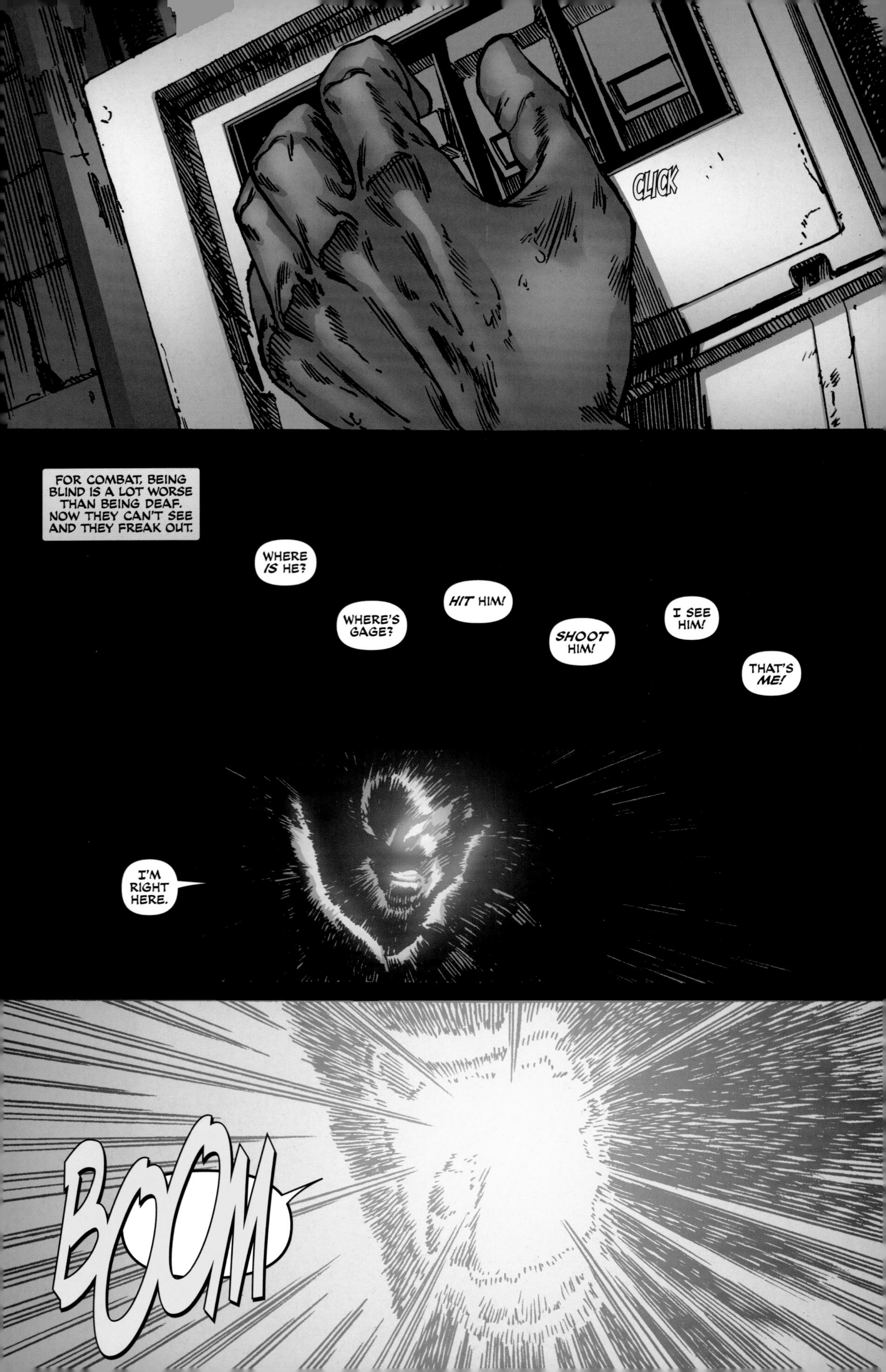
CLICK
FOR COMBAT, BEING BLIND IS A LOT WORSE THAN BEING DEAF. NOW THEY CAN'T SEE AND THEY FREAK OUT.
WHERE IS HE?
WHERE'S GAGE?
HIT HIM!
SHOOT HIM!
I SEE HIM!
THAT'S ME!
I'M RIGHT HERE.
BOOM

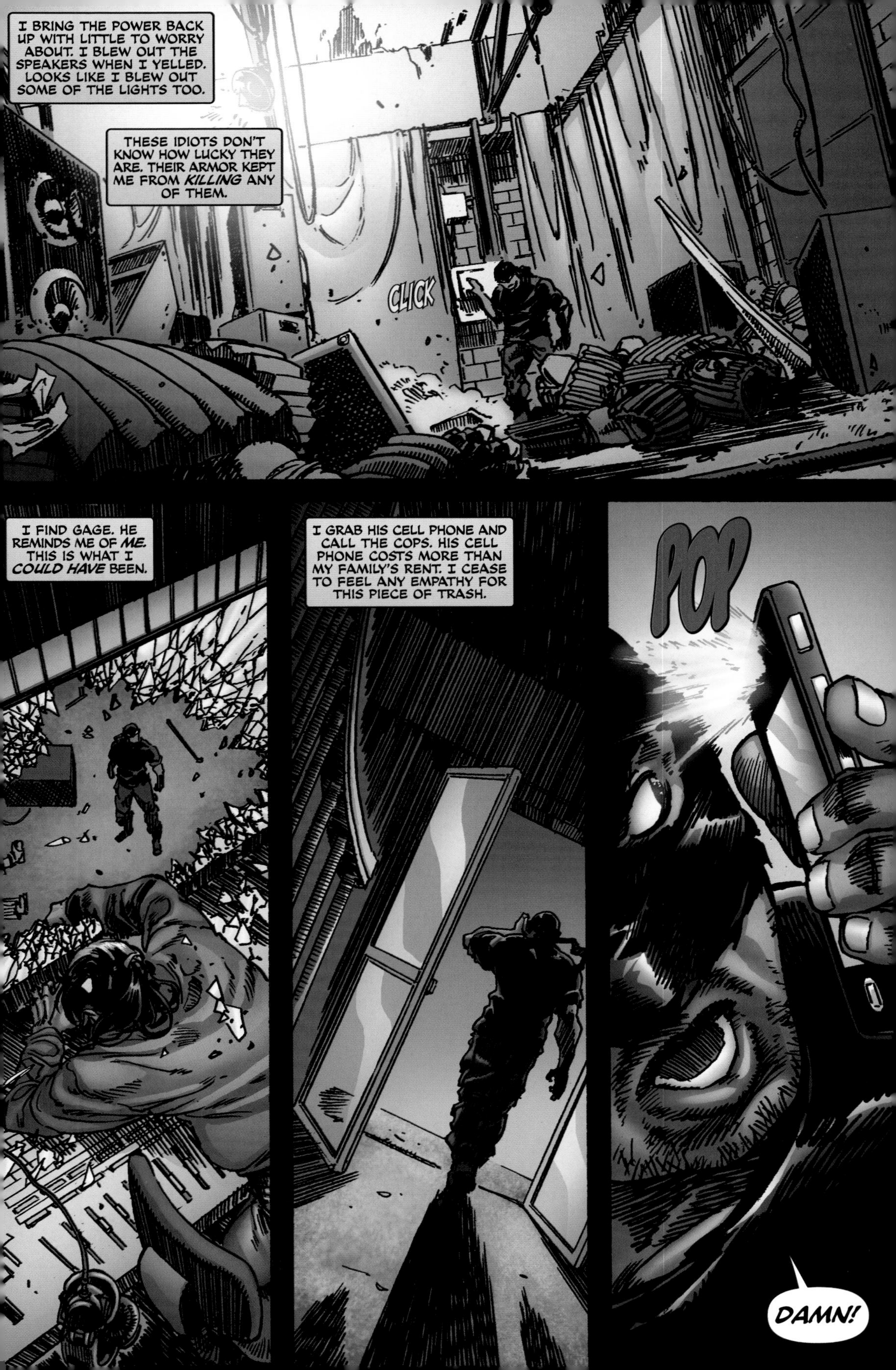
I BRING THE POWER BACK UP WITH LITTLE TO WORRY ABOUT. I BLEW OUT THE SPEAKERS WHEN I YELLED. LOOKS LIKE I BLEW OUT SOME OF THE LIGHTS TOO.
THESE IDIOTS DON'T KNOW HOW LUCKY THEY ARE. THEIR ARMOR KEPT ME FROM *KILLING* ANY OF THEM.
CLICK
I FIND GAGE. HE REMINDS ME OF *ME*. THIS IS WHAT I *COULD HAVE* BEEN.
I GRAB HIS CELL PHONE AND CALL THE COPS. HIS CELL PHONE COSTS MORE THAN MY FAMILY'S RENT. I CEASE TO FEEL ANY EMPATHY FOR THIS PIECE OF TRASH.
POP
DAMN!

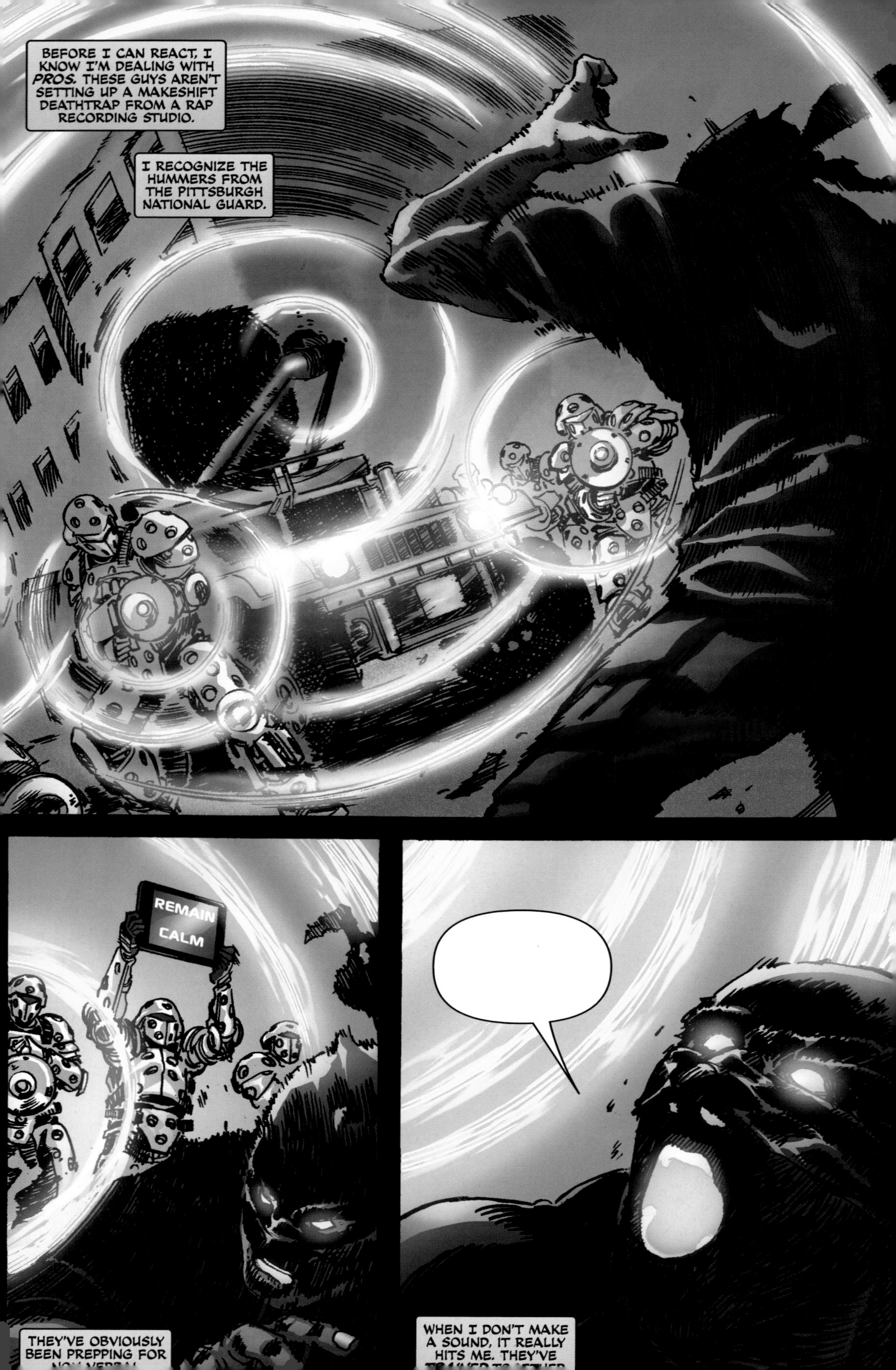
BEFORE I CAN REACT, I KNOW I'M DEALING WITH *PROS.* THESE GUYS AREN'T SETTING UP A MAKESHIFT DEATHTRAP FROM A RAP RECORDING STUDIO.
I RECOGNIZE THE HUMMERS FROM THE PITTSBURGH NATIONAL GUARD.
REMAIN CALM
THEY'VE OBVIOUSLY BEEN PREPPING FOR
WHEN I DON'T MAKE A SOUND, IT REALLY HITS ME. THEY'VE

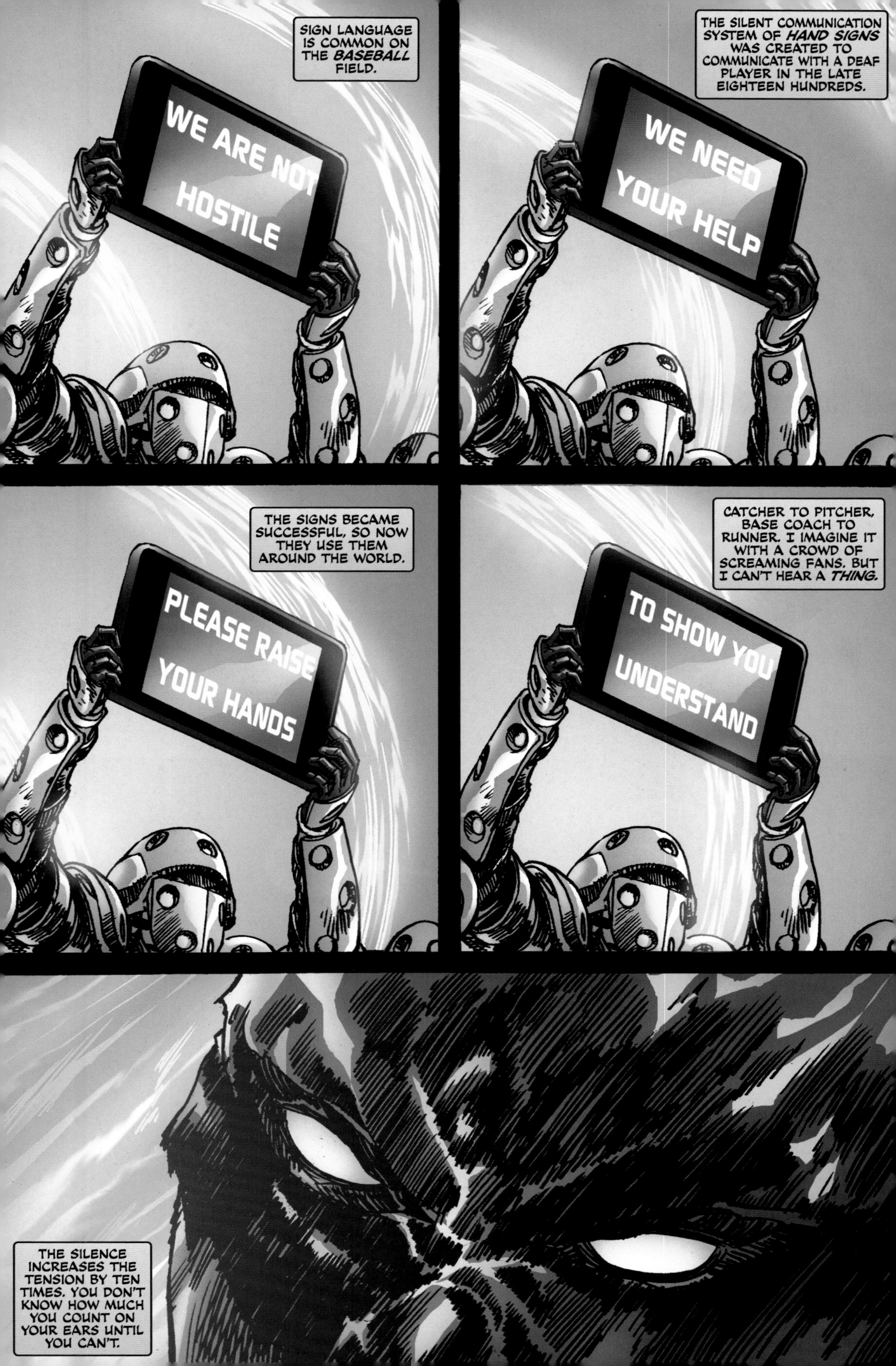
SIGN LANGUAGE IS COMMON ON THE BASEBALL FIELD.
WE ARE NOT HOSTILE
THE SILENT COMMUNICATION SYSTEM OF HAND SIGNS WAS CREATED TO COMMUNICATE WITH A DEAF PLAYER IN THE LATE EIGHTEEN HUNDREDS.
WE NEED YOUR HELP
THE SIGNS BECAME SUCCESSFUL, SO NOW THEY USE THEM AROUND THE WORLD.
PLEASE RAISE YOUR HANDS
CATCHER TO PITCHER, BASE COACH TO RUNNER. I IMAGINE IT WITH A CROWD OF SCREAMING FANS. BUT I CAN'T HEAR A THING.
TO SHOW YOU UNDERSTAND
THE SILENCE INCREASES THE TENSION BY TEN TIMES. YOU DON'T KNOW HOW MUCH YOU COUNT ON YOUR EARS UNTIL YOU CAN'T.

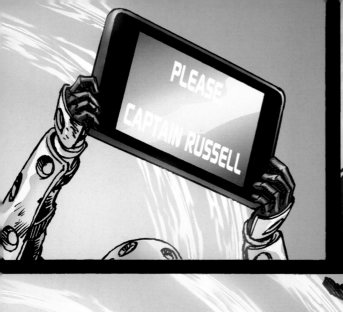

PLEASE, CAPTAIN RUSSELL

THAT SETTLES IT. THEY KNOW WHO I AM.

I DO SOMETHING I'VE *NEVER* DONE. I *SURRENDER*.

CAPTAIN RUSSELL? I'M GENERAL WASHINGTON.

SON, IT'S URGENT. WE NEED YOU AND YOUR... *TALENTS*, BACK IN AFGHANISTAN IMMEDIATELY.

YOU AREN'T THE *ONLY ONE*, SOLDIER.

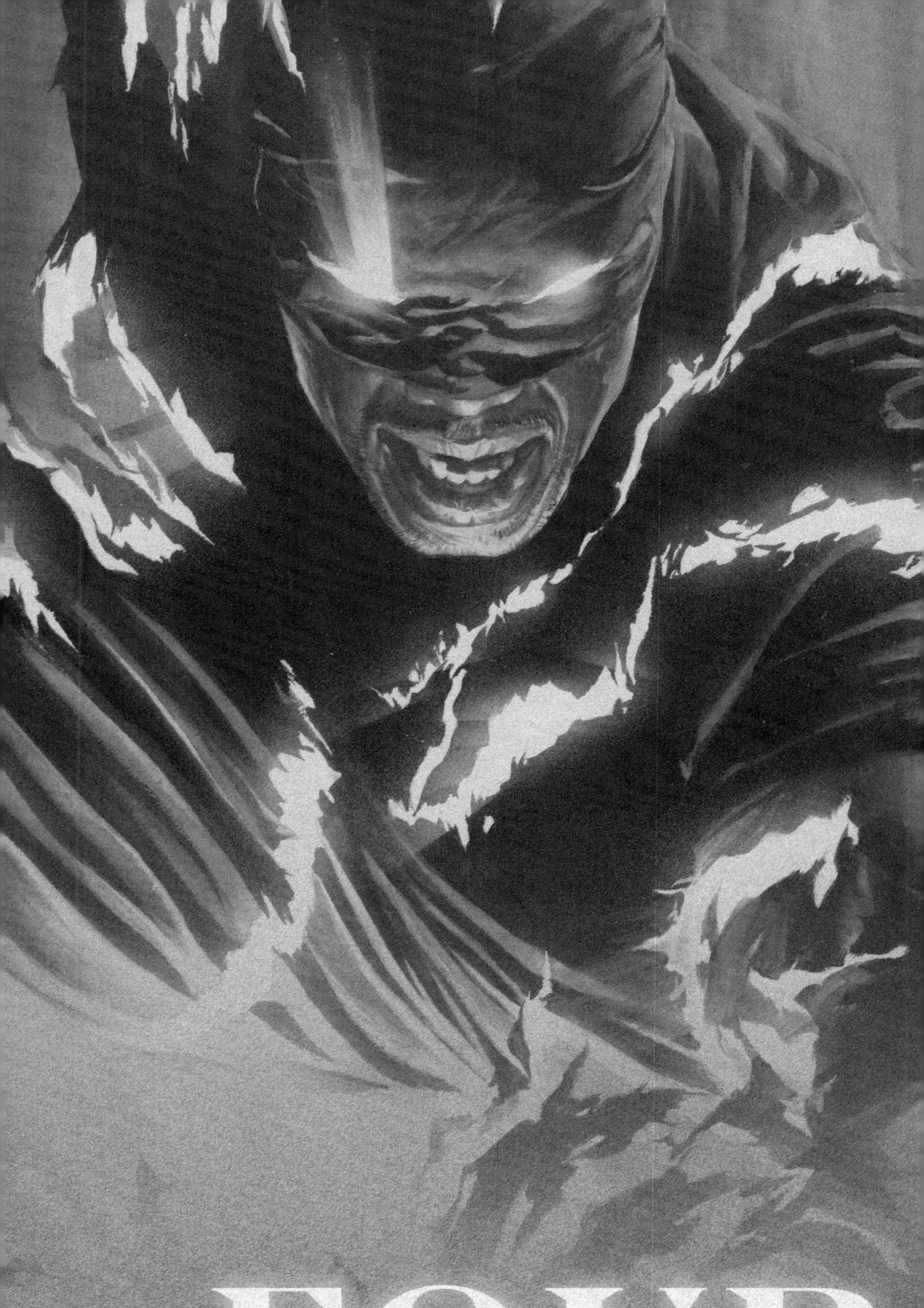

FOUR

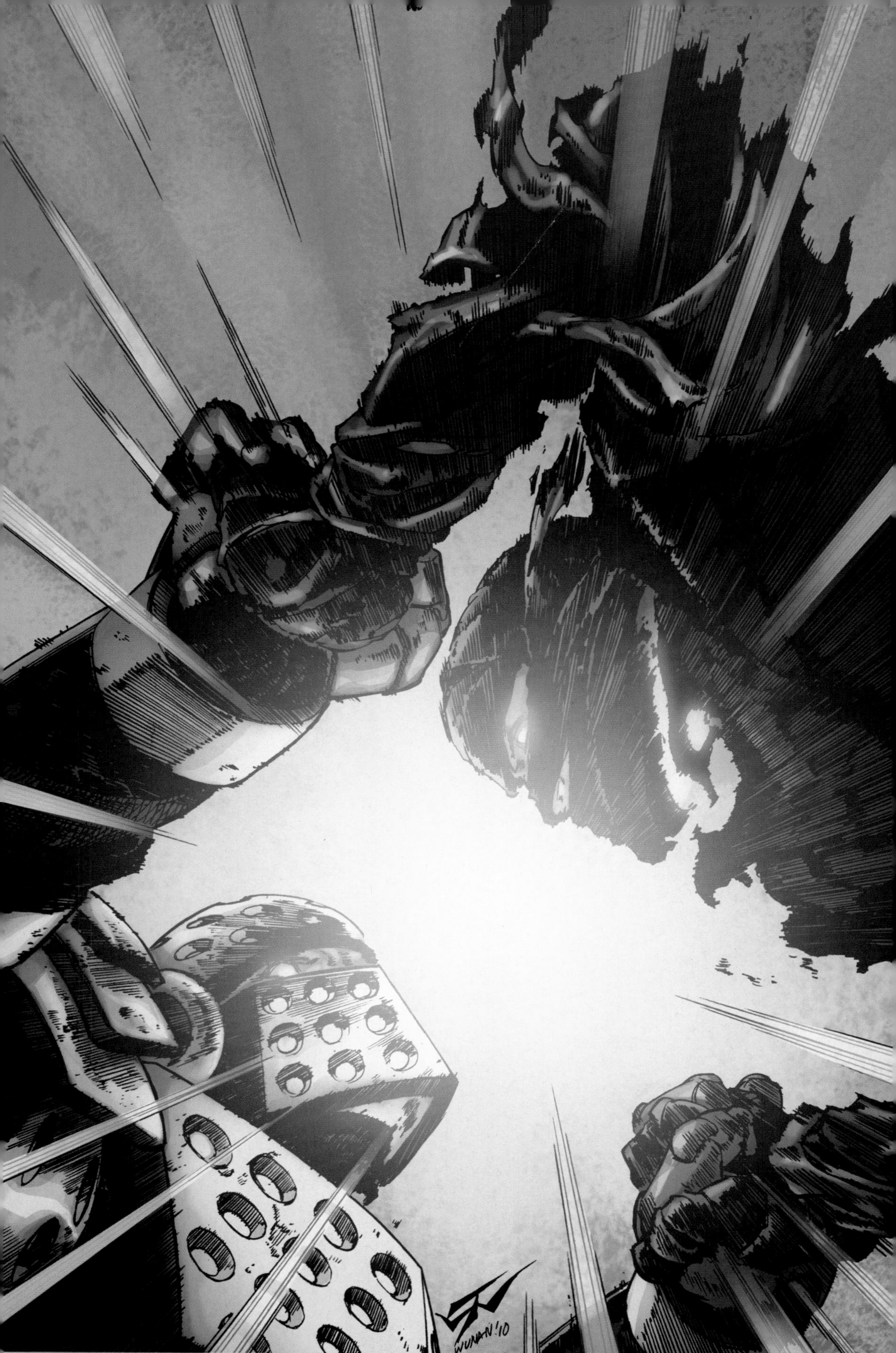
WUNAN!'10

ISSUE #4 ALTERNATE COVER BY WILSON TORTOSA

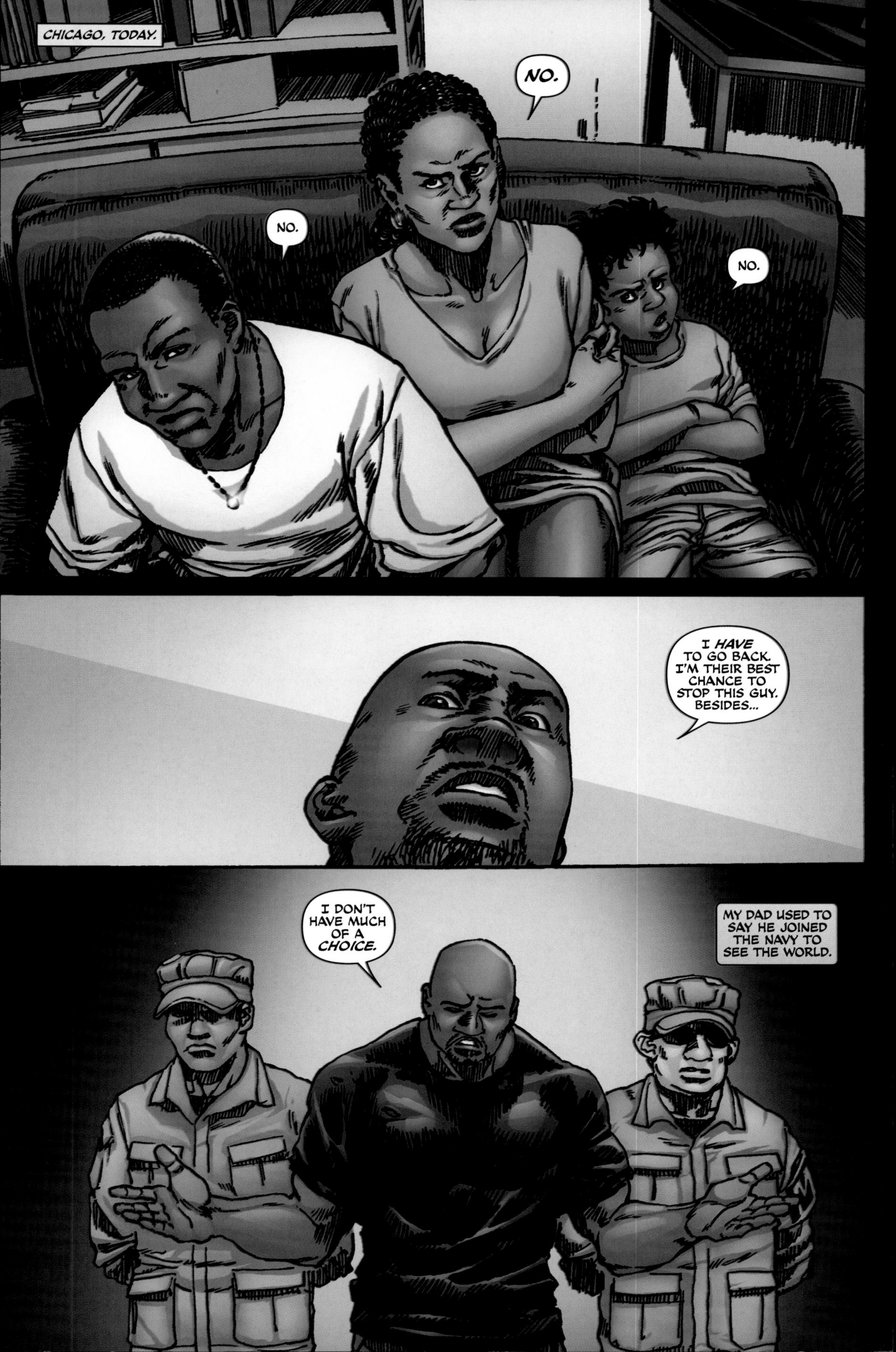
CHICAGO, TODAY.
NO.
NO.
NO.
I HAVE TO GO BACK. I'M THEIR BEST CHANCE TO STOP THIS GUY. BESIDES...
I DON'T HAVE MUCH OF A CHOICE.
MY DAD USED TO SAY HE JOINED THE NAVY TO SEE THE WORLD.

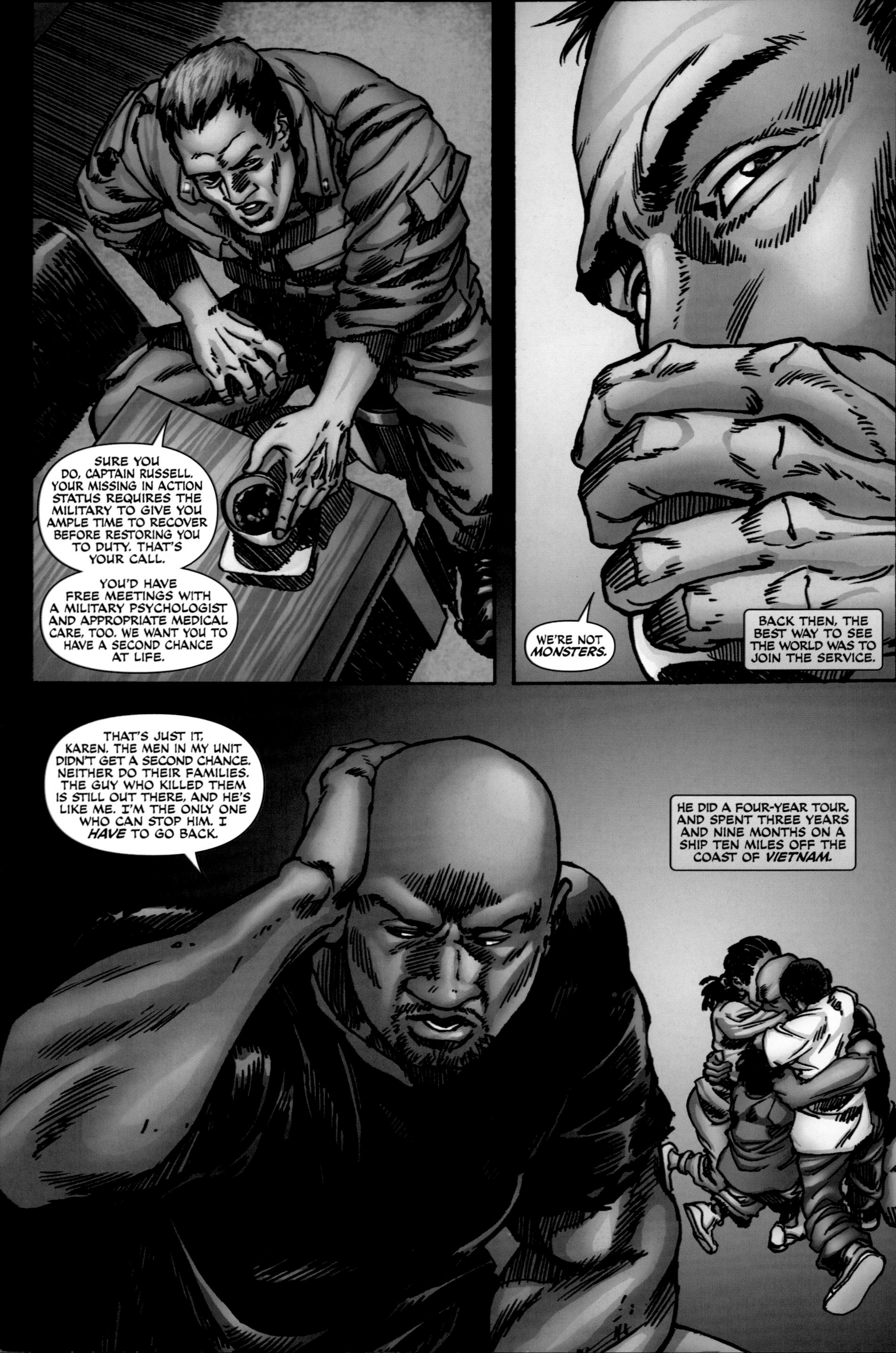
SURE YOU DO, CAPTAIN RUSSELL. YOUR MISSING IN ACTION STATUS REQUIRES THE MILITARY TO GIVE YOU AMPLE TIME TO RECOVER BEFORE RESTORING YOU TO DUTY. THAT'S YOUR CALL.
YOU'D HAVE FREE MEETINGS WITH A MILITARY PSYCHOLOGIST AND APPROPRIATE MEDICAL CARE, TOO. WE WANT YOU TO HAVE A SECOND CHANCE AT LIFE.
WE'RE NOT *MONSTERS.*
BACK THEN, THE BEST WAY TO SEE THE WORLD WAS TO JOIN THE SERVICE.
THAT'S JUST IT, KAREN. THE MEN IN MY UNIT DIDN'T GET A SECOND CHANCE. NEITHER DO THEIR FAMILIES. THE GUY WHO KILLED THEM IS STILL OUT THERE, AND HE'S LIKE ME. I'M THE ONLY ONE WHO CAN STOP HIM. I *HAVE* TO GO BACK.
HE DID A FOUR-YEAR TOUR, AND SPENT THREE YEARS AND NINE MONTHS ON A SHIP TEN MILES OFF THE COAST OF *VIETNAM.*

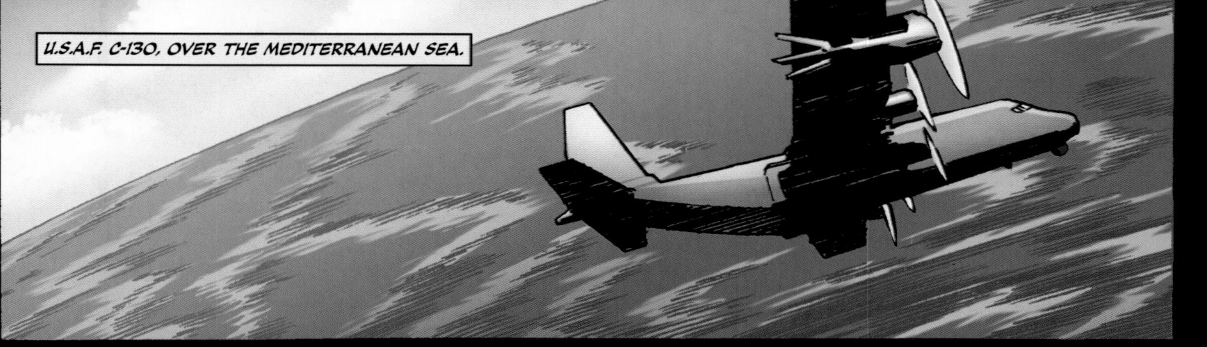
U.S.A.F. C-130, OVER THE MEDITERRANEAN SEA.

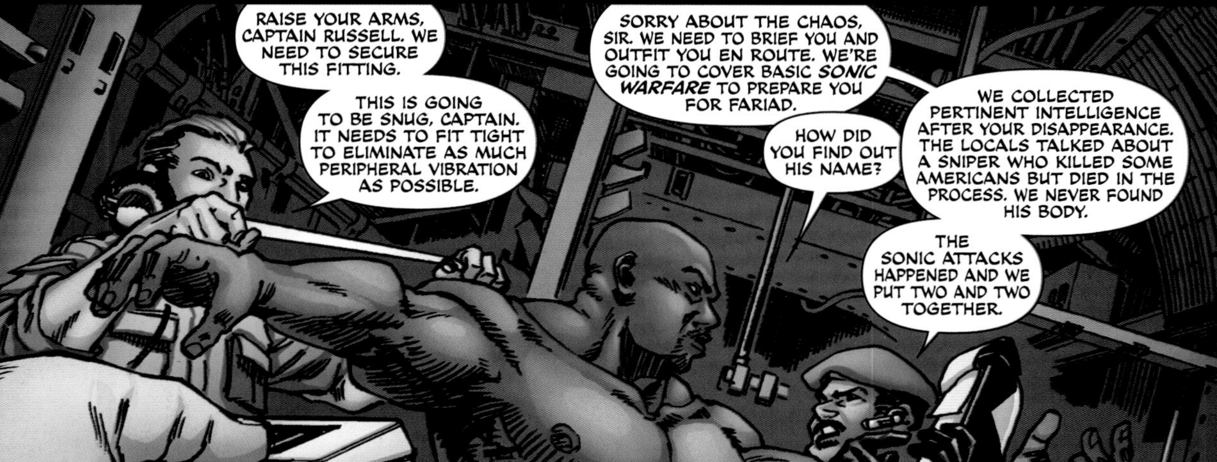
RAISE YOUR ARMS, CAPTAIN RUSSELL. WE NEED TO SECURE THIS FITTING.
THIS IS GOING TO BE SNUG, CAPTAIN. IT NEEDS TO FIT TIGHT TO ELIMINATE AS MUCH PERIPHERAL VIBRATION AS POSSIBLE.
SORRY ABOUT THE CHAOS, SIR. WE NEED TO BRIEF YOU AND OUTFIT YOU EN ROUTE. WE'RE GOING TO COVER BASIC SONIC WARFARE TO PREPARE YOU FOR FARIAD.
HOW DID YOU FIND OUT HIS NAME?
WE COLLECTED PERTINENT INTELLIGENCE AFTER YOUR DISAPPEARANCE. THE LOCALS TALKED ABOUT A SNIPER WHO KILLED SOME AMERICANS BUT DIED IN THE PROCESS. WE NEVER FOUND HIS BODY.
THE SONIC ATTACKS HAPPENED AND WE PUT TWO AND TWO TOGETHER.

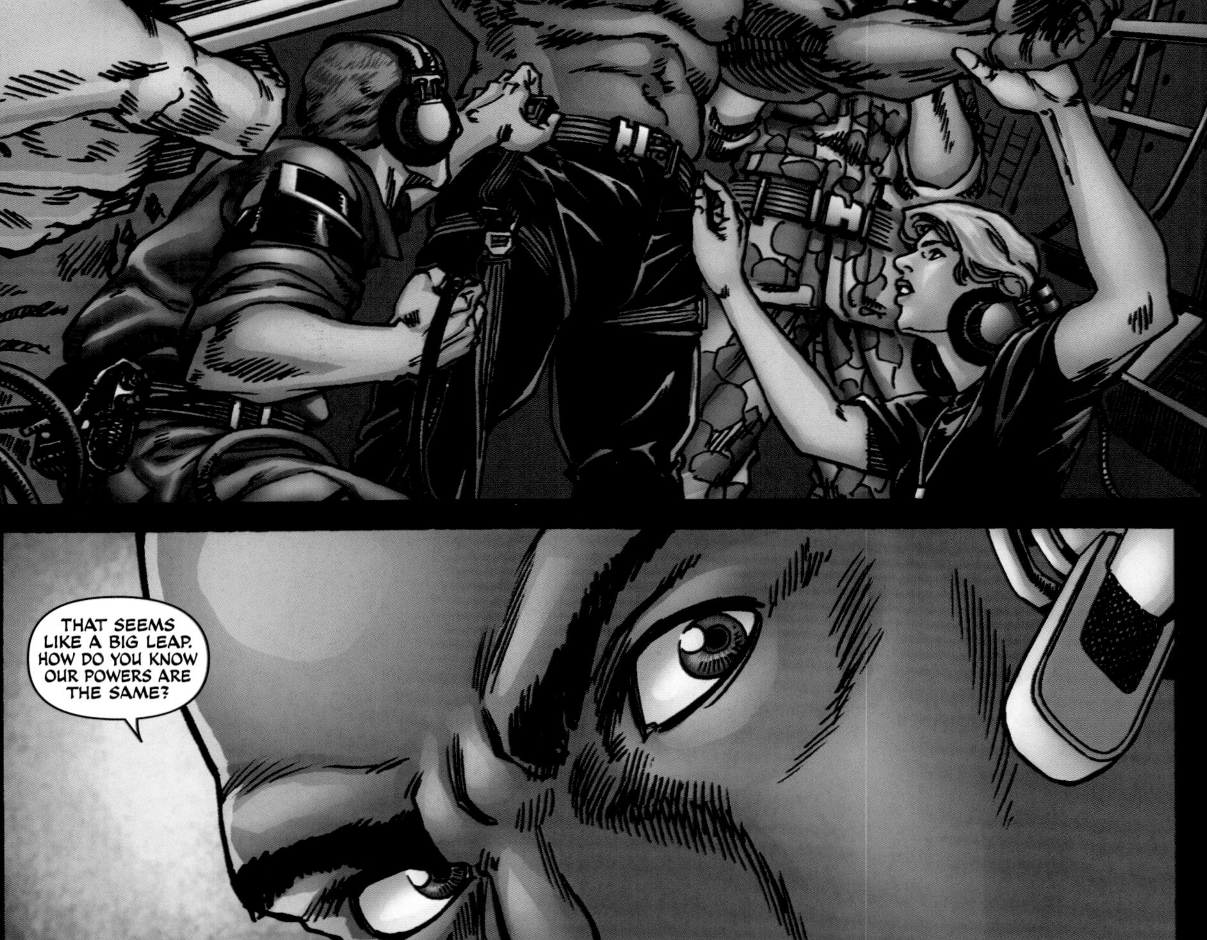
THAT SEEMS LIKE A BIG LEAP. HOW DO YOU KNOW OUR POWERS ARE THE SAME?

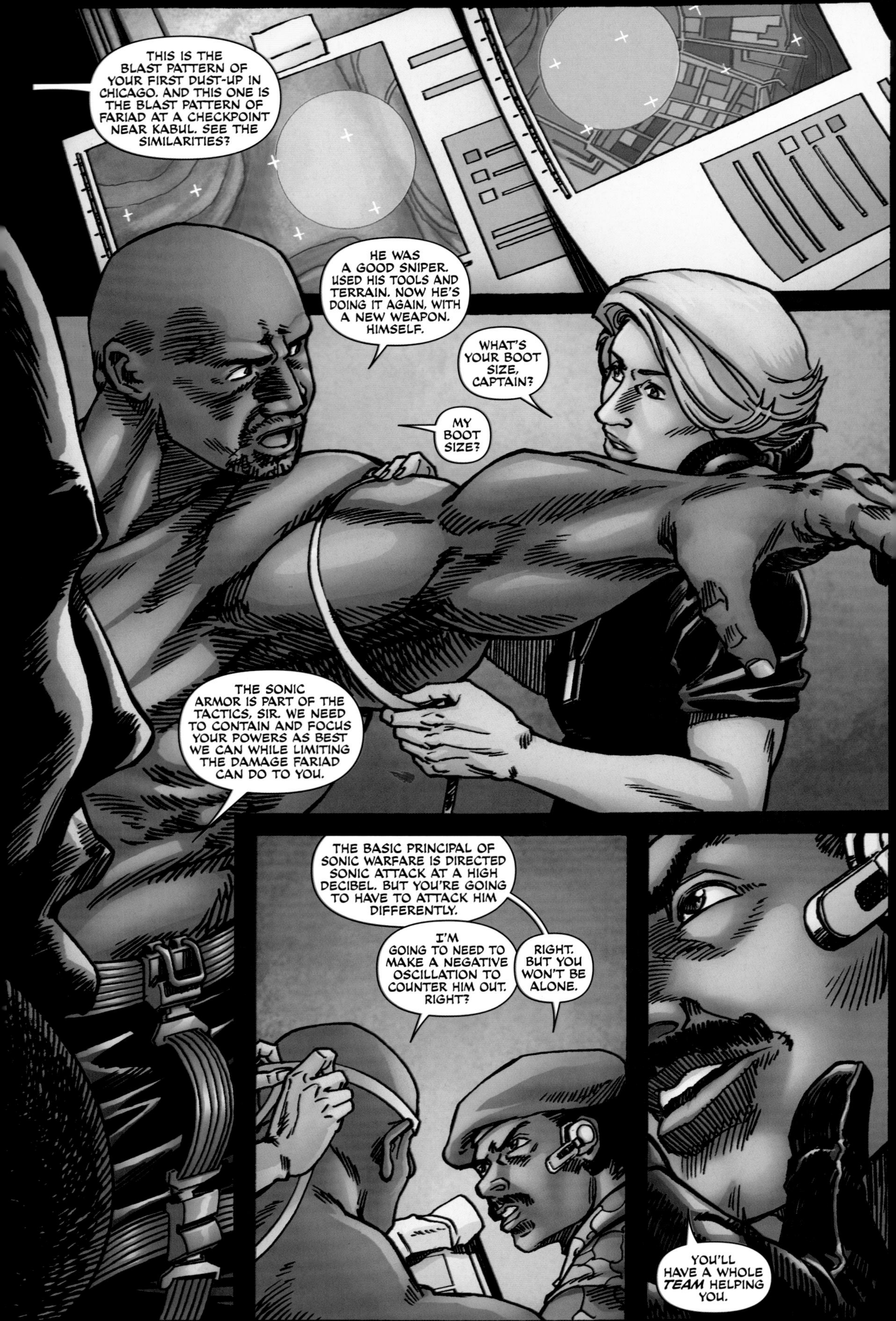
THIS IS THE BLAST PATTERN OF YOUR FIRST DUST-UP IN CHICAGO. AND THIS ONE IS THE BLAST PATTERN OF FARIAD AT A CHECKPOINT NEAR KABUL. SEE THE SIMILARITIES?
HE WAS A GOOD SNIPER. USED HIS TOOLS AND TERRAIN. NOW HE'S DOING IT AGAIN, WITH A NEW WEAPON. HIMSELF.
WHAT'S YOUR BOOT SIZE, CAPTAIN?
MY BOOT SIZE?
THE SONIC ARMOR IS PART OF THE TACTICS, SIR. WE NEED TO CONTAIN AND FOCUS YOUR POWERS AS BEST WE CAN WHILE LIMITING THE DAMAGE FARIAD CAN DO TO YOU.
THE BASIC PRINCIPAL OF SONIC WARFARE IS DIRECTED SONIC ATTACK AT A HIGH DECIBEL. BUT YOU'RE GOING TO HAVE TO ATTACK HIM DIFFERENTLY.
I'M GOING TO NEED TO MAKE A NEGATIVE OSCILLATION TO COUNTER HIM OUT. RIGHT?
RIGHT. BUT YOU WON'T BE ALONE.
YOU'LL HAVE A WHOLE *TEAM* HELPING YOU.

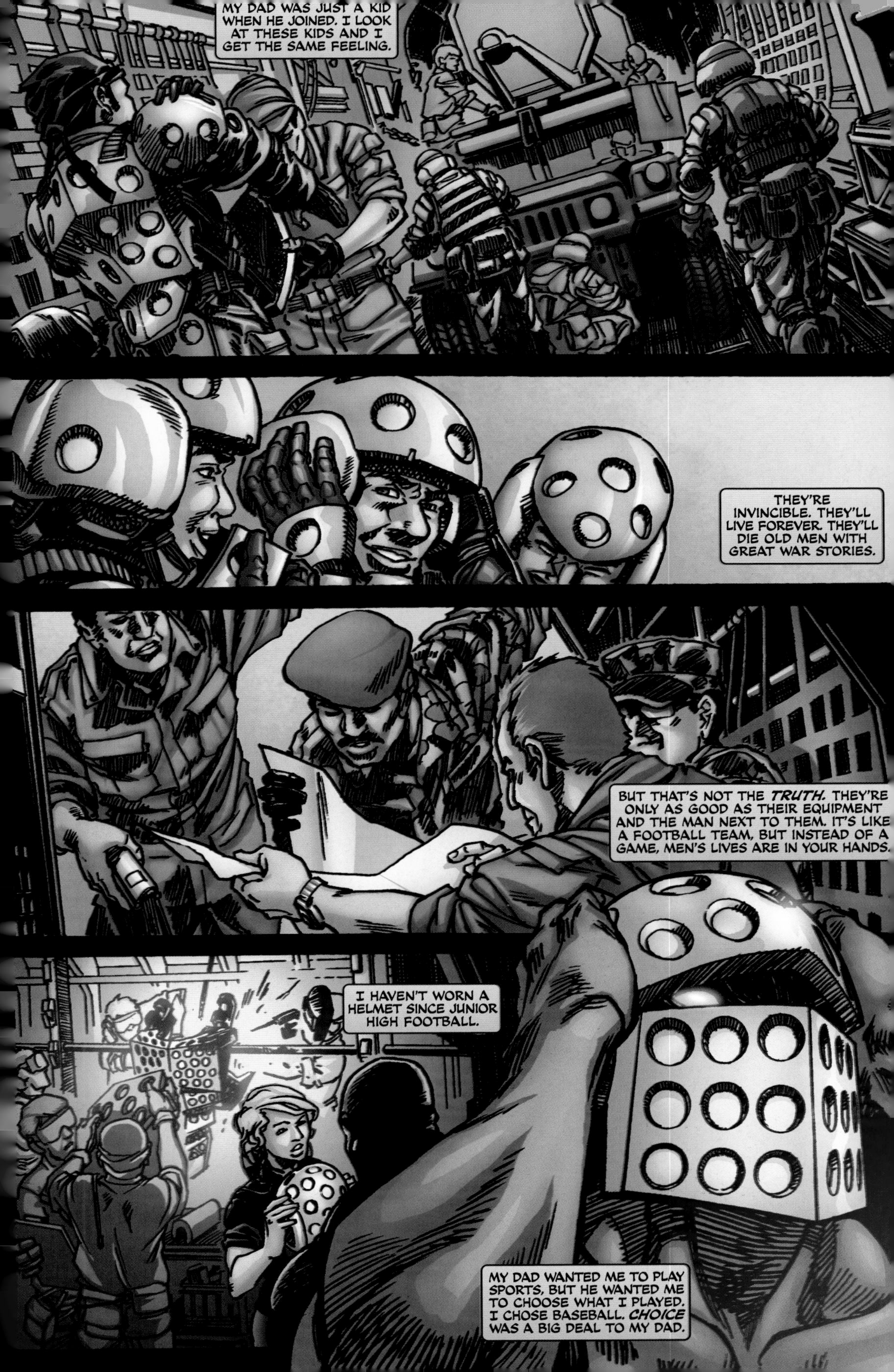
MY DAD WAS JUST A KID WHEN HE JOINED. I LOOK AT THESE KIDS AND I GET THE SAME FEELING.
THEY'RE INVINCIBLE. THEY'LL LIVE FOREVER. THEY'LL DIE OLD MEN WITH GREAT WAR STORIES.
BUT THAT'S NOT THE *TRUTH.* THEY'RE ONLY AS GOOD AS THEIR EQUIPMENT AND THE MAN NEXT TO THEM. IT'S LIKE A FOOTBALL TEAM, BUT INSTEAD OF A GAME, MEN'S LIVES ARE IN YOUR HANDS.
I HAVEN'T WORN A HELMET SINCE JUNIOR HIGH FOOTBALL.
MY DAD WANTED ME TO PLAY SPORTS, BUT HE WANTED ME TO CHOOSE WHAT I PLAYED. I CHOSE BASEBALL. *CHOICE* WAS A BIG DEAL TO MY DAD.

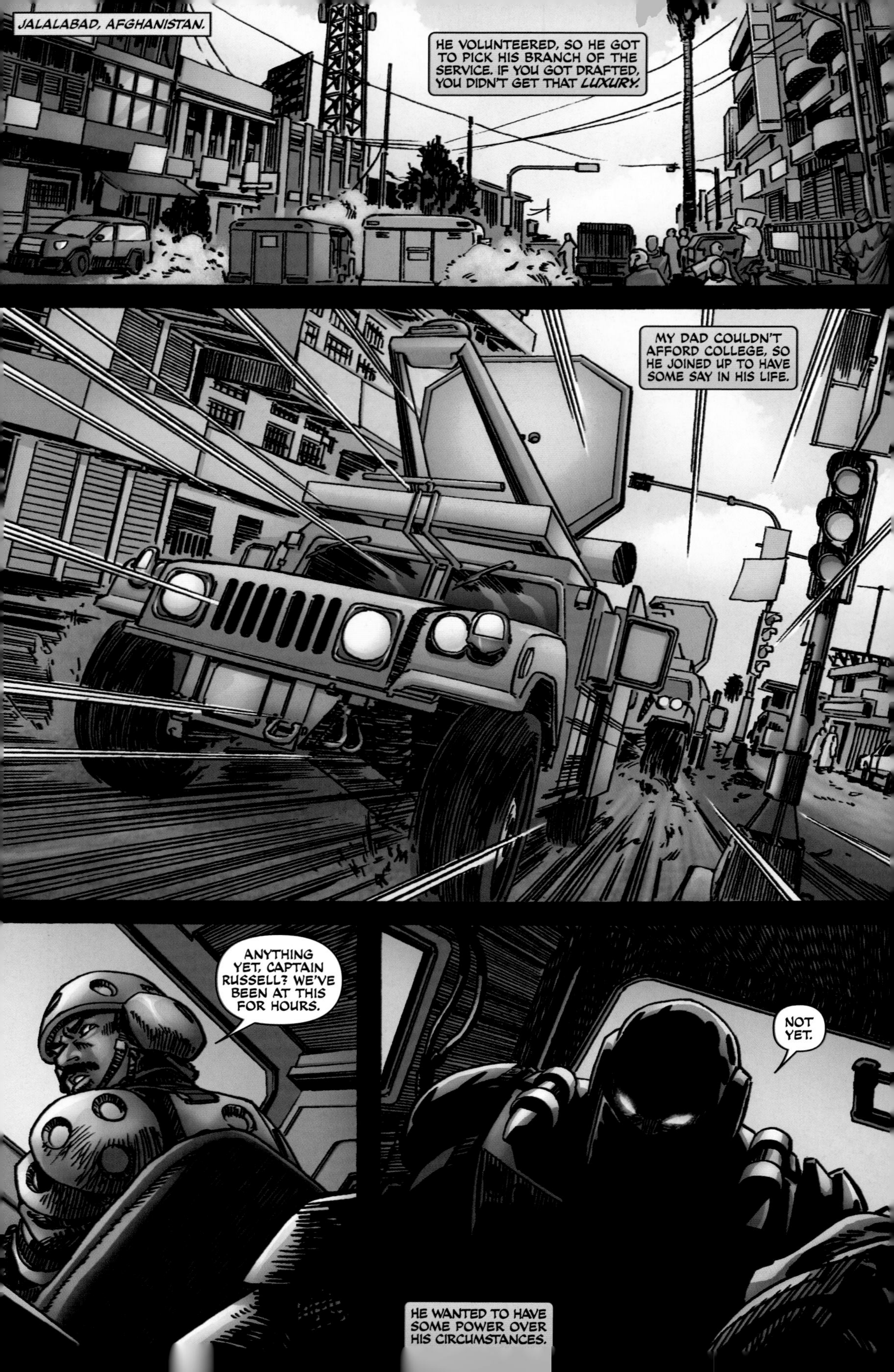
JALALABAD, AFGHANISTAN.
HE VOLUNTEERED, SO HE GOT TO PICK HIS BRANCH OF THE SERVICE. IF YOU GOT DRAFTED, YOU DIDN'T GET THAT LUXURY.
MY DAD COULDN'T AFFORD COLLEGE, SO HE JOINED UP TO HAVE SOME SAY IN HIS LIFE.
ANYTHING YET, CAPTAIN RUSSELL? WE'VE BEEN AT THIS FOR HOURS.
NOT YET.
HE WANTED TO HAVE SOME POWER OVER HIS CIRCUMSTANCES.

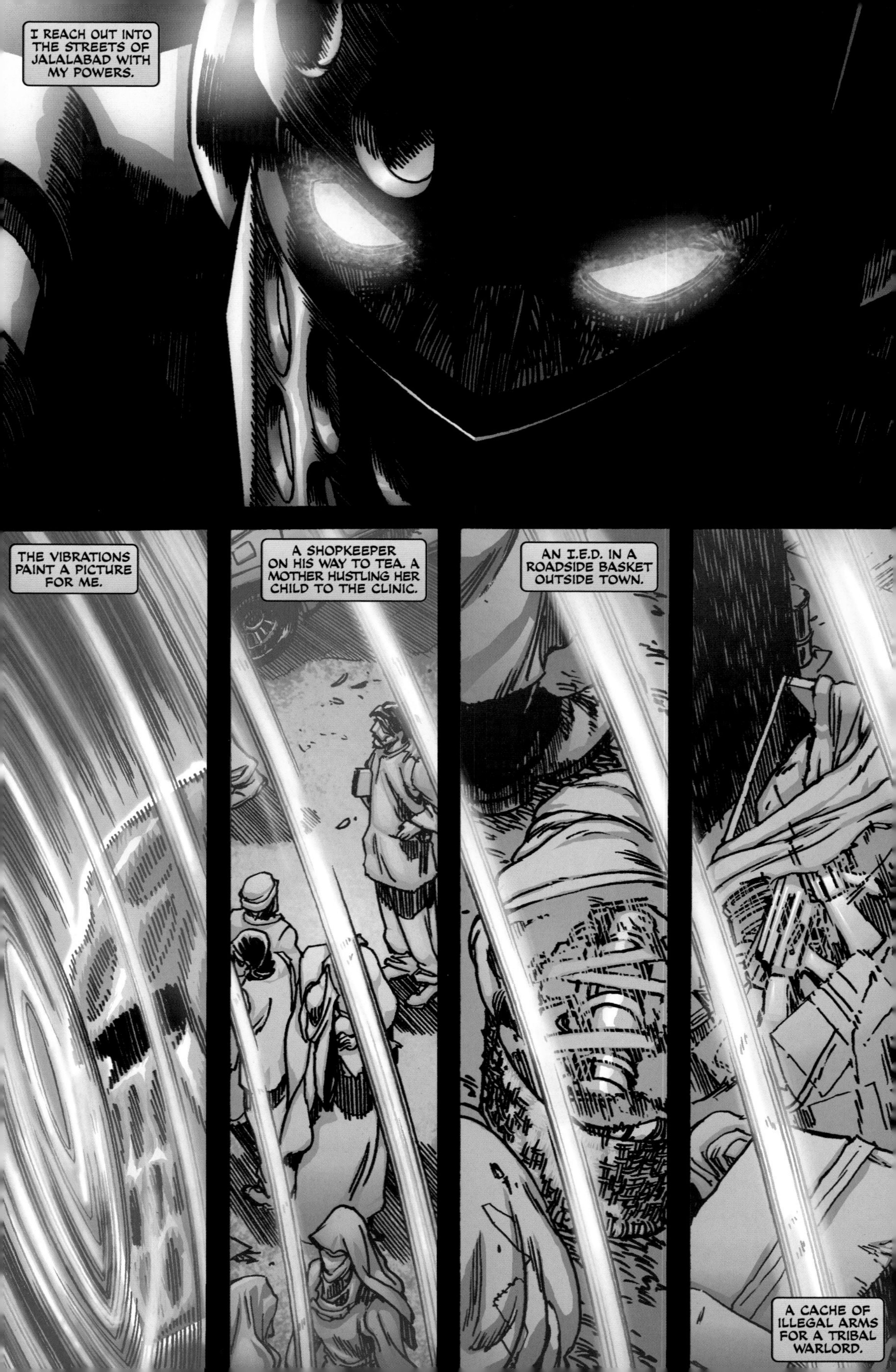
I REACH OUT INTO THE STREETS OF JALALABAD WITH MY POWERS.
THE VIBRATIONS PAINT A PICTURE FOR ME.
A SHOPKEEPER ON HIS WAY TO TEA. A MOTHER HUSTLING HER CHILD TO THE CLINIC.
AN I.E.D. IN A ROADSIDE BASKET OUTSIDE TOWN.
A CACHE OF ILLEGAL ARMS FOR A TRIBAL WARLORD.

EX-MILITARY SURVEILLANCE, PROBABLY A.S.P. AGENTS, LOOKING FOR ODD SONIC PATTERNS. PROBABLY LOOKING FOR FARIAD, TOO. OR ME.

I PING THEIR INSTRUMENTS AND THEY MOVE. THEY'RE SKITTISH. THEY PACK UP QUICKLY. THEY'LL BE GONE BEFORE WE COULD EVER GET TO THEM.

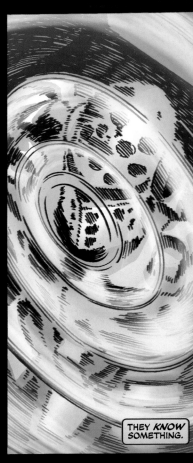

THEY *KNOW* SOMETHING.

BUT IT'LL HAVE TO WAIT.

I FOUND HIM.

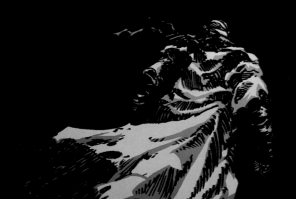

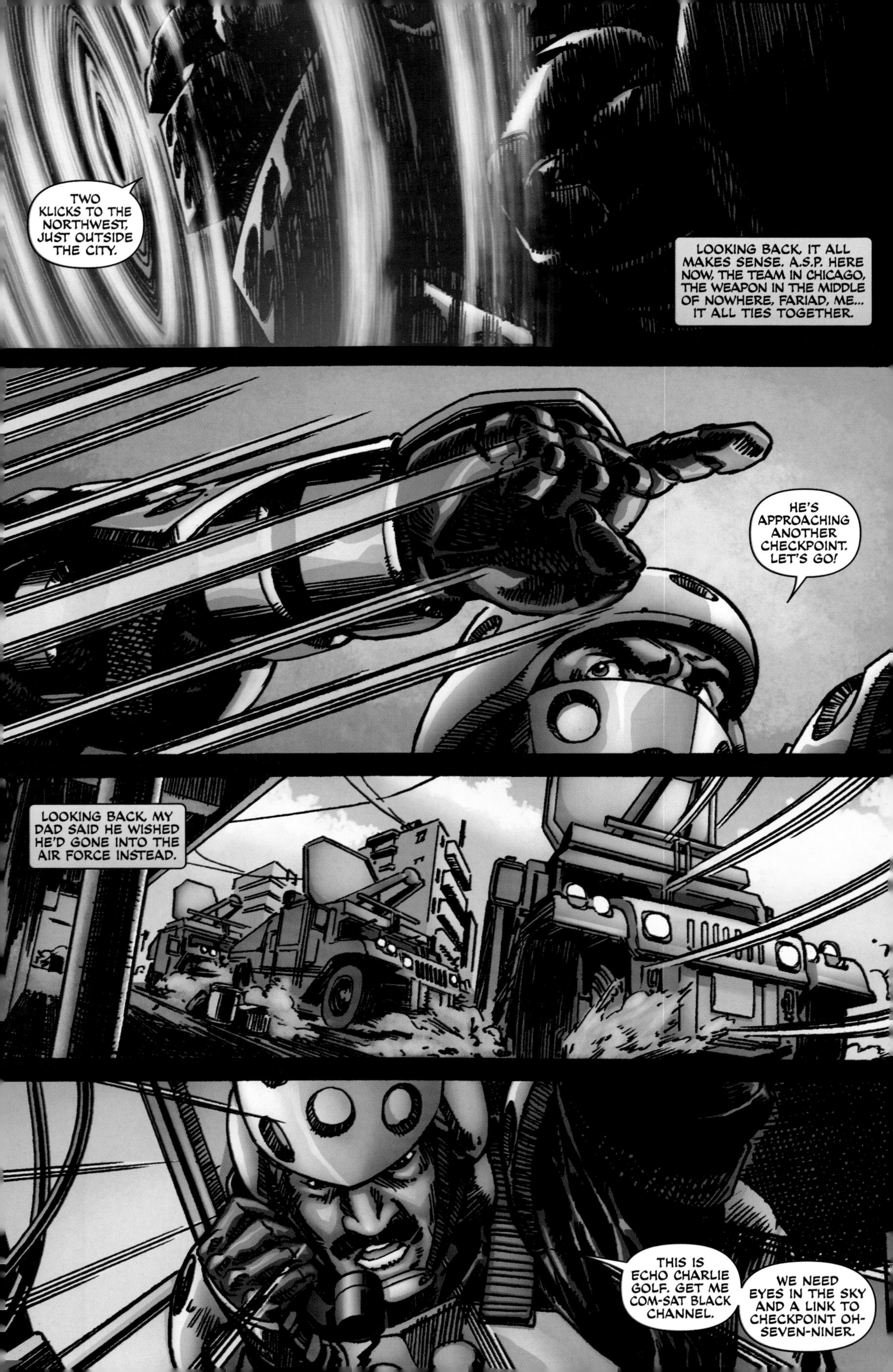
TWO KLICKS TO THE NORTHWEST, JUST OUTSIDE THE CITY.
LOOKING BACK, IT ALL MAKES SENSE. A.S.P. HERE NOW, THE TEAM IN CHICAGO, THE WEAPON IN THE MIDDLE OF NOWHERE, FARIAD, ME... IT ALL TIES TOGETHER.
HE'S APPROACHING ANOTHER CHECKPOINT. LET'S GO!
LOOKING BACK, MY DAD SAID HE WISHED HE'D GONE INTO THE AIR FORCE INSTEAD.
THIS IS ECHO CHARLIE GOLF. GET ME COM-SAT BLACK CHANNEL.
WE NEED EYES IN THE SKY AND A LINK TO CHECKPOINT OH-SEVEN-NINER.

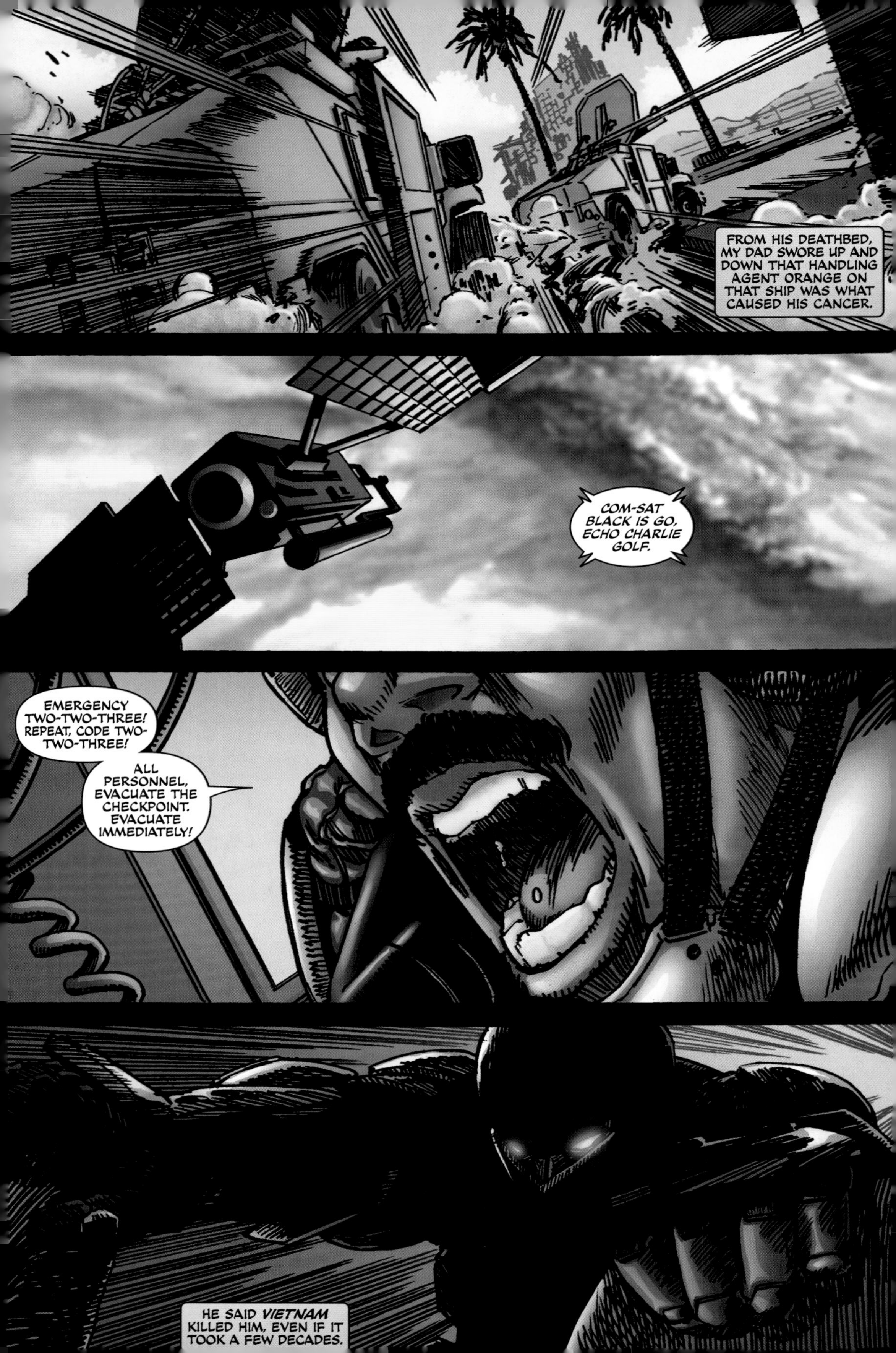
FROM HIS DEATHBED, MY DAD SWORE UP AND DOWN THAT HANDLING AGENT ORANGE ON THAT SHIP WAS WHAT CAUSED HIS CANCER.
COM-SAT BLACK IS GO, ECHO CHARLIE GOLF.
EMERGENCY TWO-TWO-THREE! REPEAT, CODE TWO-TWO-THREE!
ALL PERSONNEL, EVACUATE THE CHECKPOINT. EVACUATE IMMEDIATELY!
HE SAID *VIETNAM* KILLED HIM, EVEN IF IT TOOK A FEW DECADES.

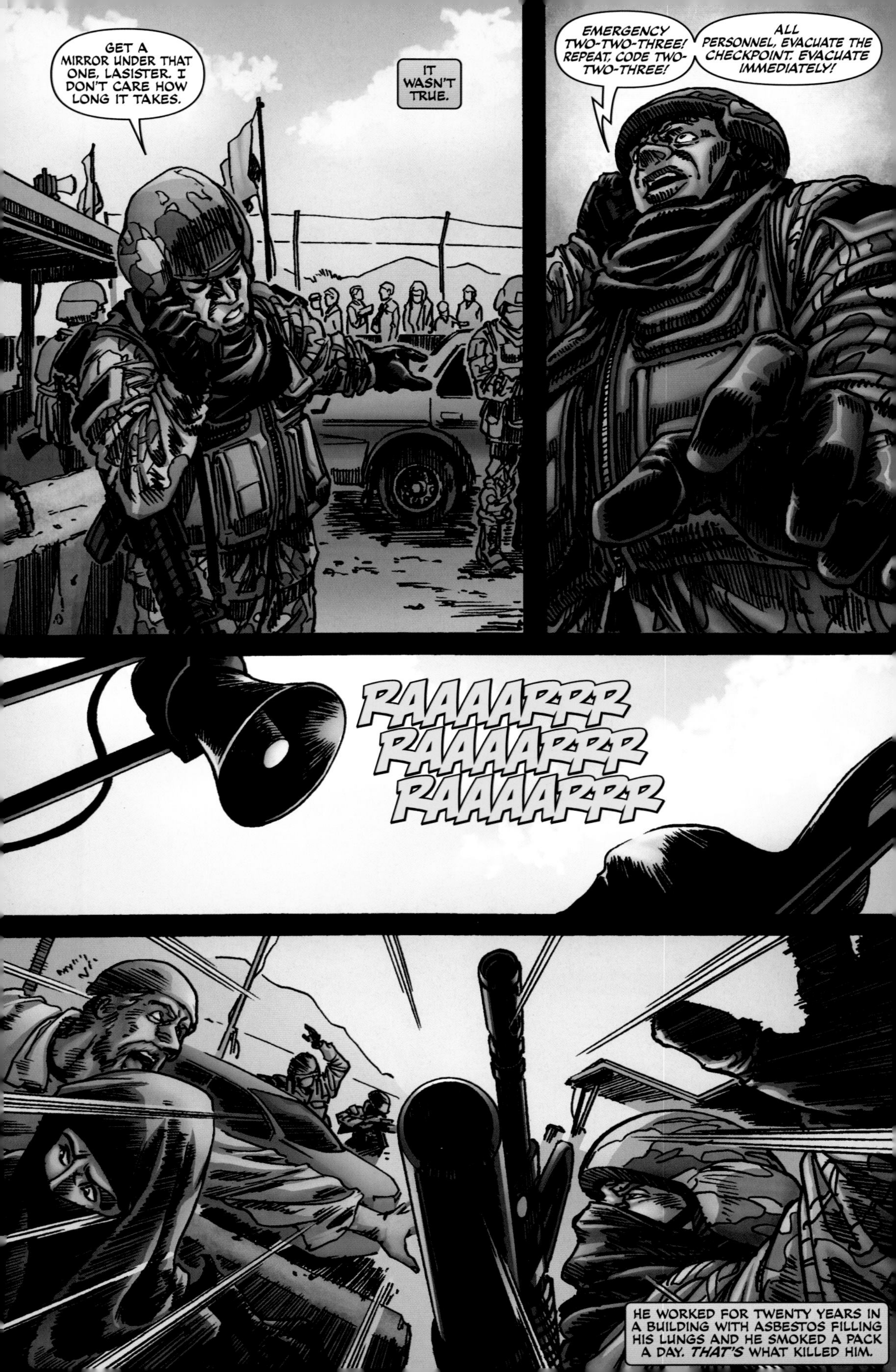
GET A MIRROR UNDER THAT ONE, LASISTER. I DON'T CARE HOW LONG IT TAKES.
IT WASN'T TRUE.
EMERGENCY TWO-TWO-THREE! REPEAT, CODE TWO-TWO-THREE!
ALL PERSONNEL, EVACUATE THE CHECKPOINT. EVACUATE IMMEDIATELY!
RAAAARRR
RAAAARRR
RAAAARRR
HE WORKED FOR TWENTY YEARS IN A BUILDING WITH ASBESTOS FILLING HIS LUNGS AND HE SMOKED A PACK A DAY. *THAT'S* WHAT KILLED HIM.

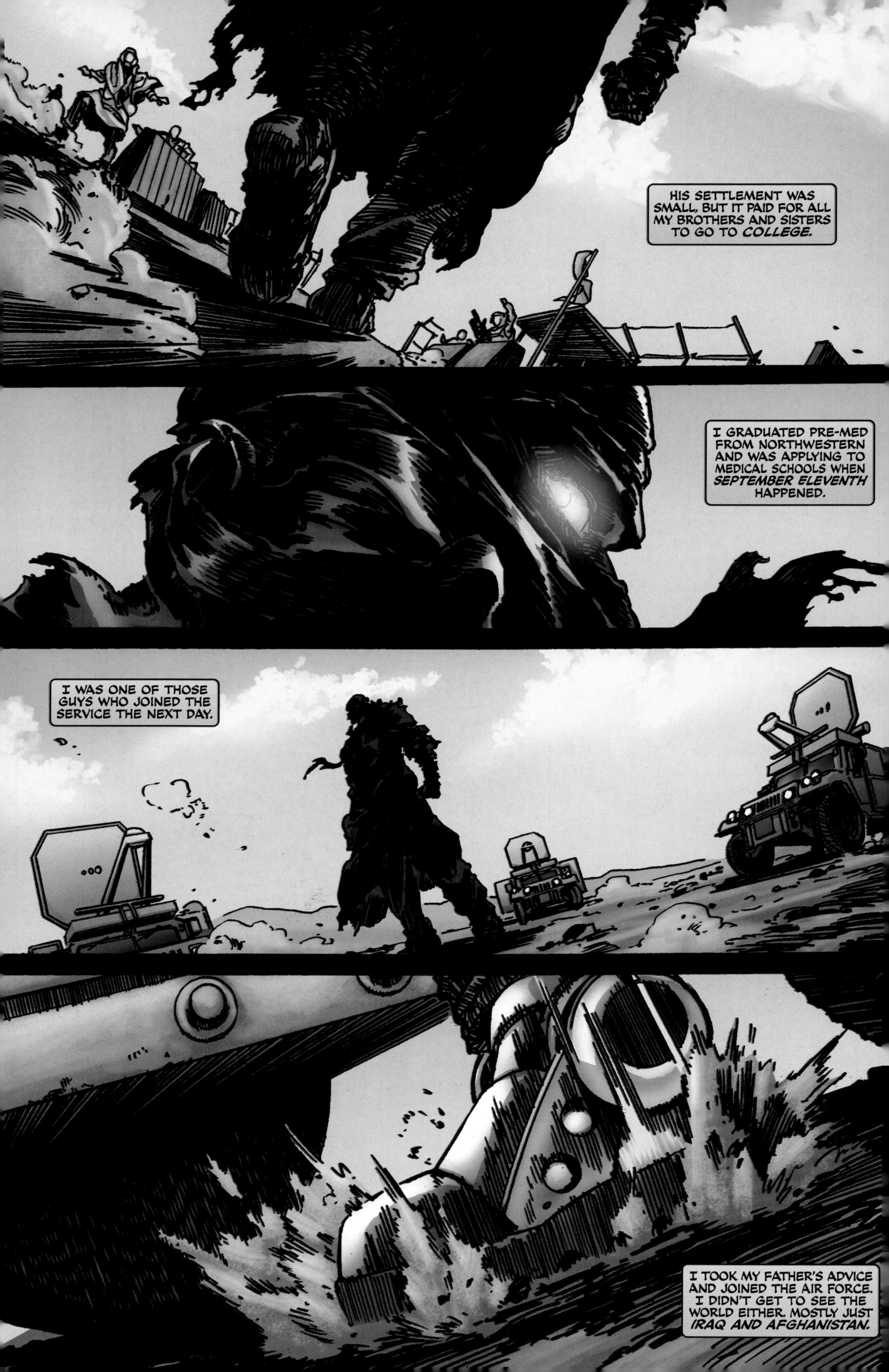
HIS SETTLEMENT WAS SMALL, BUT IT PAID FOR ALL MY BROTHERS AND SISTERS TO GO TO *COLLEGE*.
I GRADUATED PRE-MED FROM NORTHWESTERN AND WAS APPLYING TO MEDICAL SCHOOLS WHEN *SEPTEMBER ELEVENTH* HAPPENED.
I WAS ONE OF THOSE GUYS WHO JOINED THE SERVICE THE NEXT DAY.
I TOOK MY FATHER'S ADVICE AND JOINED THE AIR FORCE. I DIDN'T GET TO SEE THE WORLD EITHER. MOSTLY JUST *IRAQ AND AFGHANISTAN*.

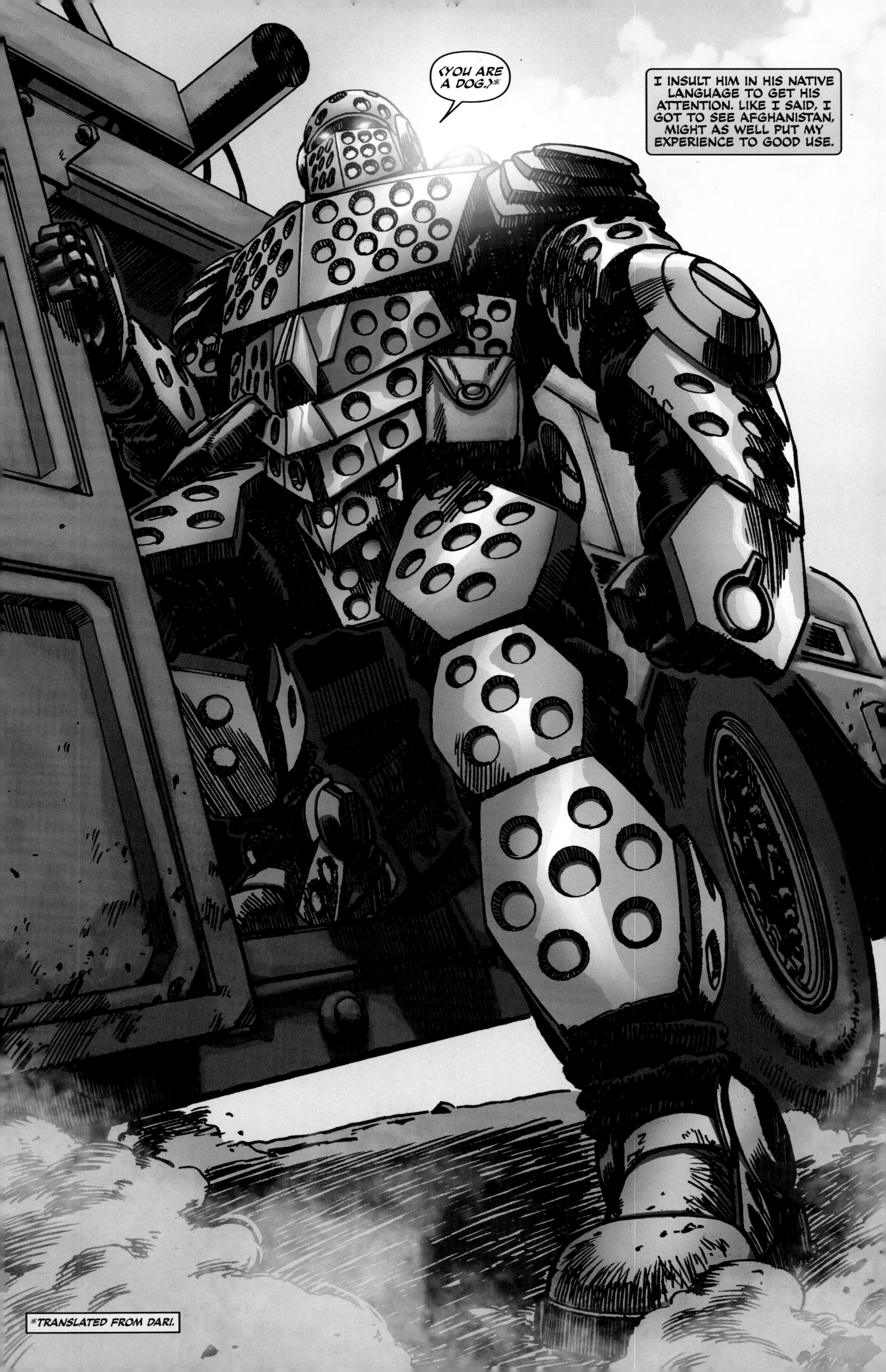
I INSULT HIM IN HIS NATIVE LANGUAGE TO GET HIS ATTENTION. LIKE I SAID, I GOT TO SEE AFGHANISTAN, MIGHT AS WELL PUT MY EXPERIENCE TO GOOD USE.
‹YOU ARE A DOG.›*
*TRANSLATED FROM DARI.

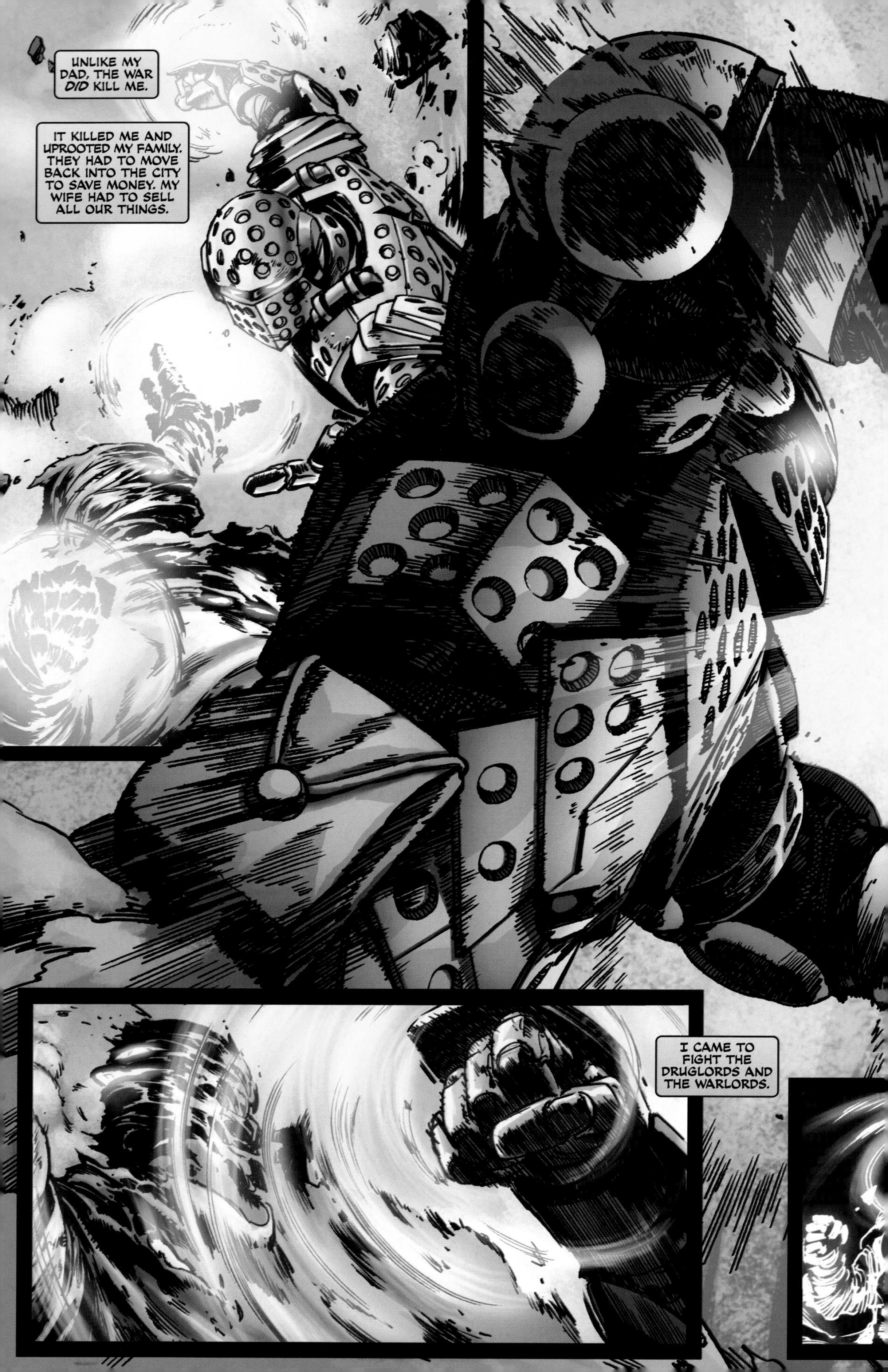
UNLIKE MY DAD, THE WAR *DID* KILL ME.
IT KILLED ME AND UPROOTED MY FAMILY. THEY HAD TO MOVE BACK INTO THE CITY TO SAVE MONEY. MY WIFE HAD TO SELL ALL OUR THINGS.
I CAME TO FIGHT THE DRUGLORDS AND THE WARLORDS.

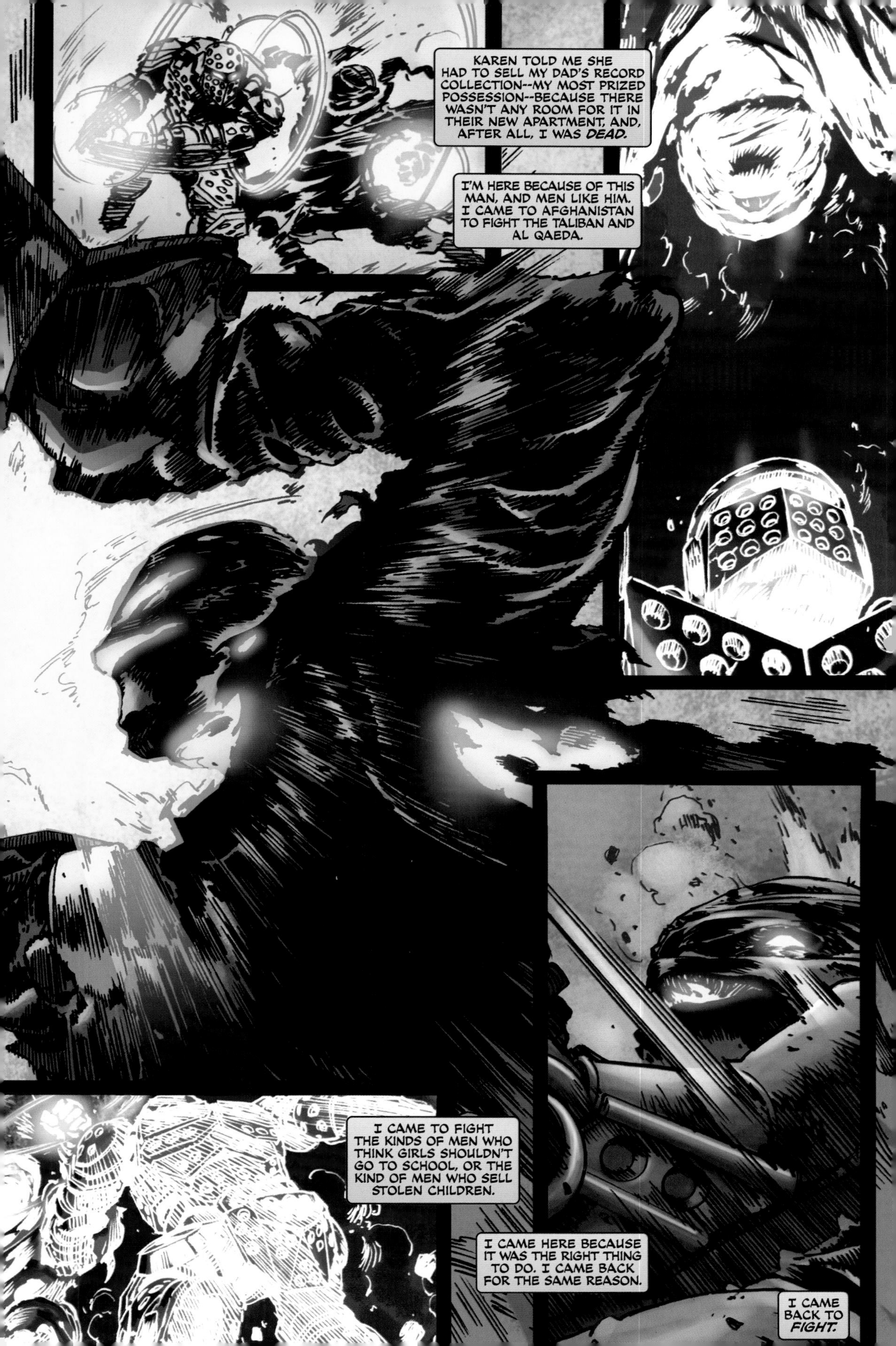
KAREN TOLD ME SHE HAD TO SELL MY DAD'S RECORD COLLECTION--MY MOST PRIZED POSSESSION--BECAUSE THERE WASN'T ANY ROOM FOR IT IN THEIR NEW APARTMENT, AND, AFTER ALL, I WAS *DEAD.*
I'M HERE BECAUSE OF THIS MAN, AND MEN LIKE HIM. I CAME TO AFGHANISTAN TO FIGHT THE TALIBAN AND AL QAEDA.
I CAME TO FIGHT THE KINDS OF MEN WHO THINK GIRLS SHOULDN'T GO TO SCHOOL, OR THE KIND OF MEN WHO SELL STOLEN CHILDREN.
I CAME HERE BECAUSE IT WAS THE RIGHT THING TO DO. I CAME BACK FOR THE SAME REASON.
I CAME BACK TO *FIGHT.*

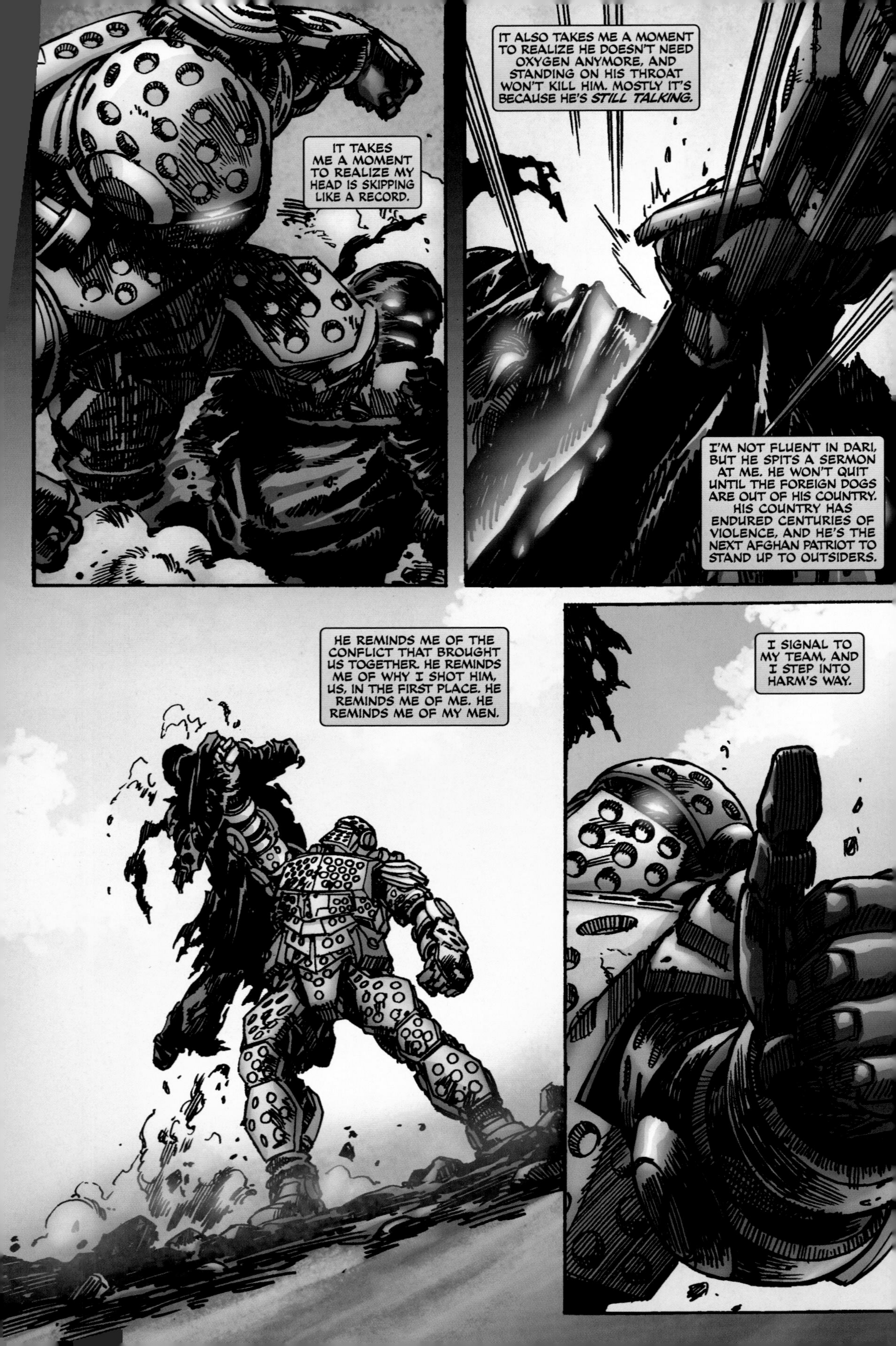
IT TAKES ME A MOMENT TO REALIZE MY HEAD IS SKIPPING LIKE A RECORD.
IT ALSO TAKES ME A MOMENT TO REALIZE HE DOESN'T NEED OXYGEN ANYMORE, AND STANDING ON HIS THROAT WON'T KILL HIM. MOSTLY IT'S BECAUSE HE'S STILL TALKING.
I'M NOT FLUENT IN DARI, BUT HE SPITS A SERMON AT ME. HE WON'T QUIT UNTIL THE FOREIGN DOGS ARE OUT OF HIS COUNTRY. HIS COUNTRY HAS ENDURED CENTURIES OF VIOLENCE, AND HE'S THE NEXT AFGHAN PATRIOT TO STAND UP TO OUTSIDERS.
HE REMINDS ME OF THE CONFLICT THAT BROUGHT US TOGETHER. HE REMINDS ME OF WHY I SHOT HIM, US, IN THE FIRST PLACE. HE REMINDS ME OF ME. HE REMINDS ME OF MY MEN.
I SIGNAL TO MY TEAM, AND I STEP INTO HARM'S WAY.

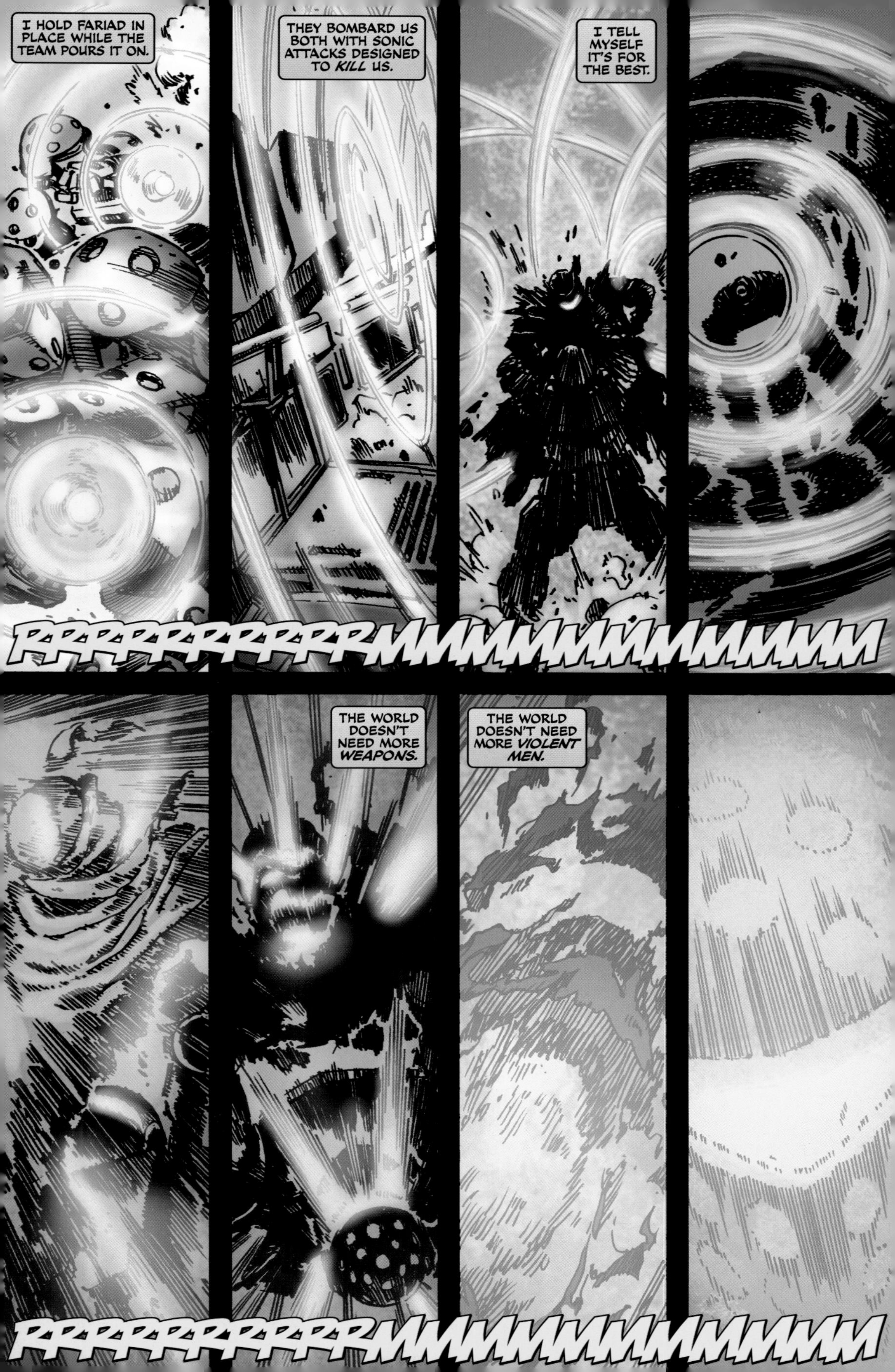
I HOLD FARIAD IN PLACE WHILE THE TEAM POURS IT ON.
THEY BOMBARD US BOTH WITH SONIC ATTACKS DESIGNED TO KILL US.
I TELL MYSELF IT'S FOR THE BEST.
RRRRRRRRRRRRRRMMMMMMMMMMMMMMM
THE WORLD DOESN'T NEED MORE WEAPONS.
THE WORLD DOESN'T NEED MORE VIOLENT MEN.
RRRRRRRRRRRRRRMMMMMMMMMMMMMMM

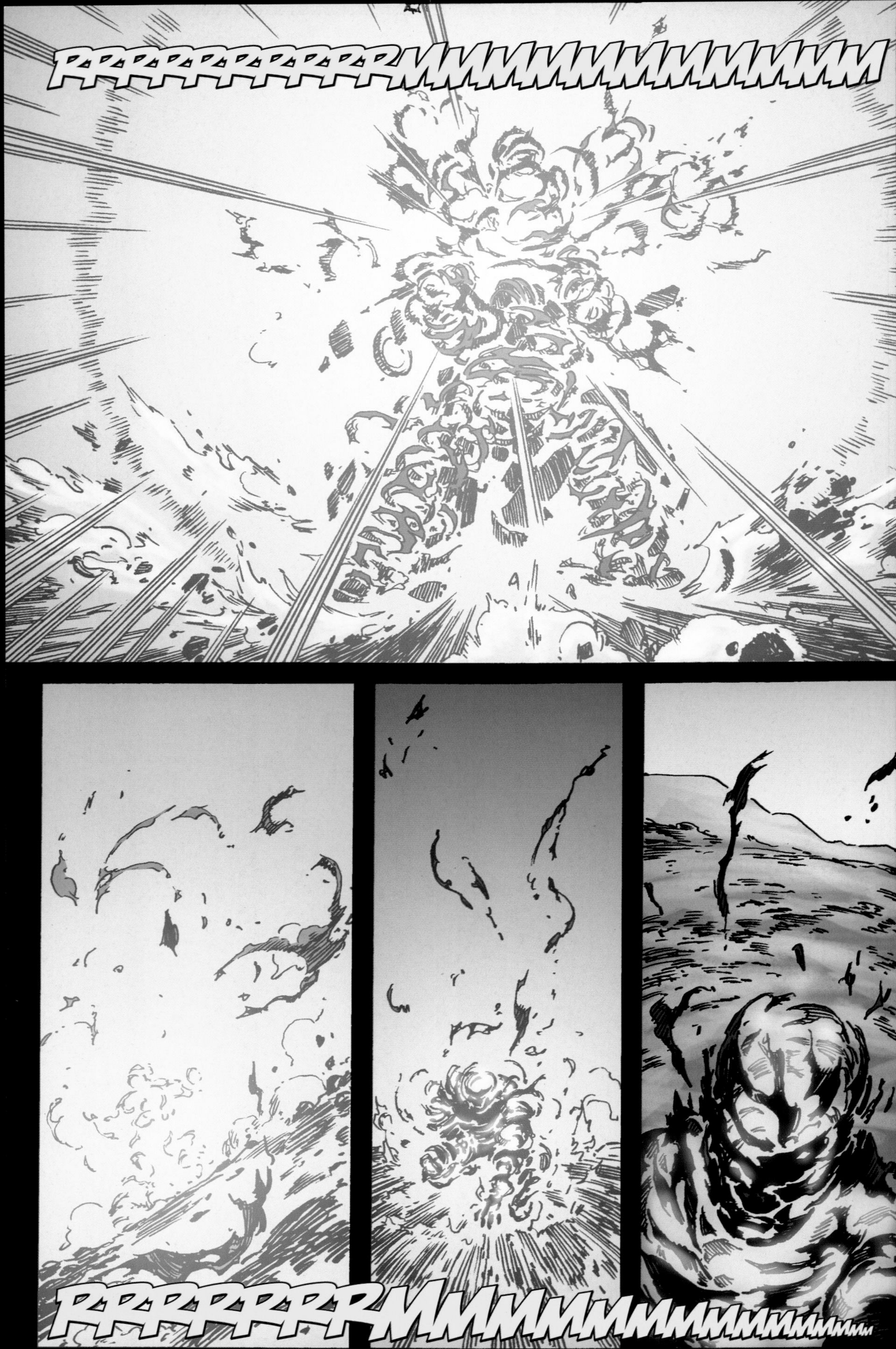
RRRRRRRRRRRRMMMMMMMMMMMMMMMM
RRRRRRRRMMMMMMMMMMMMMMMMM

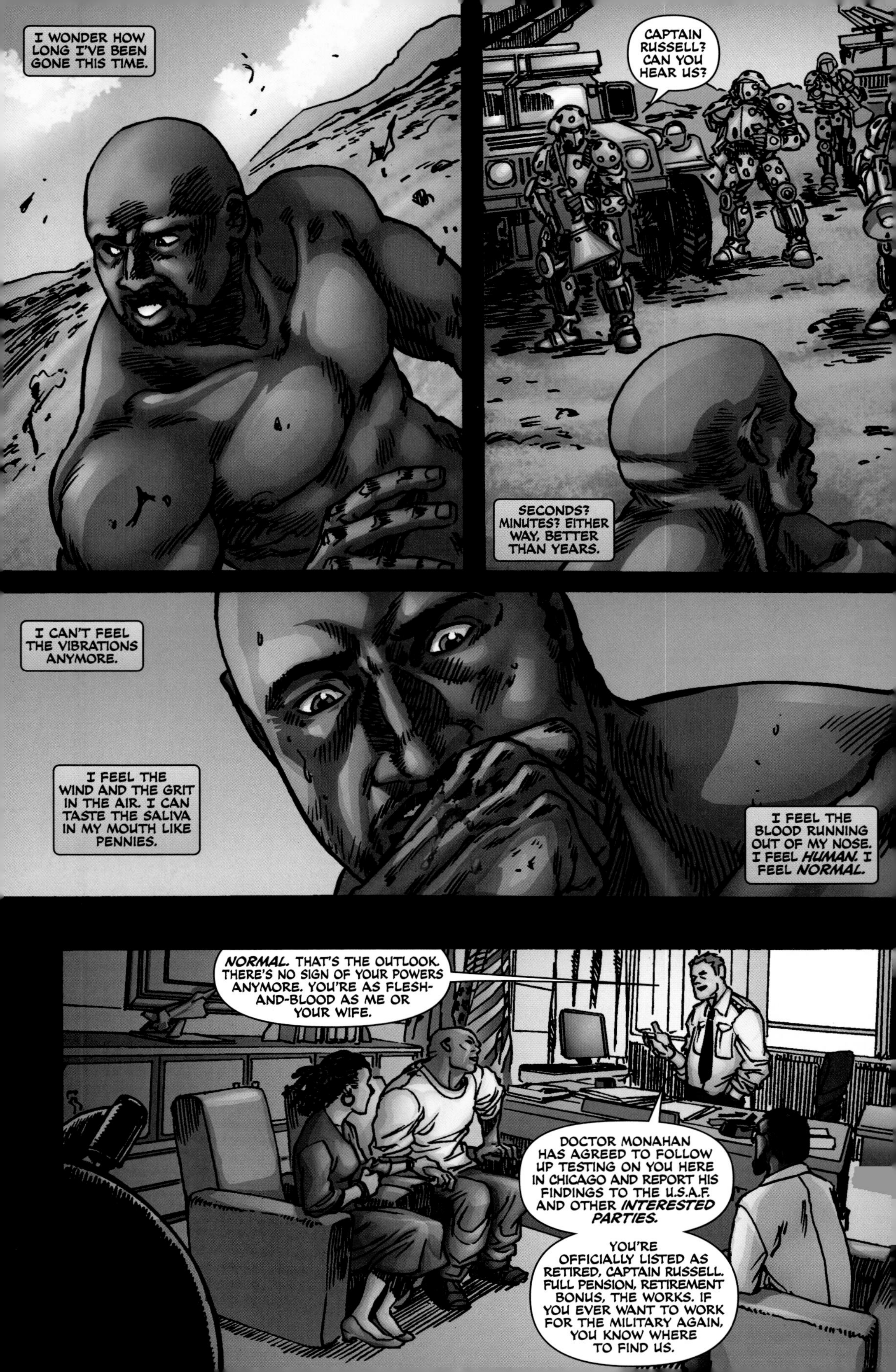
I WONDER HOW LONG I'VE BEEN GONE THIS TIME.
CAPTAIN RUSSELL? CAN YOU HEAR US?
SECONDS? MINUTES? EITHER WAY, BETTER THAN YEARS.
I CAN'T FEEL THE VIBRATIONS ANYMORE.
I FEEL THE WIND AND THE GRIT IN THE AIR. I CAN TASTE THE SALIVA IN MY MOUTH LIKE PENNIES.
I FEEL THE BLOOD RUNNING OUT OF MY NOSE. I FEEL *HUMAN.* I FEEL *NORMAL.*
NORMAL. THAT'S THE OUTLOOK. THERE'S NO SIGN OF YOUR POWERS ANYMORE. YOU'RE AS FLESH-AND-BLOOD AS ME OR YOUR WIFE.
DOCTOR MONAHAN HAS AGREED TO FOLLOW UP TESTING ON YOU HERE IN CHICAGO AND REPORT HIS FINDINGS TO THE U.S.A.F. AND OTHER *INTERESTED PARTIES.*
YOU'RE OFFICIALLY LISTED AS RETIRED, CAPTAIN RUSSELL. FULL PENSION, RETIREMENT BONUS, THE WORKS. IF YOU EVER WANT TO WORK FOR THE MILITARY AGAIN, YOU KNOW WHERE TO FIND US.

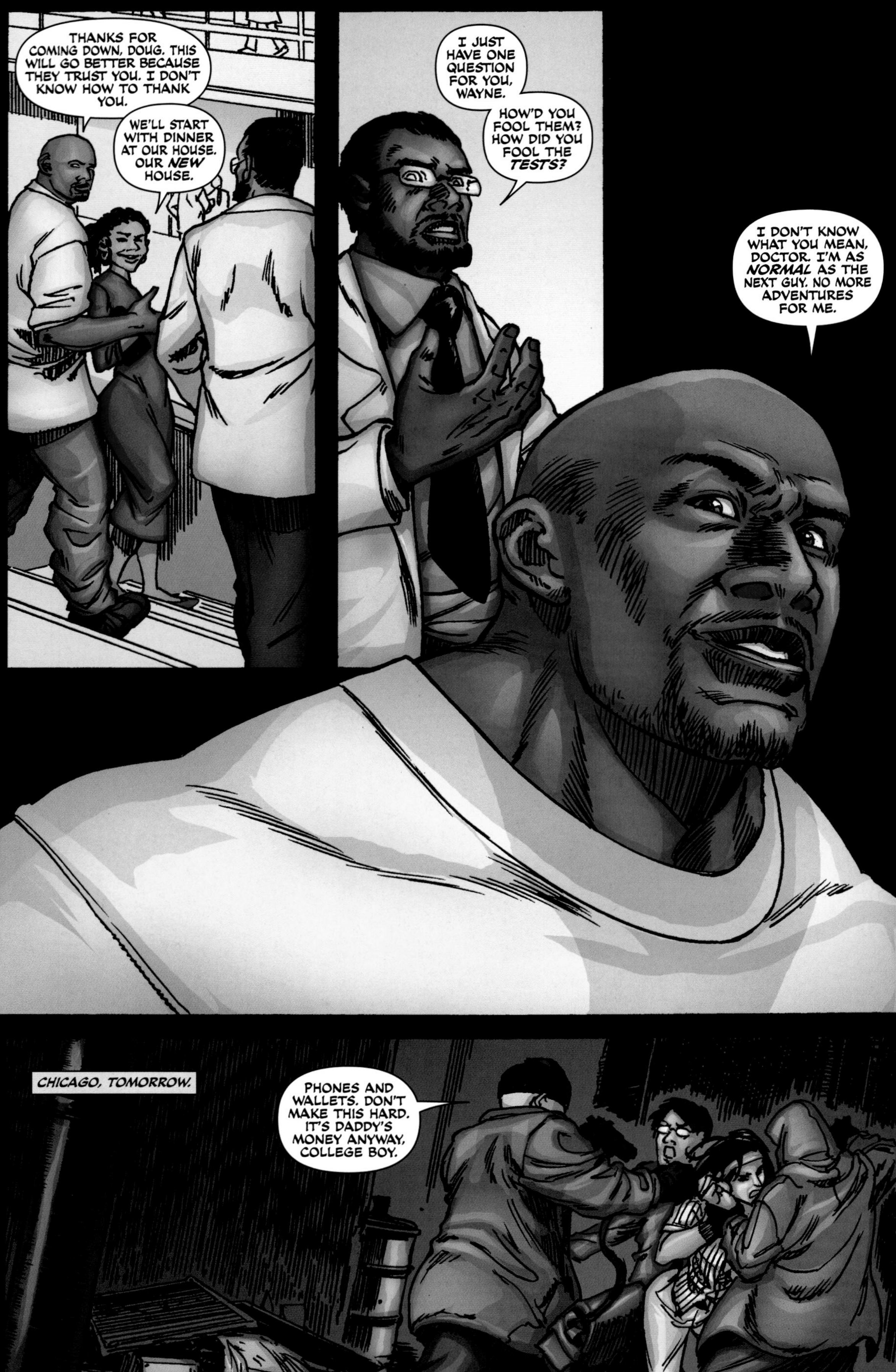
THANKS FOR COMING DOWN, DOUG. THIS WILL GO BETTER BECAUSE THEY TRUST YOU. I DON'T KNOW HOW TO THANK YOU.
WE'LL START WITH DINNER AT OUR HOUSE. OUR *NEW* HOUSE.
I JUST HAVE ONE QUESTION FOR YOU, WAYNE.
HOW'D YOU FOOL THEM? HOW DID YOU FOOL THE *TESTS*?
I DON'T KNOW WHAT YOU MEAN, DOCTOR. I'M AS *NORMAL* AS THE NEXT GUY. NO MORE ADVENTURES FOR ME.
CHICAGO, TOMORROW.
PHONES AND WALLETS. DON'T MAKE THIS HARD. IT'S DADDY'S MONEY ANYWAY, COLLEGE BOY.

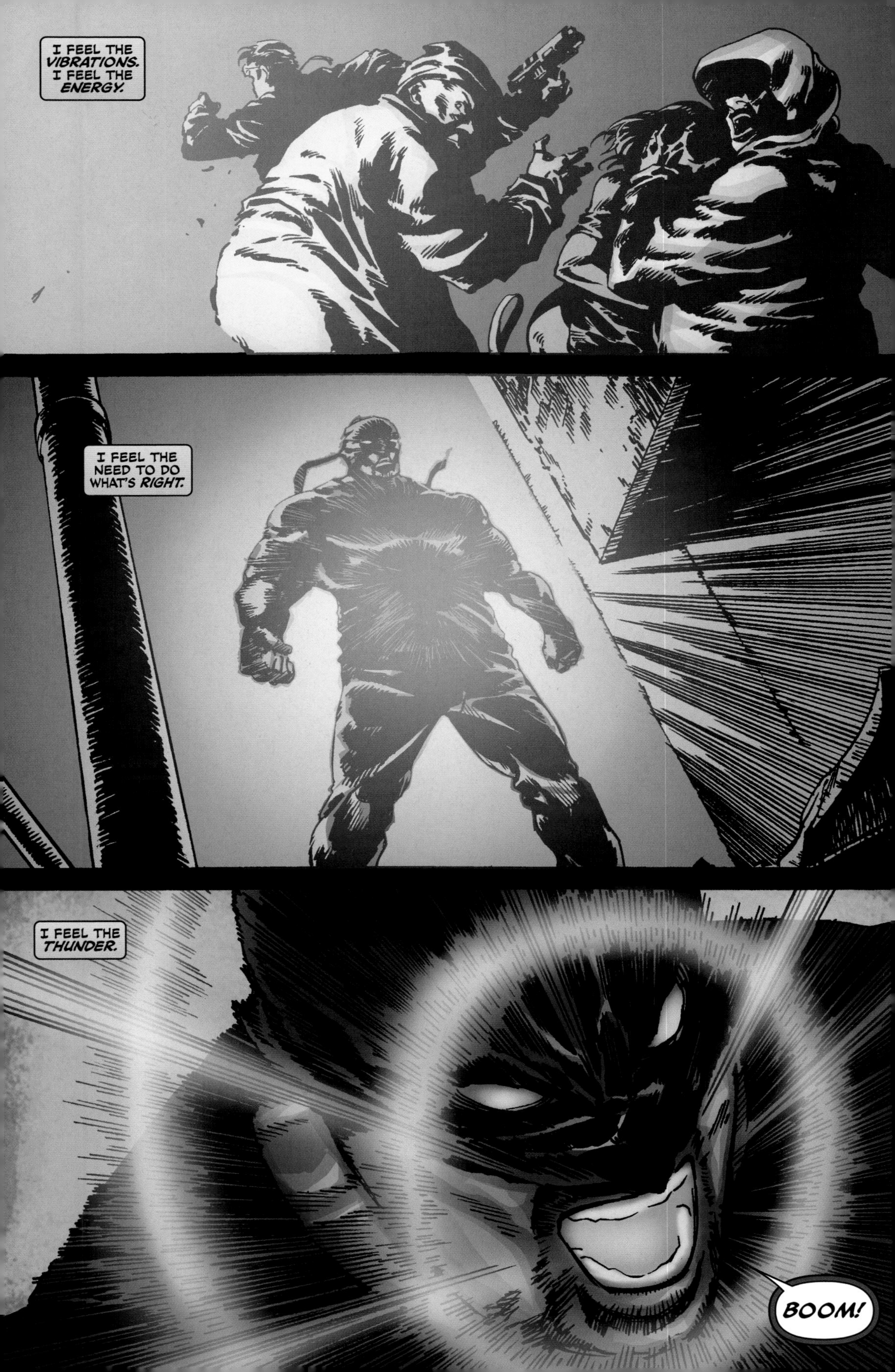

I FEEL THE VIBRATIONS. I FEEL THE ENERGY.
I FEEL THE NEED TO DO WHAT'S RIGHT.
I FEEL THE THUNDER.
BOOM!

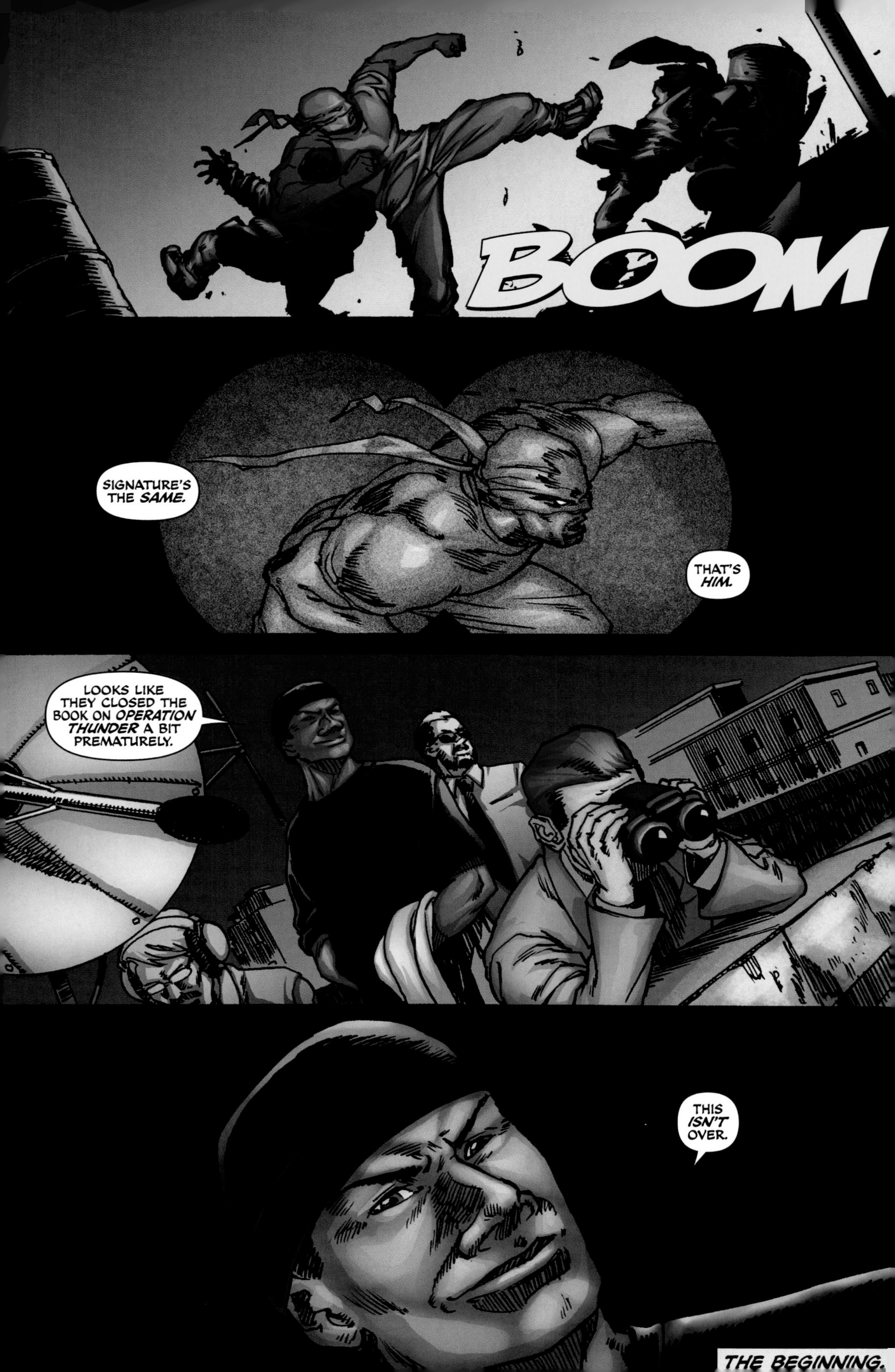
BOOM
SIGNATURE'S THE *SAME.*
THAT'S *HIM.*
LOOKS LIKE THEY CLOSED THE BOOK ON *OPERATION THUNDER* A BIT PREMATURELY.
THIS *ISN'T* OVER.
THE BEGINNING.

BONUS
MATERIALS

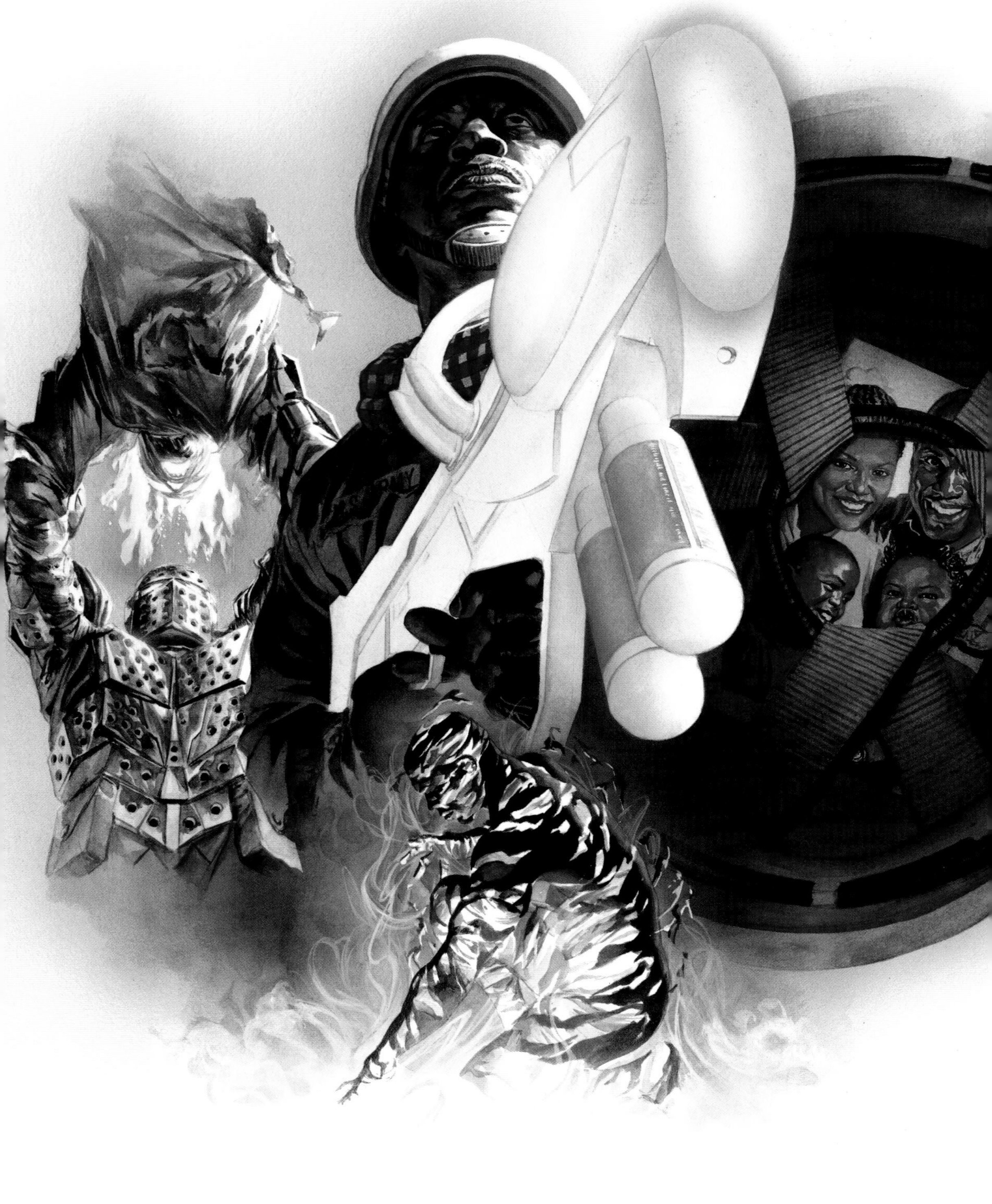

ISSUE #1 MAIN COVER BY ALEX ROSS

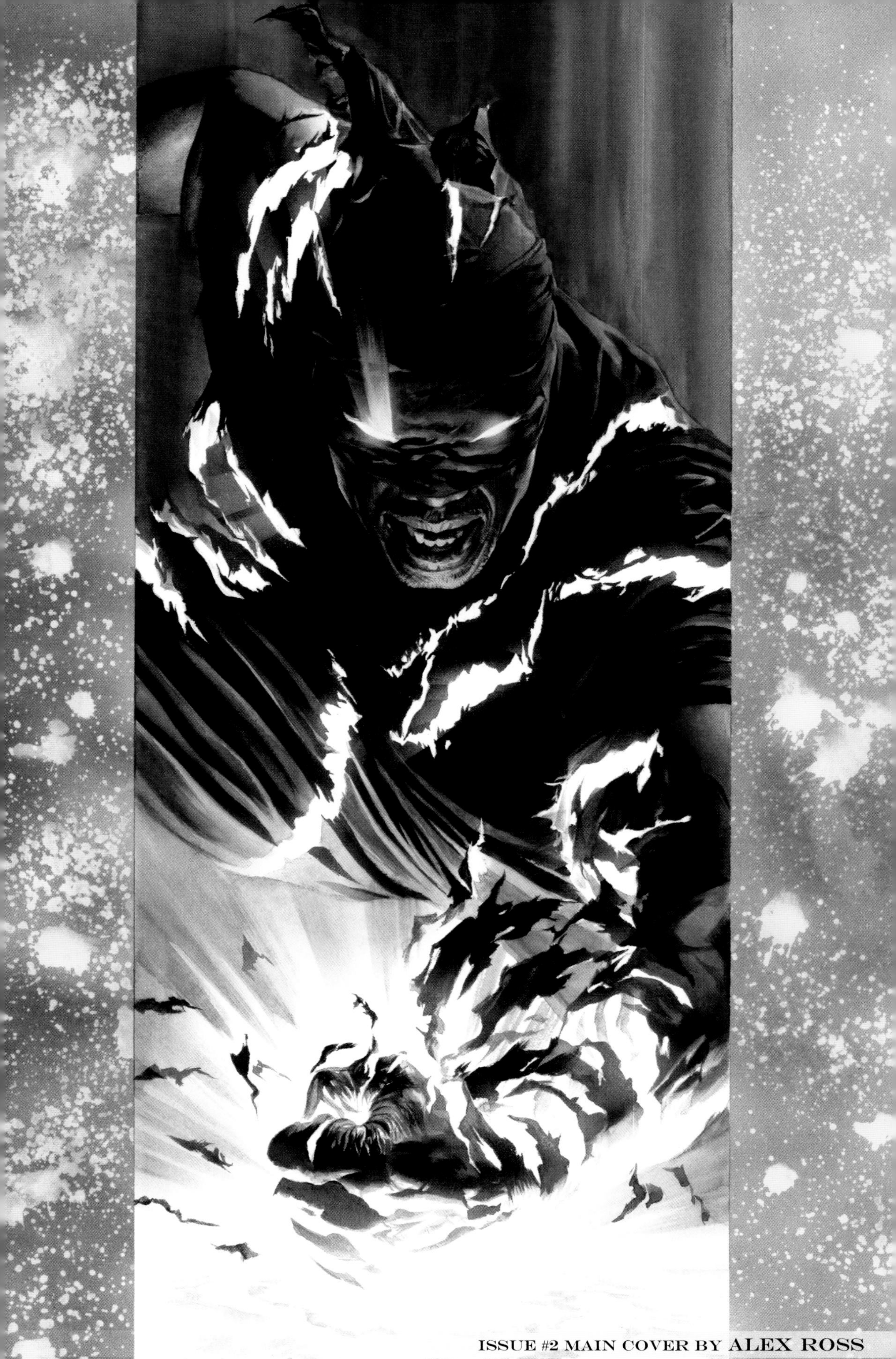

ISSUE #2 MAIN COVER BY ALEX ROSS

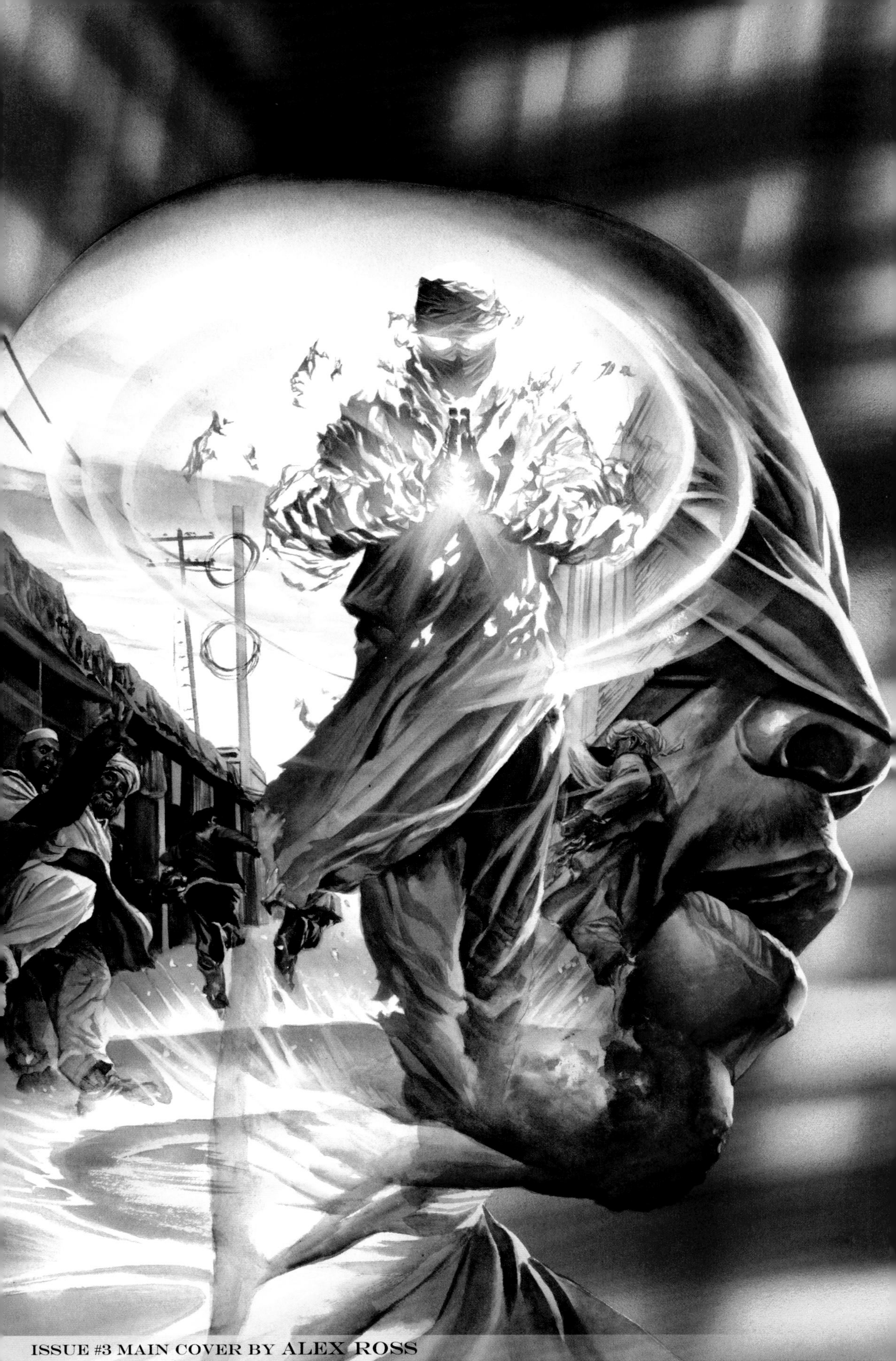

ISSUE #3 MAIN COVER BY ALEX ROSS

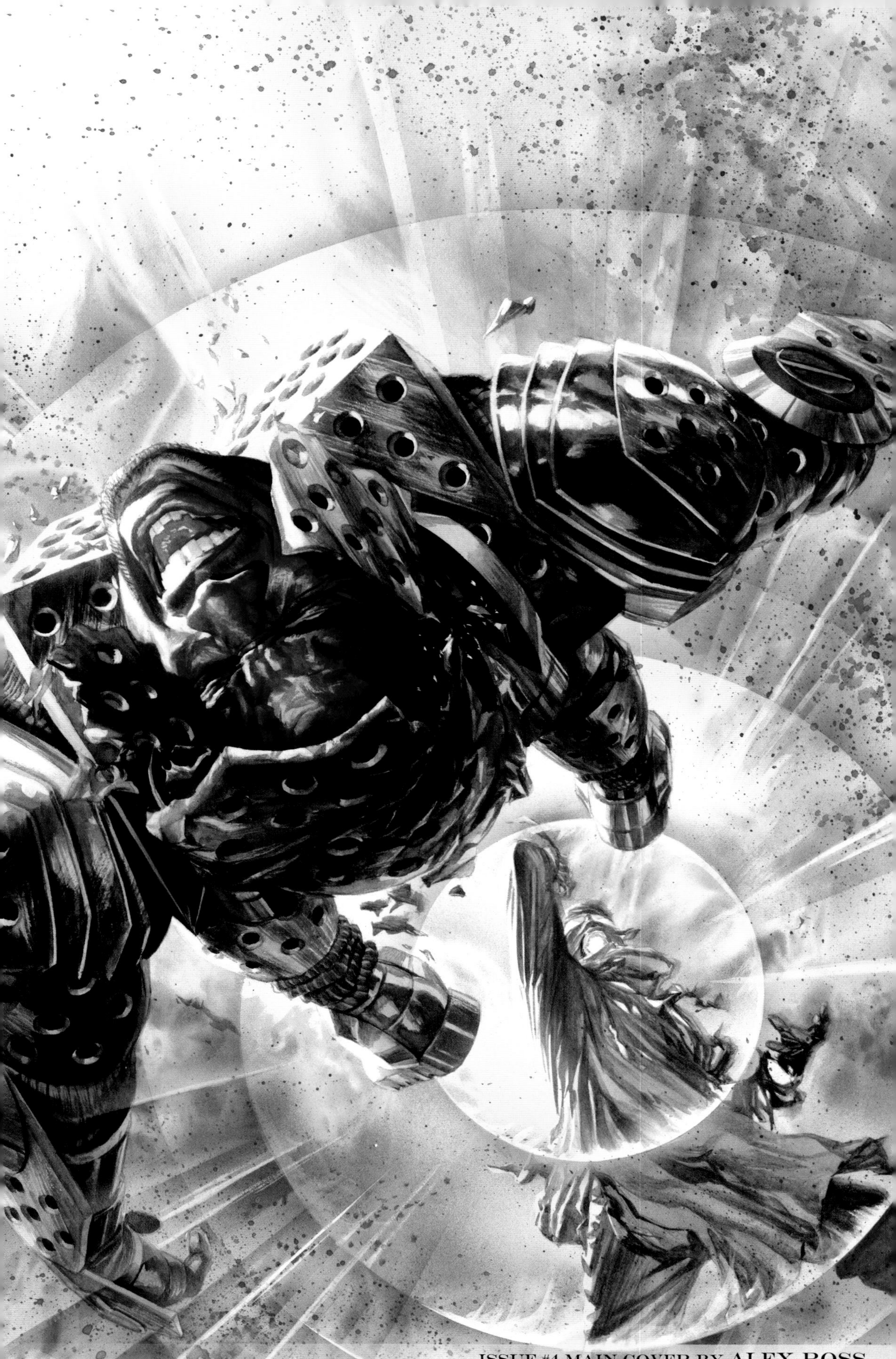

ISSUE #4 MAIN COVER BY ALEX ROSS

Rough guide for Wayne's reconstitution.

ART BY ALEX ROSS

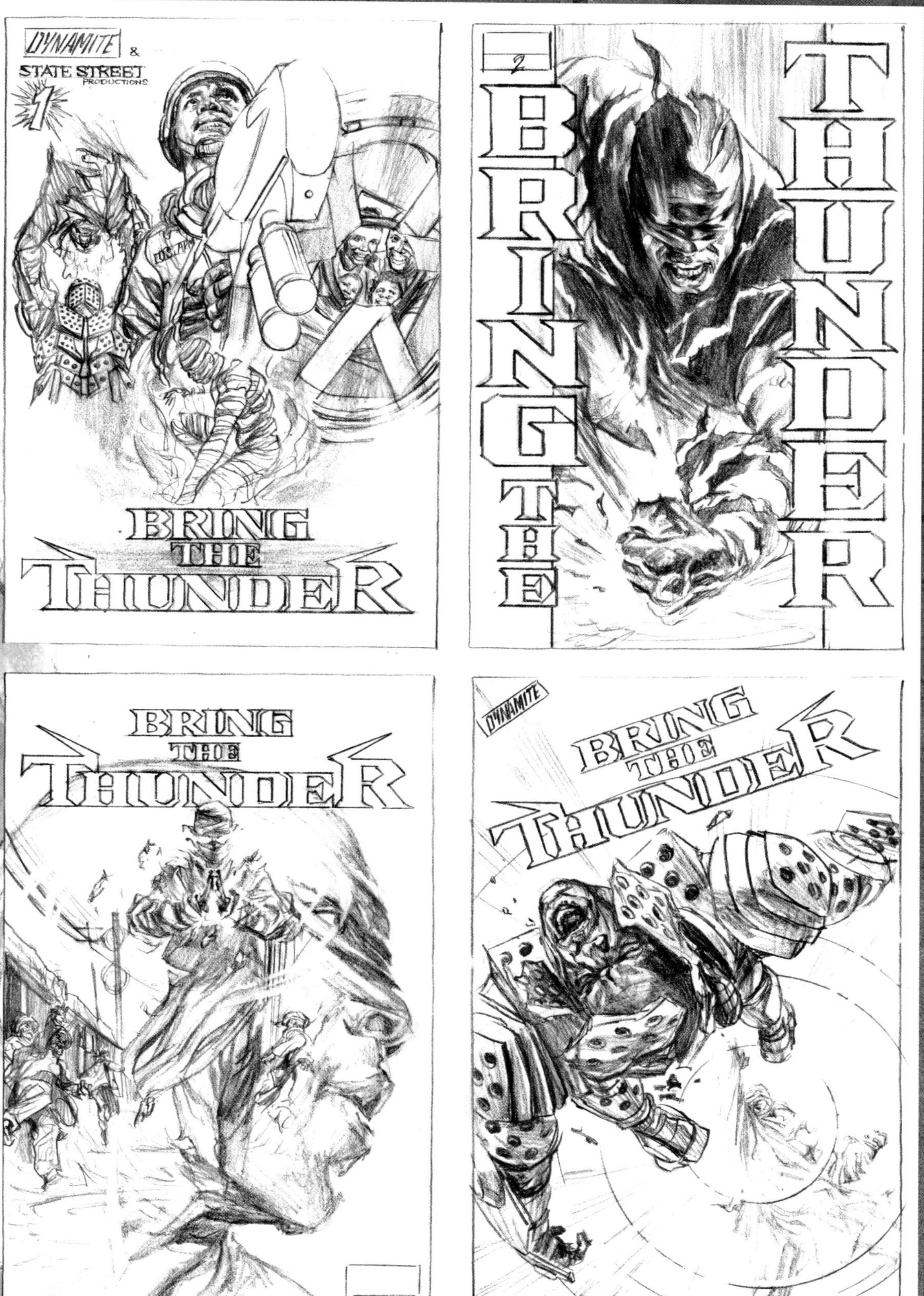
DYNAMITE &
STATE STREET PRODUCTIONS
1
BRING THE THUNDER
2
BRING THE THUNDER
BRING THE THUNDER
DYNAMITE
BRING THE THUNDER

Thumbnails for issues #1-#4.

Detail for Wayne's makeshift costume and exploding power.

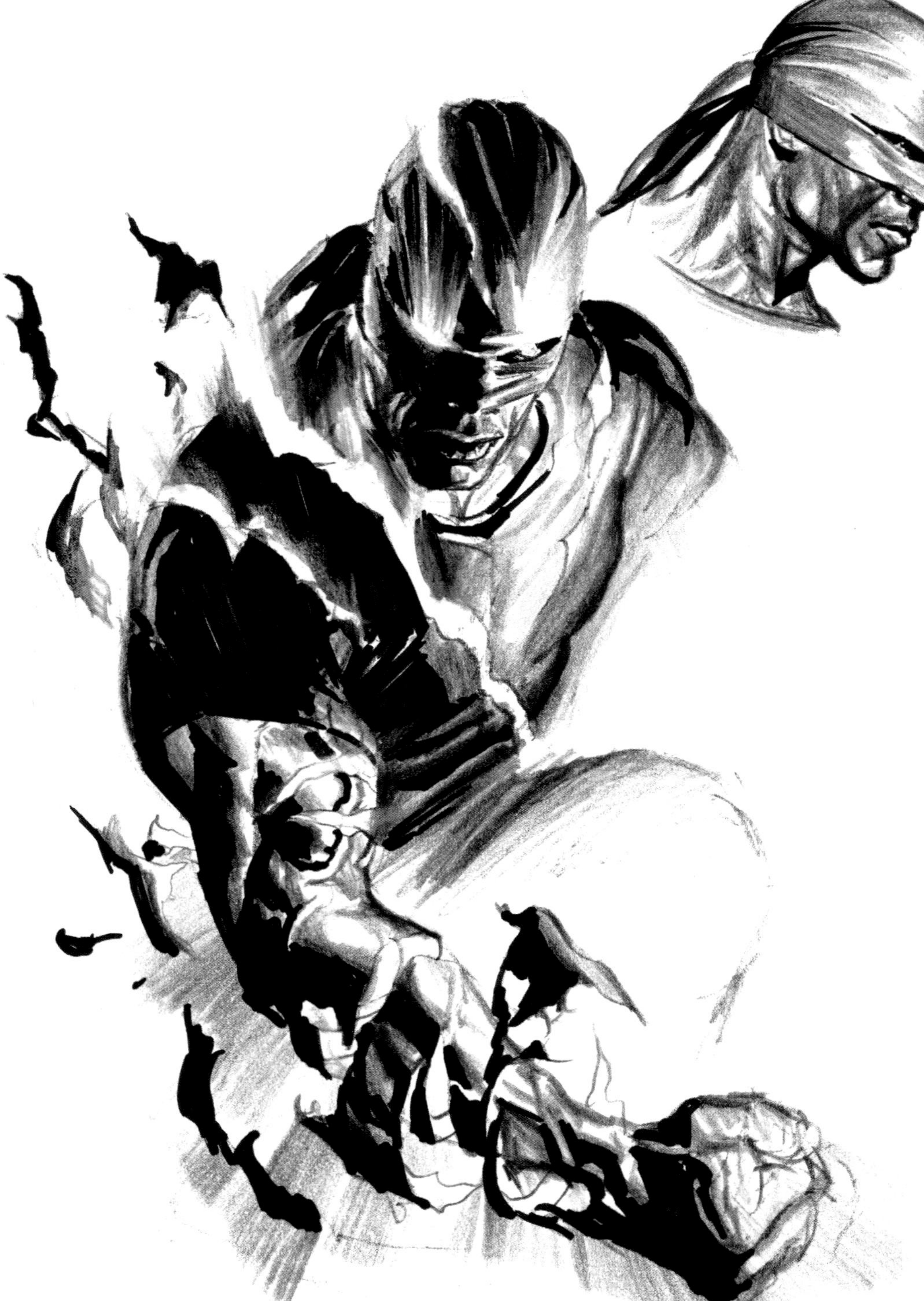

Alex's friend Terrence Hunter was the basis for Wayne Russell's likeness.

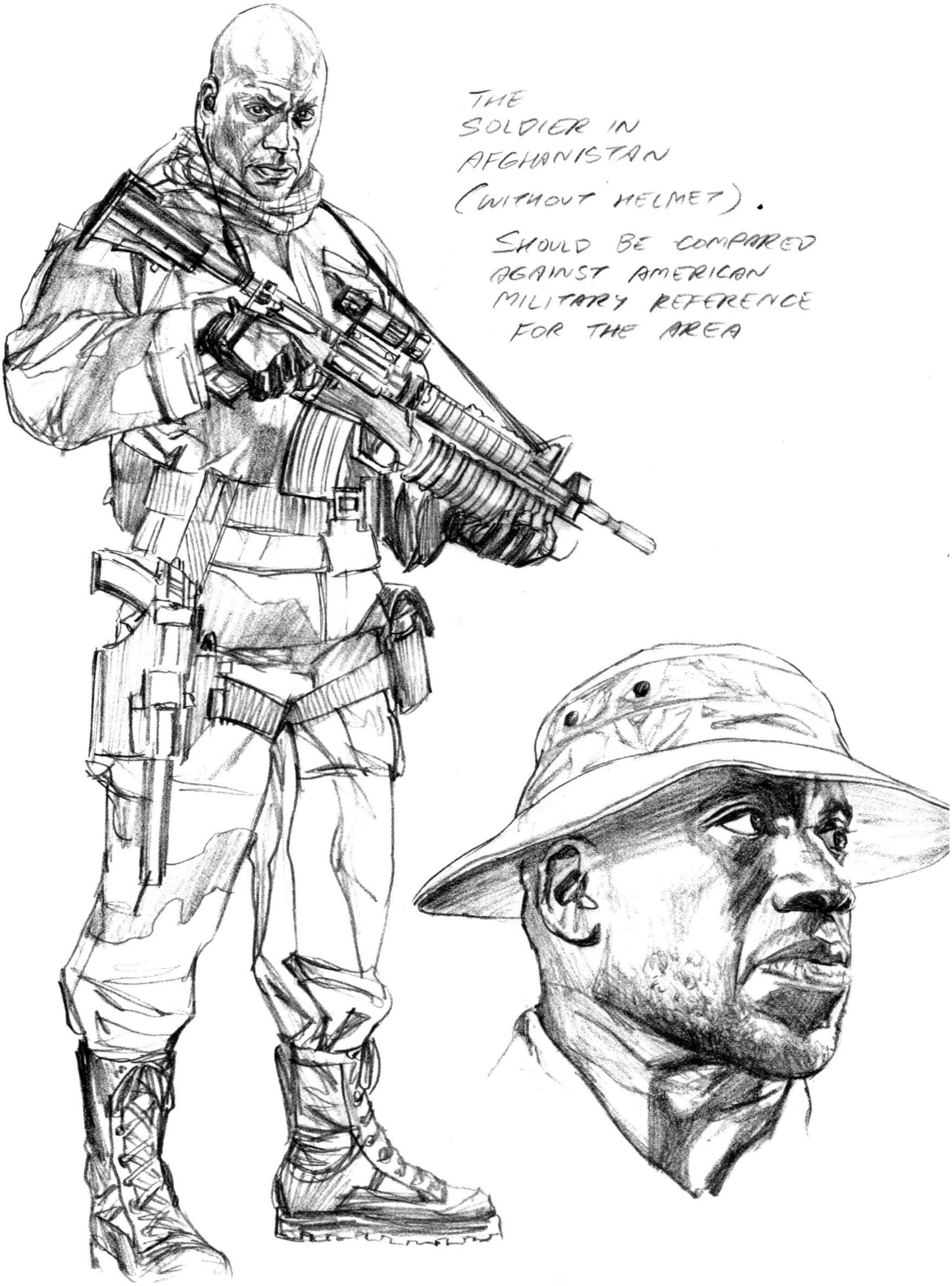
THE SOLDIER IN AFGHANISTAN (WITHOUT HELMET).
SHOULD BE COMPARED AGAINST AMERICAN MILITARY REFERENCE FOR THE AREA

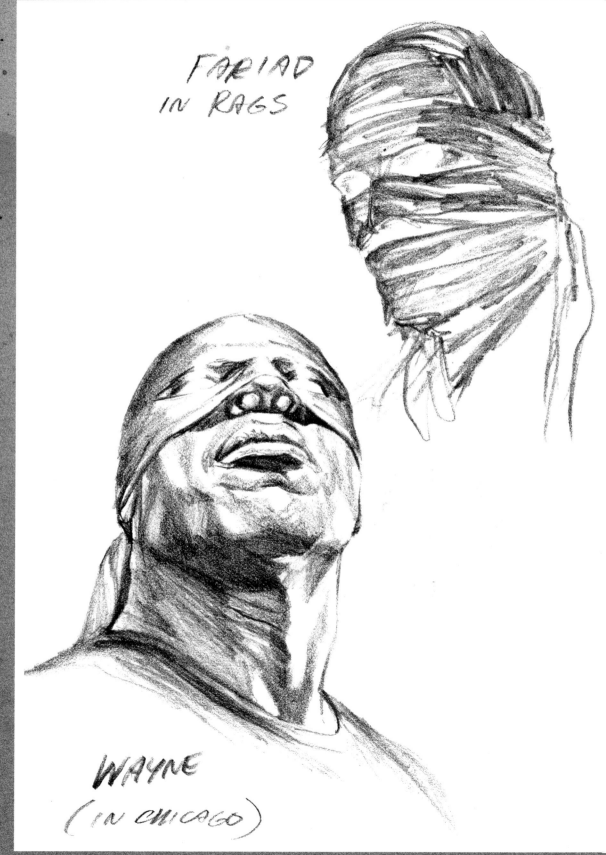

FARIAD
IN RAGS

WAYNE
(IN CHICAGO)

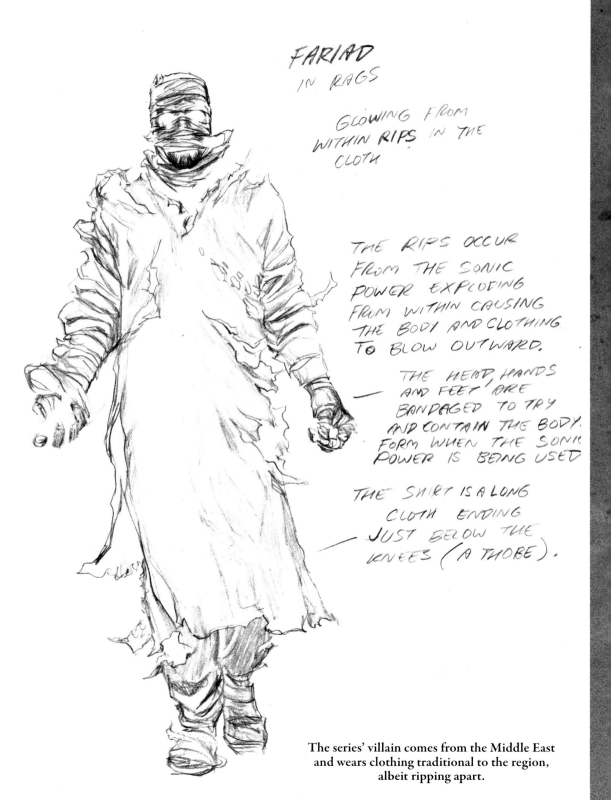

FARIAD
IN RAGS

GLOWING FROM
WITHIN RIPS IN THE
CLOTH

THE RIPS OCCUR
FROM THE SONIC
POWER EXPLODING
FROM WITHIN CAUSING
THE BODY AND CLOTHING
TO BLOW OUTWARD.

THE HEAD, HANDS
AND FEET ARE
BANDAGED TO TRY
AND CONTAIN THE BODY.
FORM WHEN THE SONIC
POWER IS BEING USED

THE SHIRT IS A LONG
CLOTH ENDING
JUST BELOW THE
KNEES (A THOBE).

The series' villain comes from the Middle East
and wears clothing traditional to the region,
albeit ripping apart.

Early design work for Wayne's armored suit and the sonic weapon that changed him.

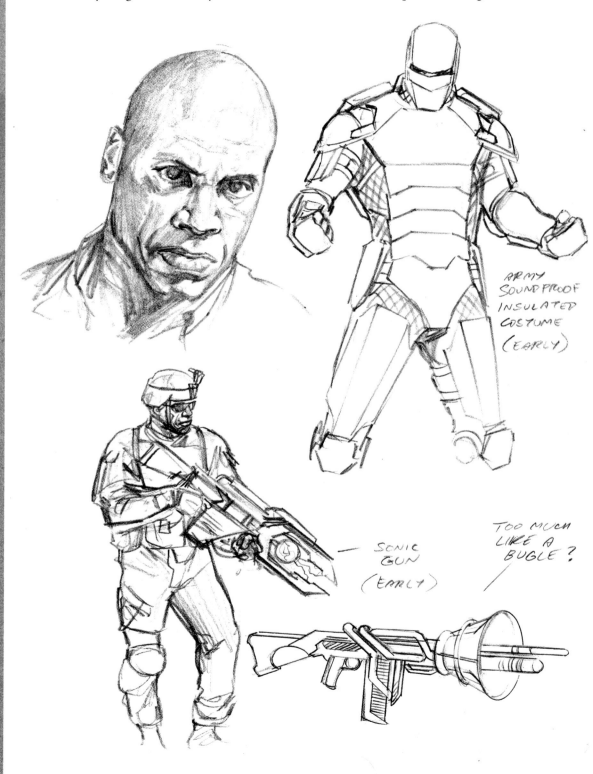

ARMY
SOUND PROOF
INSULATED
COSTUME
(EARLY)

SONIC
GUN
(EARLY)

TOO MUCH
LIKE A
BUGLE?

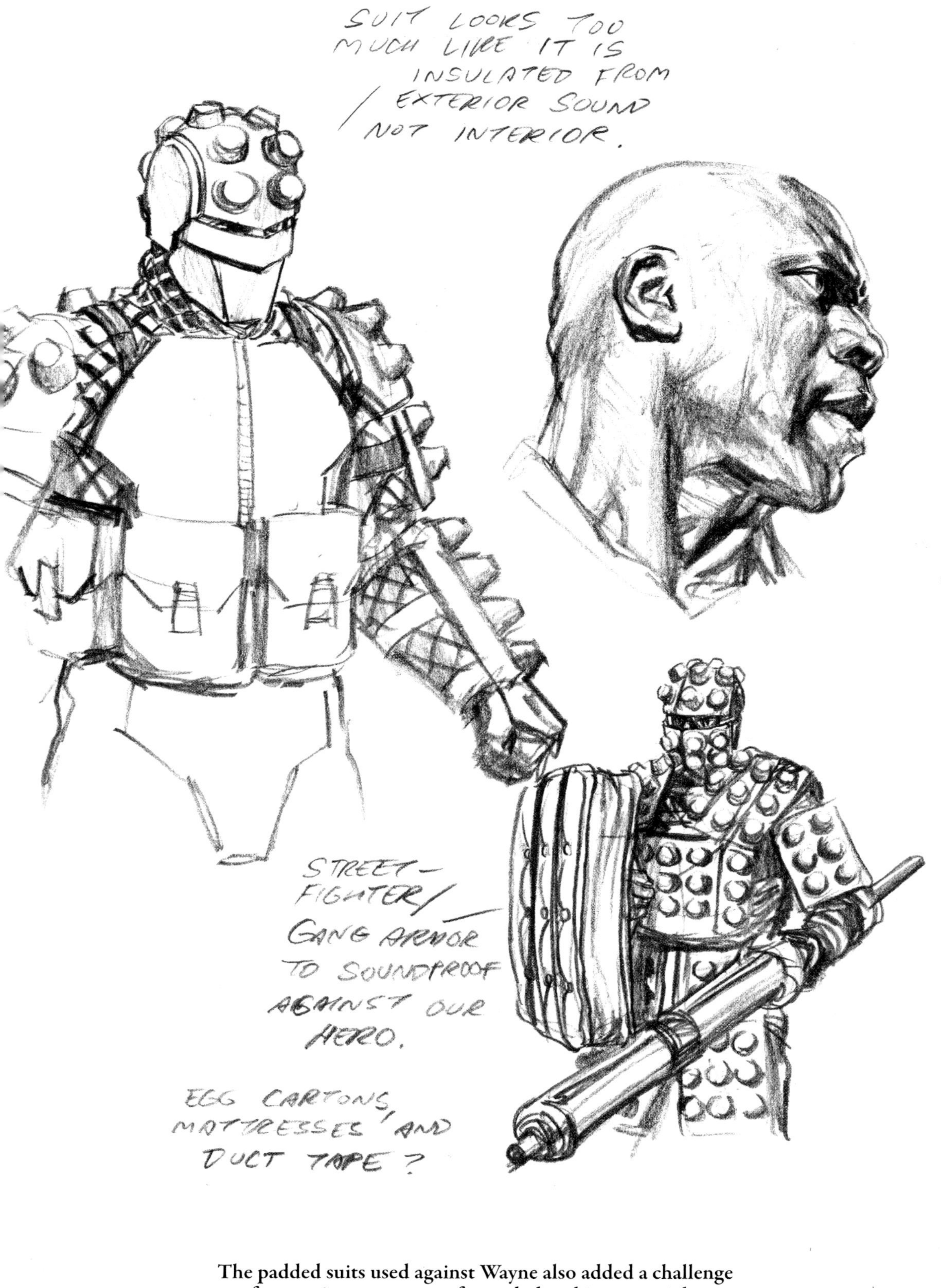
SUIT LOOKS TOO MUCH LIKE IT IS INSULATED FROM EXTERIOR SOUND NOT INTERIOR.
STREET-FIGHTER/ GANG ARMOR TO SOUNDPROOF AGAINST OUR HERO.
EGG CARTONS, MATTRESSES AND DUCT TAPE?

The padded suits used against Wayne also added a challenge for creating armor out of sound-absorbing materials.

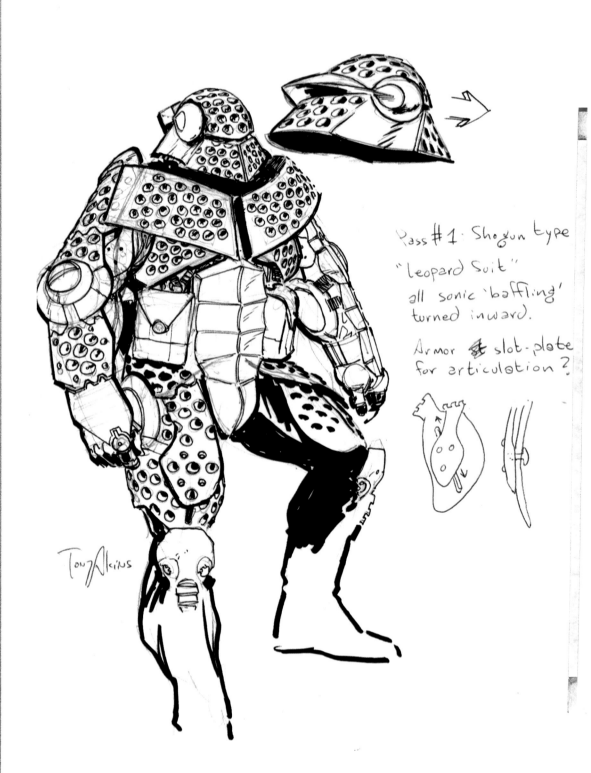

Pass #1: Shogun type
"Leopard Suit"
all sonic 'baffling'
turned inward.

Armor & slot-plate
for articulation?

TonyAkins

ART BY TONY AKINS

Fables artist Tony Akins helped in the design of Wayne's self-insulating armor. Tony's expert technical design knowledge has been helpful to Alex on previous projects like *Kingdom Come*.

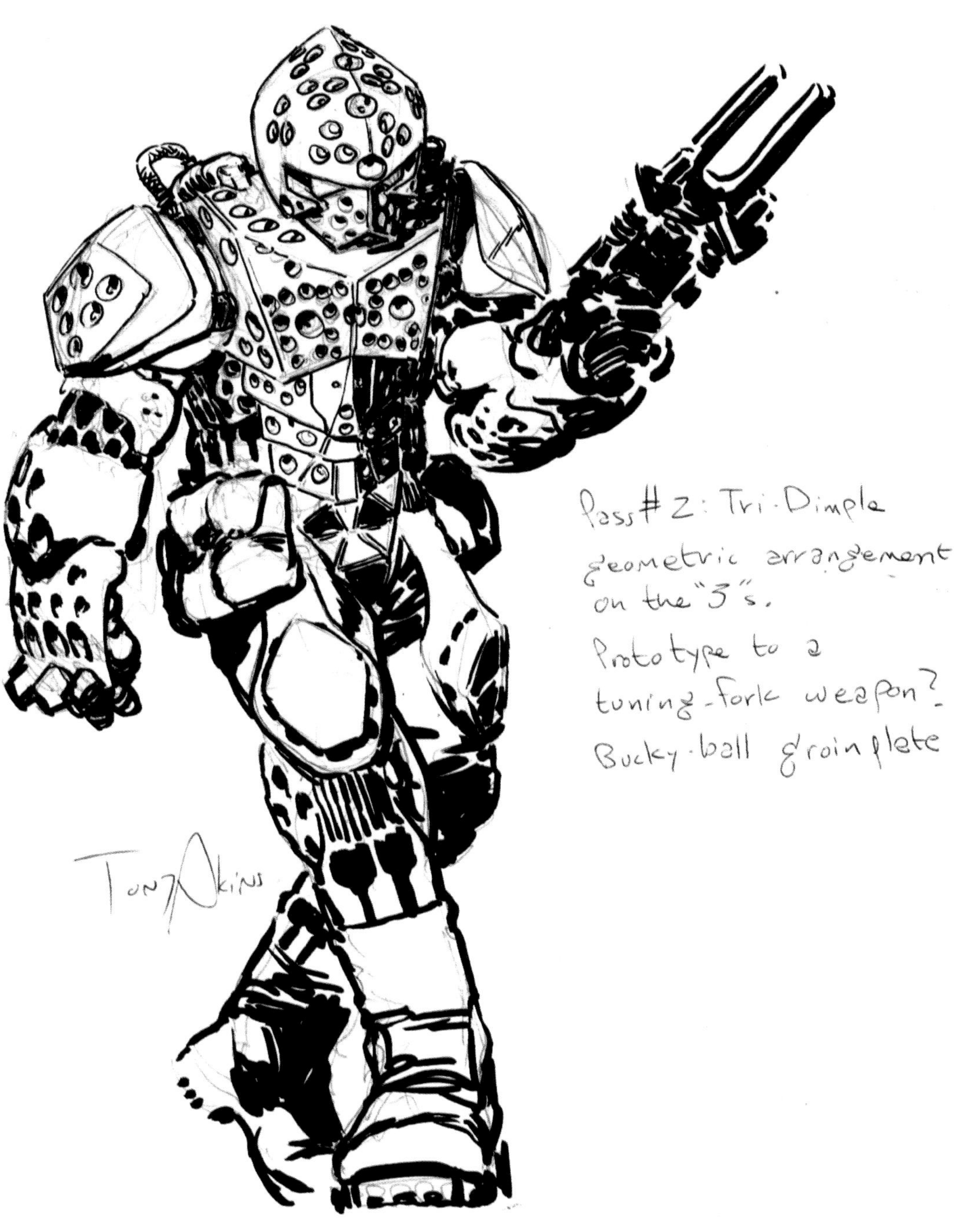
Pass #2: Tri-Dimple
geometric arrangement
on the "3"s.
Prototype to a
tuning-fork weapon?
Bucky-ball groin plate
Tony Akins

SKETCHBOOK

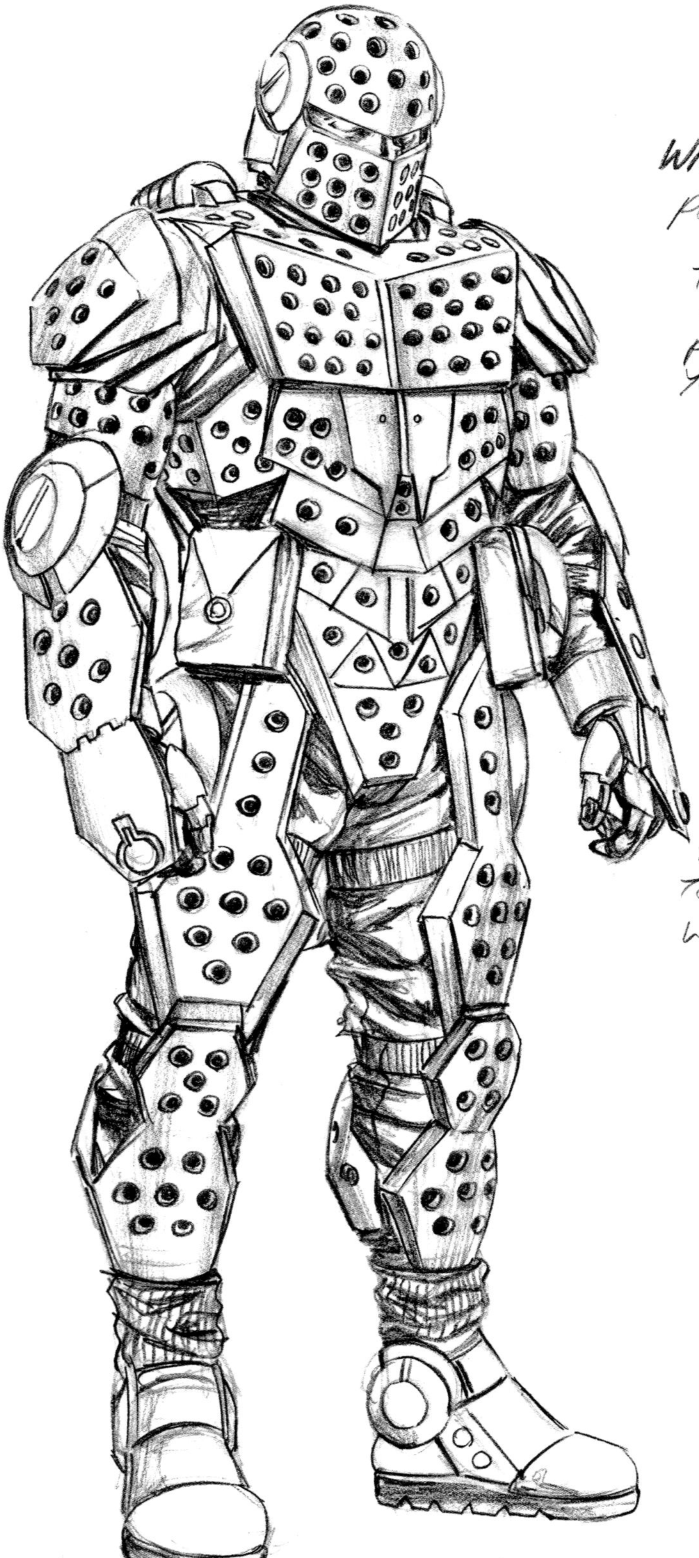

WAYNE IN
POWERSUIT

THE EYES GLOW WITHIN AS THE ONLY PART OF THE BODY YOU CAN SEE.

THE INVERTED HOLES ARE SOUND INSULATION AIMING INWARD TOWARD THE BODY, CONTAINING THE SONIC POWER FROM DISSIPATING THE BODY'S FORM.

THE ARMOR DOES DAMPEN WAYNE'S USE OF HIS SONIC POWERS IN CONTRAST TO FARIAD BEING WRAPPED IN BANDAGES.

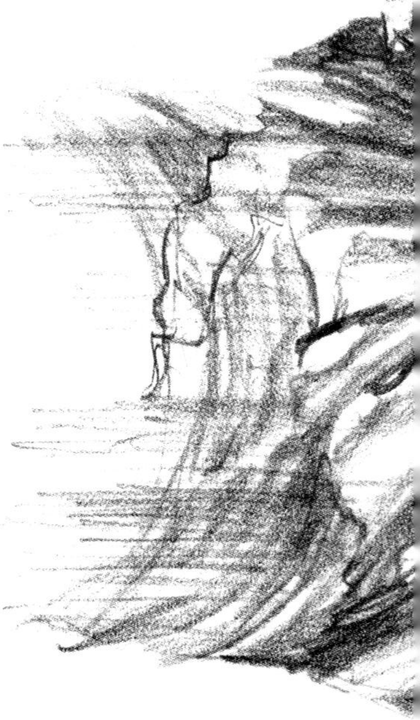

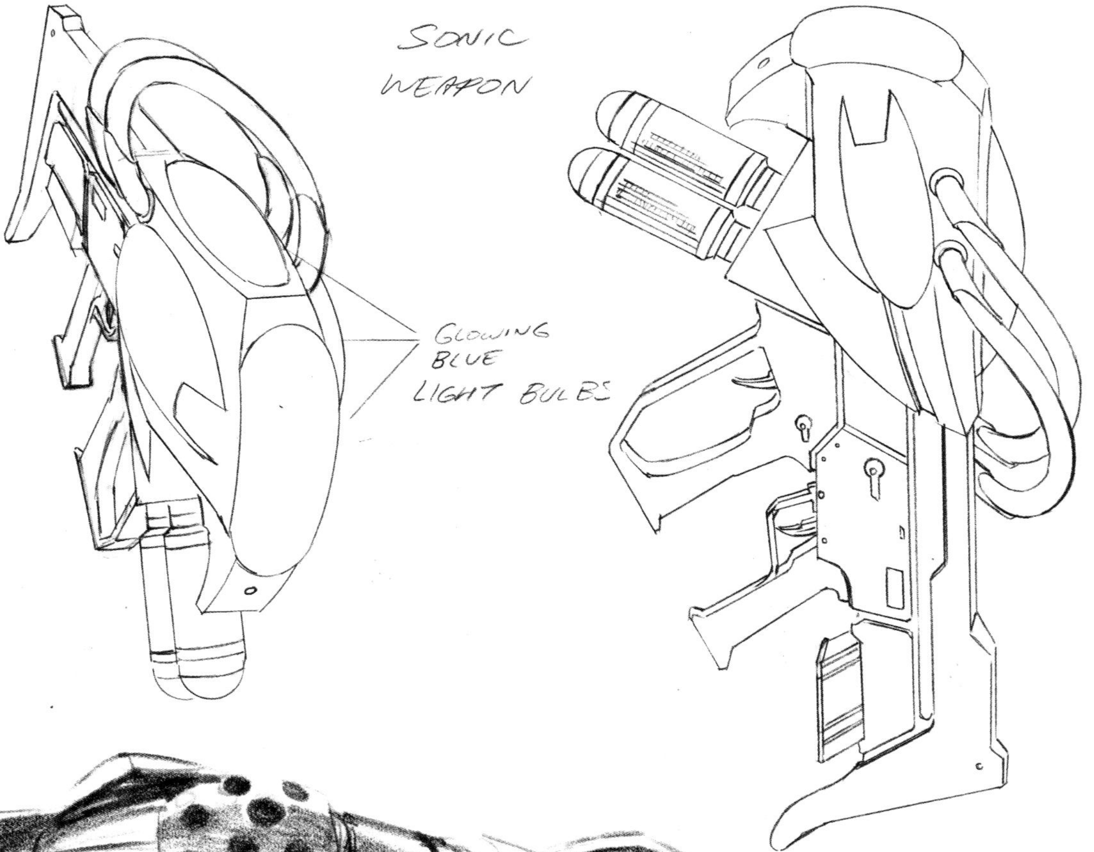
SONIC
WEAPON
GLOWING
BLUE
LIGHT BULBS

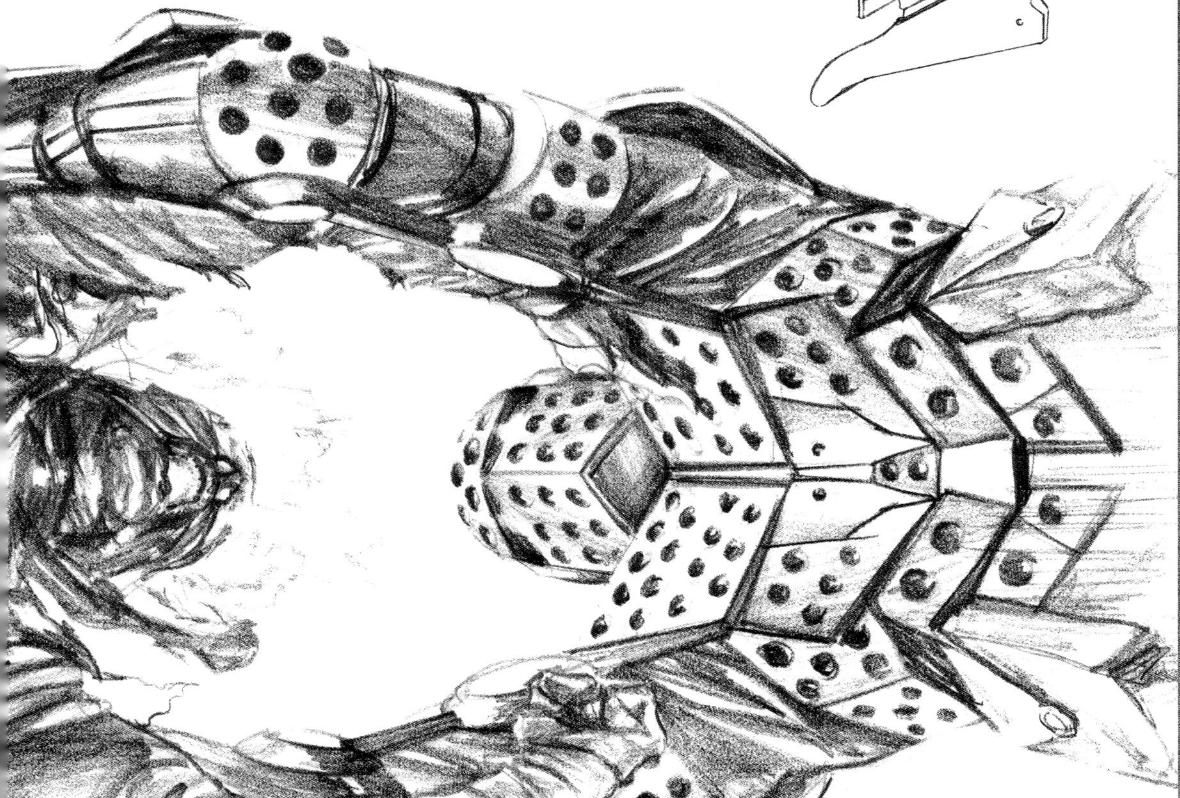

SKETCHBOOK

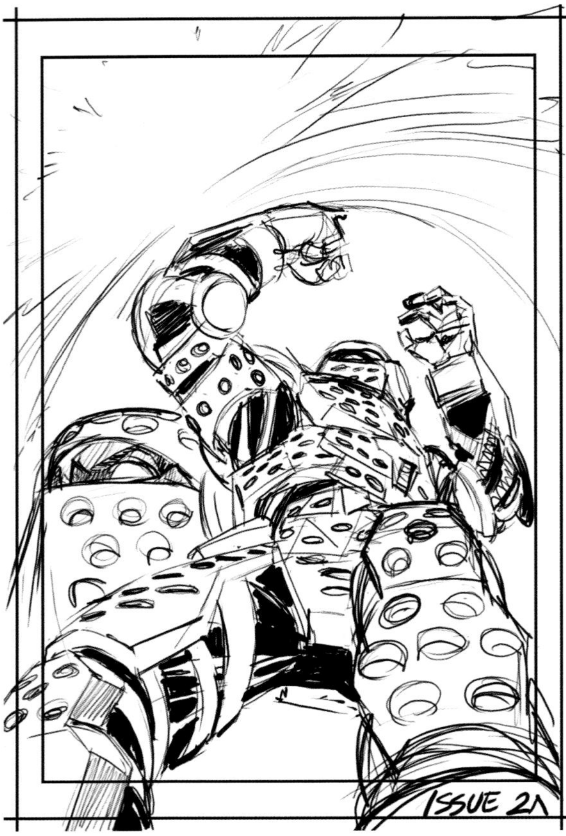
ISSUE 2A

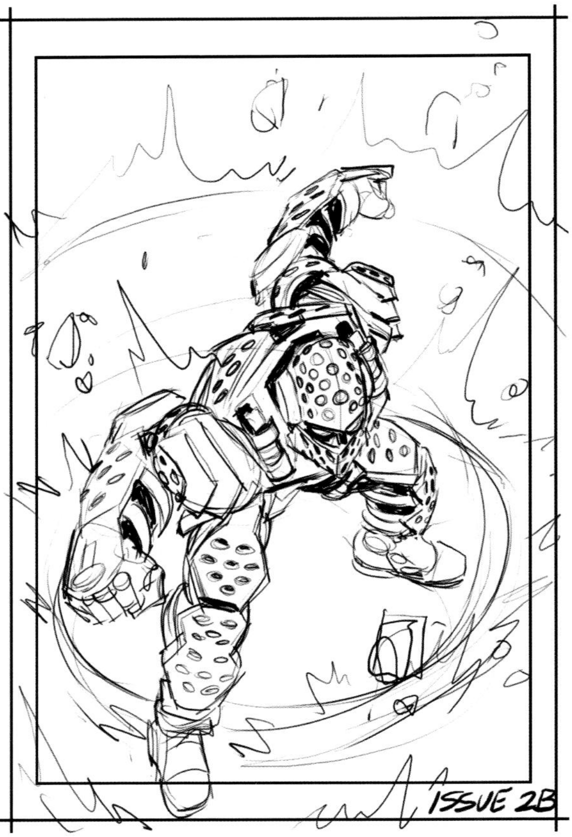
ISSUE 2B

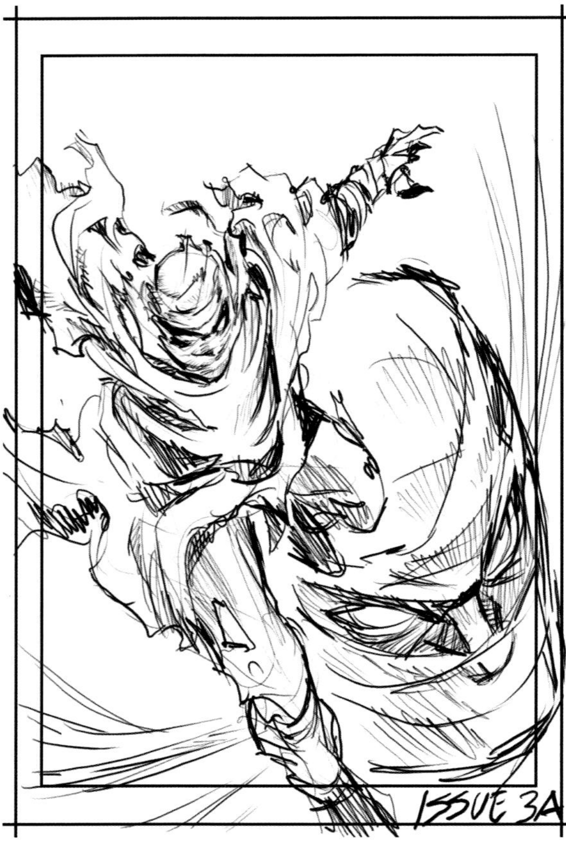
ISSUE 3A

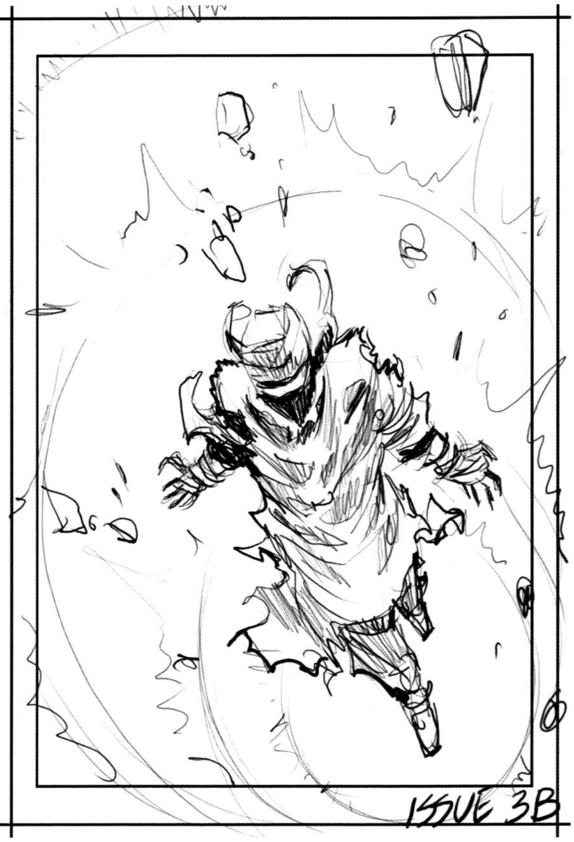
ISSUE 3B

ART BY WILSON TORTOSA

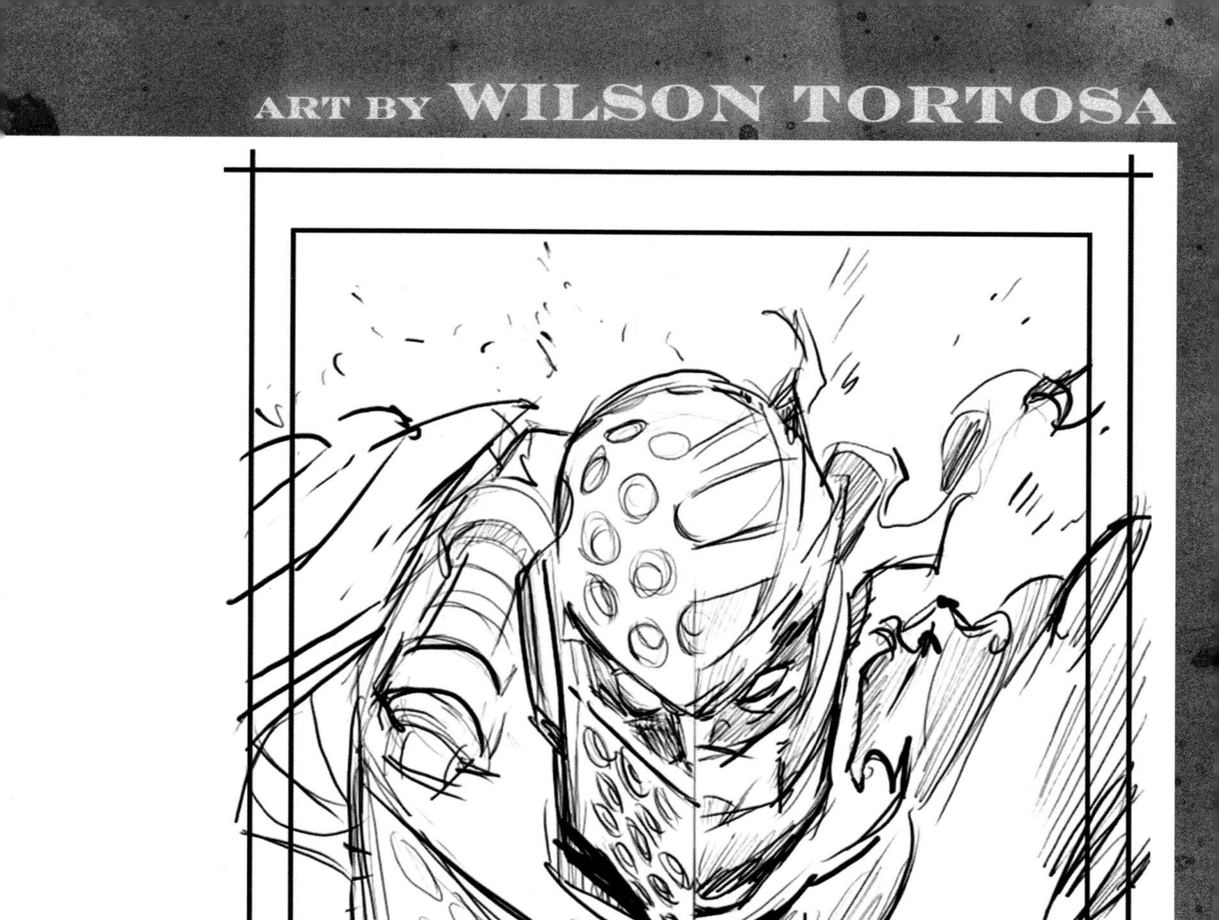
ISSUE 4B

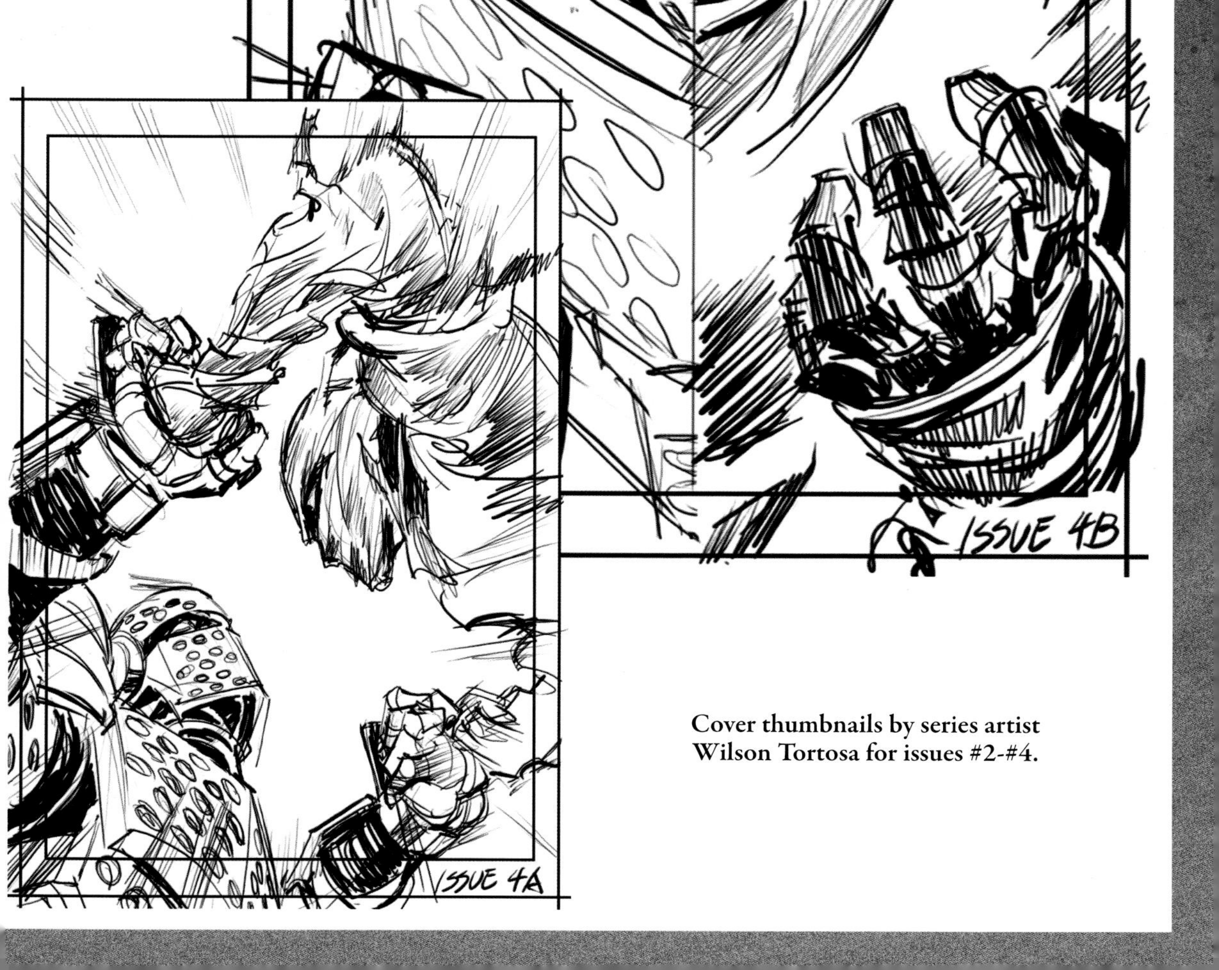
ISSUE 4A

Cover thumbnails by series artist Wilson Tortosa for issues #2-#4.

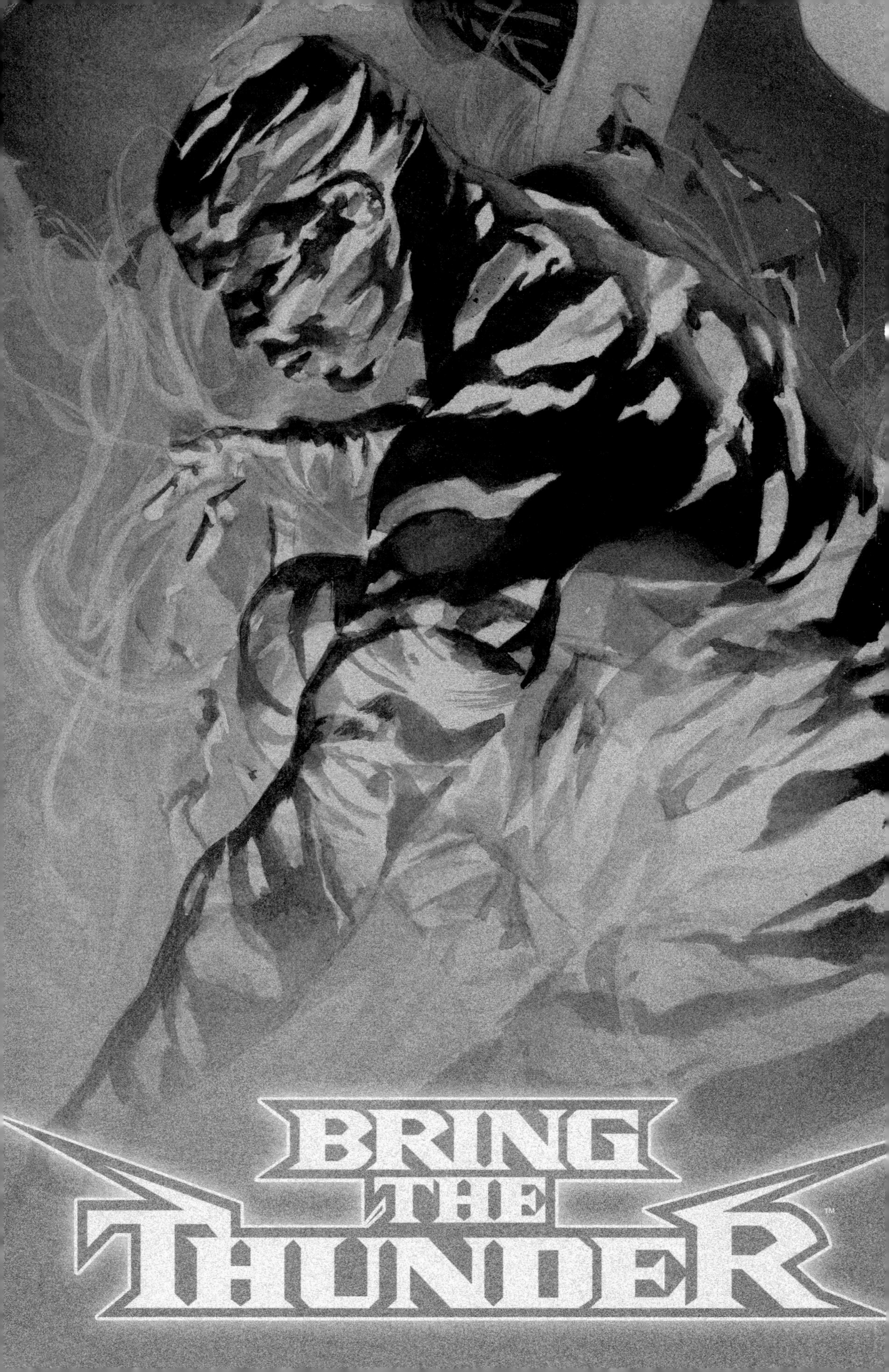
BRING
THE
THUNDER™